DOUGLAS A-1 SKYRAIDER

1945–85 (all marks and variants)

First published in December 2017

A catalogue record for this book is available from the British Library.

ISBN 978 1 78521 135 5

Library of Congress control no. 2017933524

Published by Haynes Publishing,
Sparkford, Yeovil, Somerset BA22 7JJ, UK.
Tel: 01963 440635
Int. tel: +44 1963 440635
Website: www.haynes.com

Haynes North America Inc.,
859 Lawrence Drive, Newbury Park,
California 91320, USA.

Printed in Malaysia.

Commissioning Editor: Jonathan Falconer
Copy editor: Michelle Tilling
Proof reader: Penny Housden
Indexer: Peter Nicholson
Page design: James Robertson

DOUGLAS A-1 SKYRAIDER

1945–85 (all marks and variants)

Owners' Workshop Manual

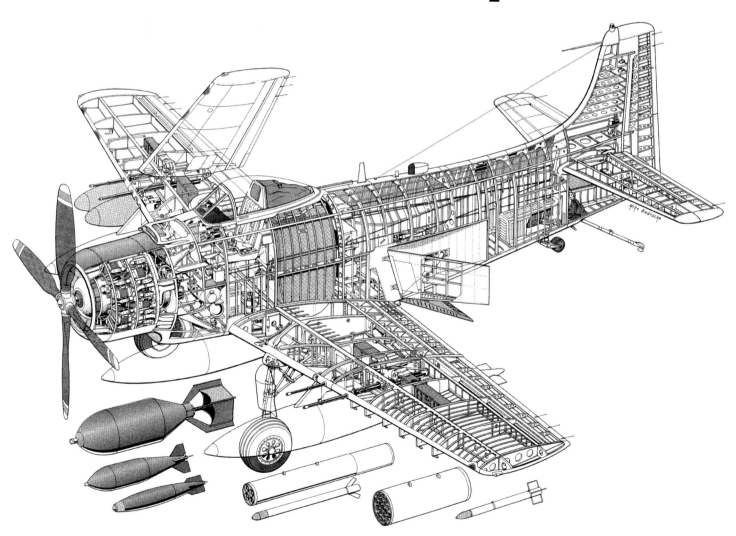

The legendary US post-war single-seat attack aircraft that found fame in the skies over Korea and Vietnam

Tony Hoskins

Contents

ABOVE A single-seat A-1H from the USAF's 6th Special Operations Squadron provides close air-support over Vietnam in 1968. *(USAF)*

OPPOSITE AD-4NA Skyraider 'JC-409' at rest before another display. *(Chad W. Veich)*

Introduction

Rapid technical developments that came about during the Second World War witnessed the emergence of naval aviation as the decisive factor in the war at sea. The Battle of Midway was fought almost entirely by US carrier-based aircraft, while the Japanese attack on Pearl Harbor that brought America into the war was also delivered by naval air power. Naval air warfare required aircraft to perform multiple roles but not all of these were suitable for launch and recovery on carriers. In many cases, flying boats carried out anti-submarine patrols, but in order to take the war to the enemy, the US Navy required dive bombers, torpedo bombers and fighters.

OPPOSITE A typical image of Second World War carrier operations – a US Navy Grumman F6F-3 Hellcat fighter makes condensation rings with its propeller as it awaits the take-off flag aboard USS *Yorktown* (CV-10), 20 November 1943. *(US Navy)*

It soon became clear that the aircraft carrier would replace the battleship as the most powerful weapon in the naval arsenal. Large battles were no longer being fought by ship-to-ship exchange of gunfire, more so over long distances by aerial bombardment with aircraft. Not only were the aircraft required for offensive tasks, but those fleets that didn't benefit from defensive air cover paid a high price. The Japanese battleship *Yamato*, seen by many as the most powerful battleship ever built, was first turned back by light escort carrier aircraft and later sunk because it lacked its own air cover.

One of the most famous offensive raids carried out with carrier-based aircraft was the Doolittle Raid of 1942, this being the launch by the US Navy of medium bombers on a one-way mission to attack Tokyo. All aircraft were subsequently lost to fuel exhaustion after bombing their targets and the experiment was not repeated. It was clear that all forces needed more carriers, but carriers can't be built quickly, so the only option to meet the high demand for air cover was a rapid development of the aircraft in service.

The solution was to develop several different naval aircraft types, many highly successful in their designed role, but not easily adaptable to the multi-role operations the US Navy so acutely required. Having multiple types in production to meet multiple requirements isn't an efficient use of your production capabilities – something had to change going forward.

Post-war reviews of operations showed that the naval air battles of the Second World War had been a steep learning curve for the US Navy. It was clear early on that a priority was for a more 'multi-role' aircraft intended to carry out both the strike and fighter aspects of carrier operations. Therefore in early 1943, the decision was made to downsize the fleet of traditional Douglas SBDs and Grumman TBMs, replacing these aircraft with a new single-seat Bomber-Torpedo (BT) aircraft. With extra fighter cover, these multi-role strike aircraft could rid themselves of their own extra protection; the associated aircrew, guns armour and equipment could then be exchanged for extra fuel and ordnance. The Naval Bureau of Aeronautics (BuAer) advised that maximum role flexibility could be achieved by carrying weapon loads externally, and by using the most powerful developed engines at that time, it was expected that this new aircraft would carry twice the ordnance payload of the existing SBD and TBM fleet.

BELOW Douglas SBD Dauntless of Bombing Squadron 8 (VB-8) on the flightdeck of the aircraft carrier USS *Hornet* (CV-8) during the Battle of Midway, 4 June 1942. *(US Navy)*

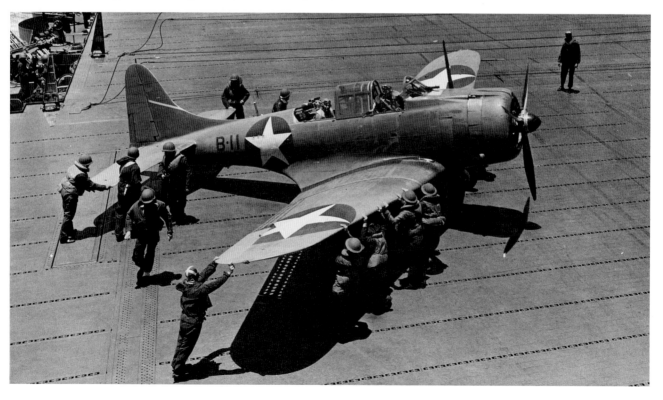

Acknowledgements

As with any book, there are always a number of individuals whose efforts behind the scenes contribute so greatly to the finished product. In particular this book would not have been possible if it wasn't for Tim Manna, the owner of the subject Skyraider aircraft G-RADR. Not only did he supply me with all the personal research into the aircraft that he has conducted over the years of ownership, but he entrusts me and my colleagues daily with the safekeeping and safe operation of this rare aircraft. It certainly is a great privilege to be awarded such a task and I will be forever grateful to him for giving me this opportunity. RADR's continued airworthiness is a team effort and my thanks go to Phil Evenden, Nick Dean, Andy Done, Mel Saggers, Dan McDonnell, Rob Turpin and Lillian Kentish for their efforts of many years that ensures RADR is in the condition it is today. Next, I must acknowledge the Chief Pilot of Kennet Aviation, the aviation legend that is John Beattie, for his notes and thoughts on operating the machine for the delights of the airshow community in the UK and Europe. Fellow European owner Christophe Brunelière has provided a terrific input on Skyraider ownership and the path required to become the pilot of such a machine today. Thanks are also due to engineer Caleb Carpenter for his thoughts on maintaining the two Skyraiders that he attends for a living. My great personal thanks are due to the veterans Mike Stanton, Cliff Johns, Dick Hall, Barry Rowland and Gary Schaffer for their accounts of military Skyraider operations in period. Thanks also to Robert Cornforth for supplying information about Douglas Aircraft manufacturing, along with his account about working there at the time of Skyraider production. During the research for this book an amazing contact was made with Jacques and Frédéric Borne, and so much is owed to them for supplying such fabulous stories and photos from the Skyraider operations in Chad and Gabon. Sincere thanks go to the photographers who willingly provided images for this book taken from their own personal archives over the years: Neil Hutchinson, Peter Arnold, Tony Clarke, Phil Glover, Lee Howard, Mark Peapell, Len Harvey, Jur van der Wees, Jelle Hieminga, Dai Ngo, Mike Freer, Clemens Vasters, Ben Hallert, Matt R. Kyle, Marc Le Beller, Ken Holston, Dries Embrechts and Chad W. Veich. Finally, my thanks have to go to Jonathan Falconer for persuading me to write this book in the first place and Mike Badrocke for his magnificent Skyraider cutaway that adorns the cover.

ABOVE Grumman TBM Avenger – together with the Dauntless formed the backbone of the US Navy's offensive aircraft in the Second World War. The Skyraider was designed to replace both of these aircraft in service. *(Phil Glover)*

Chapter One

The Skyraider story

The Douglas Skyraider was intended to be the answer to the US Navy's requirement for the ultimate multi-role aircraft. Delivered too late for the Second World War, its significance to aviation history came through its involvement in later conflicts in South East Asia and Africa, which ultimately saw the aircraft remain in active service well into the 1980s.

OPPOSITE Douglas AD-4N (NX2088G, BuNo 126935, foreground) and A-1 (N39147, BuNo 132683) Skyraider aircraft take off at Aviation Nation 2009, Nellis AFB, Nevada, on 14 November 2009. BuNo 126935 served with the US Navy before passing to the French Armée de l'Air and saw action in Chad in the 1970s, but was destroyed in a crash in 2011. BuNo 132683 served with the US Navy and South Vietnamese Air Force.
(Eugene Berman/Shutterstock.com)

The story around how the Skyraider came into being is as fantastic as the aeroplane itself turned out to be, if not a little exaggerated over time. Legend says that its designer, Edward Heinemann – the Chief Engineer of the Douglas Aircraft Company – sat in the Statler Hotel in Washington DC all night in June 1944 and created what turned out to be an iconic aircraft. That night certainly happened, but this was after some serious effort had occurred in the preceding weeks, along with two key members of his design team – Leo Devlin and Gene Root.

At the time, Douglas had produced the XSB2D-1 Destroyer, a further development of this, the XBTD-1, being a single-seat, gunnerless version, which gained a Navy order for 358 units. Heinemann didn't see the XBTD-1 being a long-term machine, most likely it would be superseded by competitor manufacturers. In the weeks leading up to the company's bid for the new Navy machine, Heinemann, Devlin and

EDWARD HEINEMANN – FATHER OF THE SKYRAIDER

Heinemann was born in Saginaw, Michigan, but moved to California as a boy and was raised in Los Angeles. A self-taught engineer, he joined Douglas Aircraft as a draughtsman in 1926, but was laid off within a year. After stints at International Aircraft, Moreland Aircraft and the first Northrop Corporation, Heinemann rejoined Douglas when it acquired Northrop. Rising to the title of Douglas's Chief Engineer in 1936, his attitude to aircraft design was simple – take the most powerful engine available and design the aircraft around it. During his long career at Douglas, Heinemann designed more than 20 combat aircraft, primarily for the US Navy, including many that became legends in aviation

history. He remained with the company until 1960, when he left to join Guidance Technology. In 1962 he joined General Dynamics as Corporate Vice President of Engineering overseeing the development of the F-16. He retired in 1973.

Heinemann's designs included the following: SBD Dauntless dive bomber, A-20 Havoc light bomber/attack aircraft, A-26 Invader light bomber/attack aircraft, A-1 Skyraider attack aircraft, A-3 Skywarrior bomber, A-4 Skyhawk light bomber, F3D Skyknight night fighter, F4D Skyray carrier-based fighter aircraft, Douglas Skystreak and Douglas Skyrocket research aircraft.

Edward Heinemann passed away on 26 November 1991 in Santa Fe, California.

Root began work on a new design to replace the XBTD-1, and therefore weren't totally unprepared when they met with BuAer officials. They recommended the XBTD-1 contract be cancelled and all funding applied to a new machine that they could present in 30 days' time. The surprise to the Douglas team was BuAer's acceptance of their proposal, but with a strict presentation time of 9.00am the next morning to unveil the ideas for the new machine – hence the famous late night hotel meeting!

The men made their 9.00am deadline, complete with blueprints for the new aircraft. By noon they had their answer. The BTD programme was cancelled with immediate effect and Douglas were to produce 25 pre-production examples of the new machine, coded XBT2D-1, and have the first in the air in 9 months.

A monumental effort was made by all at the Douglas plant and on 19 March 1945, almost 9 months to the day, the first XBT2D-1 lifted

ABOVE **A US Navy Douglas XSB2D-1 Destroyer on the flight line in 1943. Only two XSB2Ds were built plus 28 single seat versions, re-designated BTD-1.** *(US Navy – US Navy National Museum of Naval Aviation)*

LEFT The single-seat BTD-1. *(US Navy – US Navy National Museum of Aviation)*

ABOVE The Douglas XBT2D-1 Skyraider prototype in flight, with pilot LaVerne Brown at the controls. *(Douglas Aircraft Company)*

from the runway at El Segundo with Douglas test pilot LaVerne Brown at the controls. It was well known that corners had been cut to make the deadline – the landing gear was borrowed from a Vought Corsair, and only a very basic early-model Curtiss-Wright 3350 engine was

installed. This engine proved problematic, with the prototype's powerplant actually failing during a dive test on 19 April 1945, which saw the Skyraider become a glider until it made a successful landing at Mines Field. However, even with these changes, the performance met expectations, and the handling pleased those who flew the machine. A major advantage over its rivals was that it was much simpler in design and therefore quicker and cheaper to build and maintain than the competitor aircraft. After two

LEFT LaVerne Brown, Director of Flight Test at Douglas, had another career to that of airline and test pilot. Originally trained as a laywer, he switched to flying and became a commercial pilot with TWA. Spotted by a Paramount executive who was a passenger on LaVerne's DC-2, LaVerne became a Hollywood actor using the stage name John Trent. He was best known for the 'Tailspin Tommy' adventure movies in the 1930s, but he wasn't a natural and left the movie world in 1941 to take up a position with Douglas. He died of cancer in 1966 aged 59. *(Photograph courtesy of Neil Corbett, Test and Research Pilots, Flight Test Engineers)*

months of evaluation, the Navy was impressed and BuAer placed an order for 548 BT2D units.

Ultimately, though, it was just a matter of weeks before the end of the Second World War and therefore the contract order was quickly slashed to just 277 BT2D, with no prospect of further orders due to the belief of BuAer officials that the future lay with jet aircraft. It was therefore decreed that only the initial production run would be required. Regardless, manufacturing moved forward, and the first production model BT2D-1 flew to the Naval Air Test Center (NATC) for evaluation. Now with the new designation of 'Attack' aircraft, the BT was dropped for just 'A' and the AD-1 was born. This aligned with the new Douglas policy of naming new aircraft with the prefix of 'Sky', and so the Skyraider came into being.

Heinemann continued to modify the early Skyraider to improve its performance in Navy trials. An early study showed that for every 100lb reduction in weight, the take-off run was decreased by 8ft, the combat range increased by 22 miles and the rate of climb increased by 18ft per minute. By getting the design staff to reduce weight, but add strength, the first production AD-1 rolled off the production line more than 1,800lb lighter than the original XBT2D-1 prototype.

No fewer than 19 months of trials were carried out, resulting in some improvements to the undercarriage, centre section and the inclusion of an improved 3350 engine with water/methanol injection. Reports from the NATC pilots put the Skyraider as one of the best-handling machines they had tested, and the most superior dive-bombing platform ever used by the Navy. By the close of 1946 BuAer declared the aircraft ready for front-line service – Heinemann's gamble for Douglas had paid off over its competitors.

Bob Cornforth recalls life in the Douglas workshops:

I worked at Douglas from March 1952 until the summer of 1962, serving my apprenticeship at El Segundo as a Tool and Die Maker. Memories are sketchy now, but I do fondly recall the Skyraiders going down the production line. During my time we built them in several variations from the AD-2 to AD-7, and I remember very well one variant of the

AD-7 series that had accommodation inside the fuselage for several stretchers so it could be used as an aerial ambulance. The Skyraider had been in full production for several years before I was hired in, and most of my early work was naturally on that established type before I moved on to working on the F4D Skyray, and the A3D Skywarrior in the later part of the 1950s. I didn't actually work on the airfield main site, instead I was based just across the highway from what is now Los Angeles International Airport. My old plant is still there and can easily be seen in the satellite view of the area south of the modern LAX, with the tool and die room where I learned my trade located in the building next to the railway tracks. Northrop Grumman have taken over those buildings now. Over on the airfield site Douglas had a huge hangar and the planes were towed down a roadway behind the plant and across Imperial Highway to get there. It really was a massive building. We had a bus for a long time that ran outside from one end to the other; I sometimes drove a three-wheel gas scooter if I was taking a tool or test equipment to try on a plane.

ABOVE Skyraider AD-4 production line at El Segundo, 6 February 1951. At least four aircraft are AD-4W early warning aircraft (first, third, seventh and ninth aircraft), the rest being AD-4N models. *(US Navy)*

BELOW Douglas World Cruiser prototype c.1924. *(Public Domain)*

BOTTOM Douglas's famous DC-3 civil passenger liner. The military variant was one of the most versatile aircraft of the Second World War and in total over 10,700 DC-3s and C-47s were built between 1936 and 1950. *(Neil Hutchinson)*

The Douglas Aircraft Company was founded by Donald Wills Douglas Sr on 22 July 1921 in Santa Monica, California, following the dissolution of the Davis-Douglas Company. The company's initial claim to fame was the first circumnavigation of the world by air in 1924 carried out by the US Army Air Service under a programme called 'World Flight'. For the record attempt, Douglas developed an existing aircraft design previously used by the US Navy.

The modified aircraft, known as the Douglas World Cruiser (DWC), proved highly successful and following the completion of the World Flight project, the Army Air Service ordered six similar aircraft. This order established the Douglas Aircraft Company among the major aircraft companies of the world and led it to adopt the motto 'First Around the World – First the World Around'.

Douglas chose a logo that showed an aircraft circling a globe, replacing the original winged heart logo. Over the decades the logo evolved into an aircraft, a rocket and a globe. It was later adopted by the McDonnell Douglas Corporation, and then became the basis of the current logo of the Boeing Company after their 1997 merger.

The company retained its military market and expanded into amphibian aeroplanes in the mid-1920s, also moving its facilities to Clover Field at Santa Monica, California. The Santa Monica complex was so large the mail girls used roller skates to deliver the intracompany mail.

In the late 1920s the company initially built torpedo bombers for the US Navy, but it developed a number of different versions of these aircraft, including reconnaissance planes and airmail aircraft. Within 5 years, the company was building about 100 aircraft annually. Among the early employees at Douglas were Ed Heinemann, designer of the Skyraider, and Jack Northrop, who later founded the Northrop Corporation.

Of its civilian enterprises the company is most famous for the 'DC' ('Douglas Commercial') series of commercial aircraft, including what is often regarded as the most significant transport aircraft ever made: the Douglas DC-3. In 1934, Douglas produced a commercial twin-engine transport plane, the Douglas DC-2, followed by the famous DC-3 in 1936. In military terms Douglas Aircraft designed and built a wide variety of aircraft for the forces of many nationalities, but most notably for the United States services of Navy, Army Air Forces, Marine Corps, Air Force and Coast Guard.

After losing thousands of workers to military service, American manufacturers hired women for production positions, to the point where the typical aircraft plant's workforce was 40% female.

At the same time Douglas joined the BVD (Boeing–Vega–Douglas) consortium to produce the B-17 Flying Fortress. After the war, Douglas built another Boeing design under licence, the B-47 Stratojet turbojet-powered bomber, using a government-owned factory in Marietta, Georgia.

The Second World War had been a major boost for Douglas, the company ranking fifth among US corporations in the value of wartime production contracts. The company produced

almost 30,000 aircraft from 1942 to 1945, and its workforce swelled to 160,000. They produced a number of aircraft including the C-47 Skytrain, the DB-7 (known as the A-20, Havoc or Boston), the SBD Dauntless dive bomber and the A-26 Invader. By the end of the war, Douglas had facilities at Santa Monica, El Segundo, Long Beach and Torrance, California; Tulsa and Midwest City, Oklahoma; and Chicago, Illinois.

The wartime production boom was short-lived with Douglas Aircraft suffering cutbacks at the end of the war, due mainly to the end of government aircraft orders and a surplus of aircraft. It inevitably found it necessary to cut heavily into its workforce, letting nearly 100,000 workers go.

The United States Army Air Forces established 'Project RAND' (Research ANd Development) with the objective of looking into long-range planning of future weapons. In March 1946, the Douglas Aircraft Company was granted the contract to research on intercontinental warfare. Project RAND later became the RAND Corporation.

Douglas continued to develop new aircraft, including the successful four-engine Douglas DC-6 (1946) and its last propeller-driven commercial aircraft, the Douglas DC-7 (1953). At the same time the company had moved into jet propulsion, producing its first for the US Navy — the straight-winged F3D Skyknight in 1948 and then the more 'jet age'-style F4D Skyray in 1951. Douglas also made commercial jets, producing the Douglas DC-8 in 1958 to compete with the new Boeing 707.

The company was ready to enter the new missile business during the 1950s. Douglas moved from producing air-to-air rockets and missiles to entire missile systems under the 1956 Nike missile programme and became the main contractor for the Skybolt air-launched ballistic missile programme and the Thor ballistic missile programme. Douglas also earned contracts from NASA, notably for designing the S-IVB stage of the Saturn IB and Saturn V rockets.

In 1967, the company was struggling to expand production to meet demand for DC-8 and DC-9 airliners and the A-4 Skyhawk military attack aircraft. Quality and cash-flow problems and DC-10 development costs, combined with

shortages due to the Vietnam War, led Douglas to agree to a merger with the McDonnell Aircraft Corporation to form McDonnell Douglas. Douglas Aircraft Company continued as a wholly owned subsidiary of McDonnell Douglas, but its space and missiles division became part of a new subsidiary called the McDonnell Douglas Astronautics Company.

McDonnell Douglas later merged with its rival Boeing in 1997. Boeing combined the Douglas Aircraft Company with the Boeing Commercial Airplanes Division, ending more than 75 years of Douglas Aircraft Company history. Finally, the last Long Beach-built commercial aircraft, the Boeing 717 (third-generation version of the Douglas DC-9), rolled off the production line in May 2006. By 2011, the Boeing C-17 Globemaster III was the last aircraft to be assembled at the Long Beach facility; the final C-17 was built in late 2015.

BELOW Scandinavian Airlines at Bromma International Airport. The DC-7 was the last piston engine airliner produced by Douglas – but was already obsolete when it entered service. The British Comet jet airliner had already begun passenger flights the previous year, and soon Douglas developed the jet DC-8 and with it ended production of the DC-7. *(Scandinavian Airlines)*

BELOW The Boeing 717 – designed by McDonnell Douglas and derived from the DC-9. Production started after the merger with Boeing and it was the last passenger plane to be built by Douglas at the Long Beach plant in California. *(Public Domain)*

The El Segundo plant in Southern California began rolling out AD-1 Skyraiders from the production line at a rate of two aircraft per day in 1946. Just 11 years later Skyraider production ended with a total of 3,180 having been built. Popular as the aircraft had been, once the Korean War ended in 1953, the need for more machines was greatly reduced, hence the slow decline in production until it ceased altogether. As a result of the world becoming increasingly hostile in 1962, 5 years after production had moved on to other types, existing Skyraiders were redesignated A-1D–A-

1J and were later used by both the USAF and the Navy in the Vietnam War.

Such was the good feeling about the aircraft following the NATC test schedule that BuAer decided that some Skyraiders ought to be adapted for specialised roles. Of the original production order for the AD-1, the final 35 serials were modified for aerial countermeasures operations. In this role, an electronic countermeasures specialist was seated in the rear fuselage compartment, his job being to operate the radar search equipment for approaching forces and jam, using a chaff

dispenser, any transmissions the enemy made. The chaff dispenser and radar pods were underwing mounted, on the port and starboard wings respectively, a relatively easy modification considering the external mountings and hard points that featured so heavily in the design. Designated the AD-1Q, this special operations machine began joining the front-line squadrons in early 1948, at which time the Skyraider fully equipped six squadrons. It was met well by novice pilots as a carrier-based aircraft, these squadrons successfully completing their conversions to type including deck operations without serious incident. It rapidly became popular, the AD designation being quickly referred to affectionately as 'Able Dog'. The design nevertheless needed some refinements, as the repeated carrier landings highlighted that there were yet weaknesses in the undercarriage design and that the inner wing still required further strengthening.

These refinements were incorporated into the AD-2, along with a new canopy and the latest engine development, the R-3350-26W series giving a further 300hp output. BuAer immediately placed an order for 152 AD-2s, with the Navy purchasing an extra 21 AD-2Qs and a target tug version, the AD-2QU.

Delivery of the AD-2s began in mid-1948, and at the same time production began on the AD-3 which strengthened the airframe even further, as well as incorporating some gear improvements. By the close of 1949, 194 AD-3s had been delivered, but this time in three distinct variants. This order featured 15 new night fighter versions, the AD-3N, which allowed for a pilot a radar operator, plus a navigator in the rear cabin; 31 early warning versions – the AD-3W – which featured a modified upper fuselage to accommodate the equipment for the large belly radome; and 21 examples of the electronic countermeasure AD3-Qs.

ABOVE A US Marine Corps AD-2 Skyraider (BuNo 122224) of Marine Attack Squadron VMA-121 'Wolfraiders' in the early 1950s. *(USN/USMC)*

BELOW A US Navy Douglas AD-3W Skyraider being inspected by its crew at Naval Air Station Quonset Point, Rhode Island (USA), on 3 May 1951. The radome is clearly seen in this image. *(USN/USMC)*

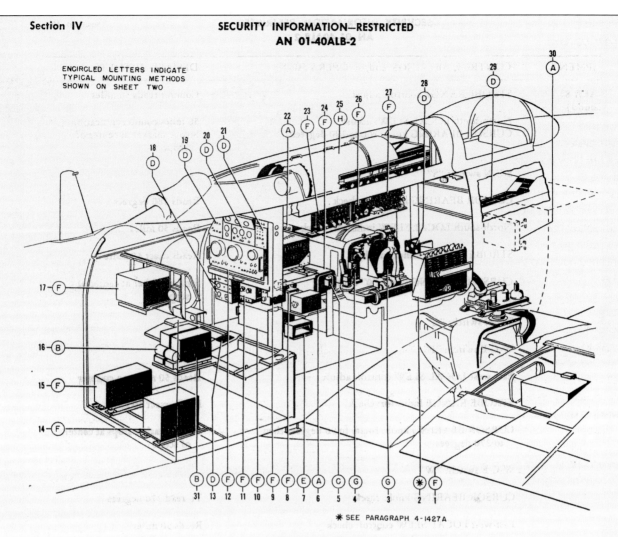

ENCIRCLED LETTERS INDICATE
TYPICAL MOUNTING METHODS
SHOWN ON SHEET TWO

✳ SEE PARAGRAPH 4-1427A

AD-3W Airplanes

Ref.	Name	Ref.	Name
1.	RT-18/ARC-1, transmitter-receiver	16.	R4A/ARR-2A, receiver
2.	TD-9/APS-20A, rectifier-timing central	17.	T-179/ART-26, relay transmitter
3.	T-120A/APS-20A, radar transmitter	18.	C-390/ARC-28, control panel
4.	R-142A/APS-20A, radar receiver		C-115/ARC-1, control panel
5.	HD-14/U, dehydrator (airplanes 122877-122897 incl.)		Control panel, 2267585 Douglas
	HD-59/APS-20A, dehydrator (airplanes 122898-122907 incl.)	19.	Master radar switch panel, 4253191 Douglas
6.	TF-107/APS-20A, variable autotransformer	20.	C-295/APS-20A, control meter box
7.	40E02, voltage regulator	21.	C-222/APX-13, control unit
8.	HD-27/U, air pump (airplanes 122877-122897 incl.)	22.	J-168/APS-20A, junction box
	HD-58/APS-20A, air pump (airplanes 122898-122907 incl.)	23.	SN-22A/APS-20A, synchronizer
9.	AM-40/AIC, interphone amplifier	24.	RT-18/ARC-1, transmitter-receiver
10.	RT-7A/APN-1, transmitter-receiver	25.	MD538/APS-20A, modulator
11.	RE-51/ARC-28, relay unit	26.	T-124A/APX-13, radar transmitter
12.	C-294/APS-20A, control indicator	27.	R-144A/APX-13, radar receiver
13.	Console assembly, 5265826 Douglas	28.	ID-131/APS-20A, pressure gauges
14.	RT-22A/APX-1, receiver-transmitter	29.	Pilot's control panel
15.	PP-268/ART-26, rectifier power unit	30.	C-219A/APS-20A, antenna control
		31.	R-23A/ARC-5, receiver

Figure 4-198 (Sheet 1 of 4 Sheets). Radio and Radar Equipment—Typical Installation
RESTRICTED

OPPOSITE The radio and radar layout in the
AD-3W *(US Navy)*

As soon as the AD-3 appeared, it was already
being superseded by the AD-4, built in N, W and
Q variants. This was to be the last of the Skyraider
orders placed by BuAer, the intention being to
equip 16 Navy and 2 Marine Attack squadrons
with the type by completion of deliveries in 1950.
That plan changed on 25 June 1950, when North
Korea invaded South Korea.

The Navy needed as many Skyraiders as
they could get into service, therefore production
continued non-stop throughout the conflict. By
the end of 1952, 1,051 AD-4s of all variants
had been built, including 165 AD-4Bs, a type
designed to carry four 20mm cannon and a
nuclear weapon, the first single-seat naval
aircraft to do so. By the close of hostilities in
July 1953, the Skyraider had more than proved
itself in combat and, as a result, BuAer not
only requested production to continue, but to
develop more variants.

The next type to emerge from the Douglas
drawing office was the AD-5, a wide body,
twin occupancy cockpit, multi-role machine.
Originally intended for anti-submarine warfare,

ABOVE AD-4B
Skyraider (BuNo
132325) of the Naval
Air Weapons Station
China Lake, California,
dropping a Mk 44
torpedo on 3 March
1959. *(USN/USMC)*

LEFT A VMA-331 AD-5
in flight. *(US Navy – US
Navy National Museum
of Naval Aviation)*

ABOVE In this superb study a US Navy AD-6 Skyraider (BuNo 134538) from Attack Squadron VA-105, 'Mad Dogs', carries out an air-to-air refuel of a North American FJ-3M Fury (the navalised F-86 Sabre) of Fighter Squadron VF-62, 'Boomerangs'. *(US Navy)*

ABOVE A US Navy AD-7 Skyraider (BuNo 142051) from Attack Squadron VA-95 'Skyknights' on the aircraft carrier USS *Ranger* (CVA-61). VA-95 was assigned to Carrier Air Group 9 (CVG-9) aboard the *Ranger* for a deployment to the Western Pacific from 6 February to 30 August 1960. 142051 was later in service with VA-115 'Arabs', CVW-11, and crashed into the Gulf of Tonkin after launching from USS *Kitty Hawk* (CVA-63) on 19 May 1966. The pilot was rescued. *(USN/USMC)*

LEFT An AD-6 and AD-5 in flight in the early 1960s, accentuating the great difference between the two series on what was essentially the same airframe. *(US Navy)*

the AD-5 was able to be modified to a 12-seat transport aircraft, air ambulance, cargo aircraft, or target tug. There were 212 day attack versions produced, plus a further 218 early warning and 239 night fighter versions, 54 of which were later modified to electronic countermeasure aircraft.

The AD-6 first flew in 1953 and soon began replacing the combat-weary AD-4s. Essentially, they were a copy of the refinements made on the AD-4B and 713 were built and delivered before the last model, the AD-7 (which was a more powerful and strengthened AD-6), came into being. The last AD-7 rolled off the El Segundo production line on 18 February 1957, and with it ended new-production Skyraiders.

Just to confuse matters more, when the tri-service designation system was adopted in September 1962, Skyraiders remaining in Navy service became A-1s in the following variants: AD-5 became the A-1E; AD-5W the EA-1E; AD-5Q the EA-1F; AD-5N the A-1G; AD-6 the A-1H; AD-7 the A-1J.

In action, the Skyraider was renowned for being able to take repeated hits and still fly on, mostly thanks to its incredible armour protection. However, with the jet age taking over, by the mid-1960s, Skyraiders were beginning to be replaced by the Douglas A-4 Skyhawk and Grumman A-6 intruder, the Navy's new primary attack aircraft. The Vietnam War, however, gave the Skyraider a new lease of life as America mobilised its military forces once more. Updating the design yet again for the new conflict, USAF Skyraiders were fitted with the Stanley Yankee extraction system, which rocket-launched the pilot from the cockpit, in a similar fashion to a conventional ejector seat system.

BELOW AD-5Q (EA-1F) Skyraiders of Tactical Electronic Warfare Squadron 33 (VAQ-33) on board USS *John F. Kennedy* in 1969. *(US Navy)*

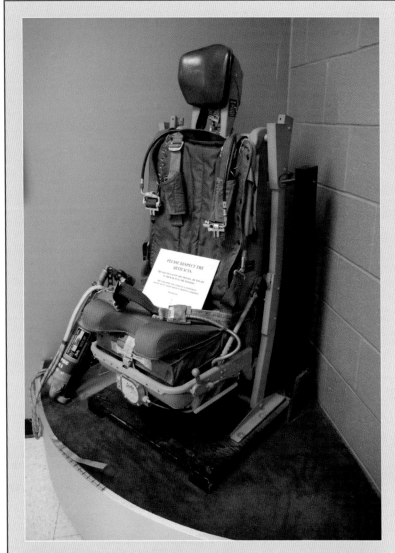

LEFT Stanley Yankee extraction system seat on display at the Wings over the Rockies Museum in Denver, Colorado. *(Ken Holston)*

THE STANLEY YANKEE EXTRACTION SYSTEM

Just as in the Second World War, the ability for the crew to exit the aircraft in an emergency was one that concerned both the designers and the aircrew alike. While conventional parachute systems were considered the normal method of escaping to safety, alternative methods were designed and implemented.

Perhaps one of the most bizarre systems designed was the Stanley Yankee system, essentially a primitive ejector seat arrangement, which was included as a modification to some Skyraiders that flew in Vietnam.

The system was activated following the jettisoning of the canopy, when a rocket would fire from the rear wall of the cockpit, pulling the pilot out of the aircraft by means of a pair of rope-like straps. The pilot's seat was designed to allow the seat back to rise up a set of rails and the lower pan was articulated to position the pilot as close to a vertical position as possible in order to allow the rocket to extract him. His parachute was rigged to an automatic opening system, therefore hopefully ensuring the safe extraction of the pilot and deployment of his parachute without human intervention. The system was designed to work at speeds of 30kts and above with the aircraft in a wings-level attitude. It was innovative enough to be considered for the Space Shuttle programme, but following testing it was rejected owing to weight and physical available space issues.

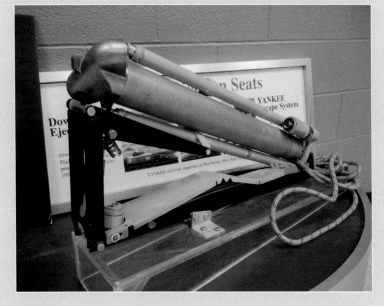

LEFT The Yankee rocket assembly mounted behind the armoured headrest. A complete system is installed in an actual section of A-1H 52-139788, which the USAF used as a training aircraft at Hurlburt Field, Florida. *(Ken Holton)*

Use by other air forces

South Vietnamese Air Force

At the time of the Vietnam conflict, the South Vietnamese Air Force (VNAF) was equipped with ageing F8F Bearcats, many of which were due for replacement. In September 1960, the US Navy started to transfer A-1 Skyraiders to replace the older aircraft, and by 1962, the VNAF had 22 Skyraiders, rising to 153 aircraft by 1968. In total 354 Skyraiders were transferred by the USA to the VNAF, peaking in 1965 with seven fully complemented squadrons. The experience requirement for VNAF trainees to convert to the Skyraider was between 800 and 1,200 hours on the Bearcat aircraft, with the successful candidates being trained by the US Navy in the United States.

Training the VNAF

The USAF training of VNAF pilots took place at Hurlburt Field, Florida (sometimes referred to as Eglin AFB, Aux 9), at the 4407th Combat Crew Training Squadron (CCTS). All the instructor cadre were combat veterans, many of whom had completed multiple tours of duty in South-east Asia. Gary Schaffer, who retired a captain after 7 years in the USAF remembers:

I was an instructor at Hurlburt Field from June 1971 until October 1972 when the nine remaining aircraft were flown to McClellan AFB, California, and the squadron was deactivated. At McClellan the aircraft were 'pickled' and transferred to a cargo ship for transfer to Vietnam.

The VNAF students I worked with did not begin their careers in the Vietnamese Armed Forces as pilots. Many of them were combat infantry veterans selected by their commanders for pilot training. Some of the students had basic flight training in Vietnam and others completed training at Sheppard AFB, TX. From my personal experience the VNAF students were dedicated and focused throughout the training. Their adherence to checklists and procedures was absolute. If the procedural steps were A-B-C-D & E, after being shown the first time, they repeated the steps exactly flight after flight. In contrast to USAF pilots and their 1-year

assignment, the VNAF pilots were going home to fly and fight for the duration of the war. Our goal as instructors was to give the VNAF students enough knowledge and experience to allow them to survive the first year of combat. If they made it through the first year, they would learn enough to survive and fly many thousands of missions. Many VNAF Skyraider pilots flew in excess of 5,000 close air support missions.

In the field, US Navy mechanics maintained the new Skyraiders and trained the ground crews with dedicated courses. Over time the responsibility of training the VNAF personnel transferred to the USAF. VNAF Skyraider pilots became some of the most experienced on type in the world – unlike the American pilots whose combat tour typically lasted 12 months; the VNAF crews flew thousands of hours and were particularly skilled with the aircraft. Slowly the older Skyraider airframes were withdrawn from VNAF service during the Vietnamisation period between 1968 and 1972, to be replaced by the remaining inventory of US aircraft as the USA ended its direct involvement with the war.

United Kingdom

The United Kingdom had also noticed the new machine being used by the US Navy and expressed an interest in acquiring a number. Its endurance and ability to carry heavy equipment

BELOW Surviving AEW.1 WT121 at the Fleet Air Arm Museum Reserve Collection, Yeovilton. Originally built as BuAr 124121, this aircraft flew with VC-11 and VC-12 before joining the Royal Navy in 1953. She last flew in September 1960 and came to Yeovilton as an underslung load beneath a Sea King. *(Phil Glover)*

suited it perfectly for early warning defence of the country during the Cold War. As such, the Royal Navy acquired 50 AD-4W early warning aircraft in 1951 through the Military Assistance Program. All 50 passed into the hands of 849 Naval Air Squadron, which with the type now designated as Skyraider AEW.1, provided four-plane detachments for the British carriers. Training on to the type was provided by 778 Naval Air Squadron at RNAS Culdrose.

The Skyraider in naval service saw a limited career – other than some seeing action in the Suez Crisis in 1956, by 1960 the Fairey Gannet AEW.3 began to replace the AEW.1 and all Skyraiders were retired by 1962. However, their equipment proved useful longer-term; the APS-20 radar units from the Skyraiders were removed and were later hung under RAF Avro Shackleton AEW.2s. These saw service through to their retirement in 1991.

Sweden

Obviously, when the UK retired their complement of 50 aircraft, they were looking to other countries to see if there was a market to pass them on, and they found a solution for this with Sweden. Fourteen ex-British AEW.1 Skyraiders were sold to Svensk Flygtjänst AB in 1962. Stripped of all equipment, these aircraft were used as target-towing aircraft and the type finally retired in 1976.

France

In 1959, France purchased 20 AD-4s, 5 AD-4NAs and 88 AD-4Ns representing 113 ex-US Navy Skyraiders. All the aircraft were

brought to AD-4NA status by SFERMA in Bordeaux. The first of these completed aircraft were taken on charge in February 1960 by the 20ᵉ Escadre based in Algeria to fight against the FLN (Front de Libération Nationale) in the Algerian War of Independence. The aircraft were used by the 20ᵉ Escadre de Chasse (EC 1/20 'Aures Nementcha', EC 2/20 'Ouarsenis' and EC 3/20 'Oranie') and EC 21 in the close air-support role, armed with rockets, bombs and napalm. They stayed until 1963, following the independence of Algeria.

Although the Algerian campaign was short, the aircraft proved itself well and although mostly having a quiet service life, they were heavily involved in the civil war in Chad, at first with the Armée de l'Air, and later with a nominally independent Chadian Air Force

staffed by French mercenaries. The aircraft also operated under the French flag in Djibouti and on the island of Madagascar. French crews frequently used the aft station to carry maintenance personnel, spare parts and supplies to forward bases. In Chad they even used the aft station for a 'bombardier' and his 'special stores' – empty beer bottles! These were considered as non-lethal weapons, thus not breaking the government-imposed rules of engagement during operations against Libyan-supported rebels in the late 1960s and early '70s. In 1975 six further aircraft were sent to fight in Chad, then on to clash with Libyan forces and following a demand by General Felix Maaloum, eight Skyraiders were transferred to the Gabon Air Force where a squadron was formed in 1976.

ABOVE SFERMA's apron at Bordeaux. After their transatlantic ferry flights, Skyraiders were modified at Bordeaux prior to joining the Armée de l'Air. Visible here are a mixture of AD-4s, some awaiting modification, and the silver aircraft that are complete and ready for delivery to the Escadrilles.
(Public Domain)

LEFT French SkyraiderAD4-NA F-AZHK seen at Duxford in July 2010. Originally built as BuNo 127002, she wears the markings worn with EC 01.020 of the Armée de l'Air in Algeria. She later served alongside 126922 in Gabon.
(Peter Arnold)

Chapter Two

Skyraider at war

Designed to fight the Japanese in the Pacific theatre during the Second World War, it was nearly another decade before the Skyraider finally saw combat. If the Korean War had not broken out in 1950, development would probably have ceased with the AD-4 version, but Skyraider production boomed and the remaining versions were designed and built. Production had already ceased by the time that war flared in Vietnam, but the Skyraider was still deemed the most suitable aircraft for the Navy and Air Force to take to war once again.

OPPOSITE A-1H Skyraider '579' of VA-25 on board USS *Midway* in 1965 armed with Mk 82 500lb GP freefall bombs underneath the wings (out of shot) and a centreline Mk 83 1,000lb GP bomb with 'daisy cutter' proximity fuse attached to its nose.

For an aircraft whose main design feature decades before was to carry more destructive firepower than any flying machine before it, the Skyraider became the only single-piston-engine, single-crew aircraft ever to carry a nuclear warhead. The Skyraider was a welcome sight to advancing ground forces and gave reassurance to downed crews in enemy territory that a rescue was imminent. However, the destruction the Skyraider could deliver should never be forgotten. The terrifying effect this had on those on the receiving end, together with the memories crews who delivered their payloads still keep with them today, should be foremost in our minds when we think of the Skyraider at war.

We are fortunate that the last airworthy Skyraider in the UK symbolises, possibly more than any other Skyraider, the story of the type in conflict. From its first 'blooding' in Korea, the Kennet Aviation Skyraider saw military missions, accidents and uprisings. Fighting in the Algerian War of Independence, and conflicts in Chad

and Gabon, had G-RADR flown in Vietnam it would have taken part in every major aerial conflict that involved the Skyraider. Today we live in different times, and G-RADR is fortunate to have only cameras shooting her and not guns. Some of her old crew have been traced and their stories, along with those of other veterans, follow here. Although these are just a mere snapshot of the roles the Skyraider undertook, it is hoped that G-RADR will symbolise the operational history of the type in the 20th century.

History of G-RADR

Although 126922 was one of 1,051 AD-4s built between 1948 and the end of 1951, little is known of her early months; however, we do know she rolled off the production line towards the end of 1948. Allocated initially to VA-728, which was originally a reserve attack squadron from NAS Glenview, Illinois, the squadron was prepared to be called up for active service in Korea when required. During 1952, VA-728 transferred to be based at NAS Moffett Field, California, and began to train up their crews for war. Departing via NAS Alameda, VA-728 boarded USS *Princeton* on 24 January 1953. On board, the reserve squadrons became redesignated as frontline units, VA-728 becoming VA-155.

From the archives we know that 922 flew somewhere in the region of 72 combat sorties during the Korean War, including close air-support of ground troops and anti-submarine patrols. As part of the great show of power on the last day of the war, 922 took to the skies to patrol as hostilities ended. With the pulling back of forces post-war, 922 was selected to be left at NAS Attsugi in Japan, but was force-landed in a rice paddy in bad weather en route. Recovered and transported to the Douglas factory for repair, upon completion of this, it was transferred to storage at NAS Litchfield Park, Arizona.

With the dispersal of the US inventory of Skyraiders to foreign forces, 922 was sold to the French Armée de l'Air in 1960 and was ferried to NAS Norfolk, Virginia, for collection. She left US service with just 1,214 flight hours

and made the long crossing of the Atlantic. Upon arrival in Bordeaux, 922 was modified for French service by SFERMA and was allocated SFERMA line No. 42. Its first deployment was to EAA 601, based at Châteaudun Air Base arriving on 25 October 1960, and over the next 15 years 922 went on to serve with 11 French units. Blood was seen again with 922 spending 3 years fighting in Algeria until 1963.

ABOVE G-RADR in early service, is second in line for launch on the USS *Princeton*.
(Mike Stanton)

LEFT Skyraiders under modification at SFERMA, Bordeaux.
(Public Domain)

LEFT 126922 with the Presidential Guard over Gabon *(Jacques Borne)*

Reaching the end of its useful service life, it was one of eight aircraft selected for transfer to the Armée de l'Air Gabonaise, taking on registration TR-KMO on 9 February 1976. The aircraft served in Gabon and with the GAP (Groupement Aérien Présidentiel) in Chad, and was damaged by colliding with trees during a low-level bombing mission, before being taken off charge in 1985 and ferried back to France. Overhauled by Aeroretro in 1985, 922 was sold to Amicale Jean-Baptiste Salis and following being registered F-AZED on 27 August 1986, the aircraft was repainted to depict an aircraft from VA-152. The Fighter Collection at Duxford acquired the aircraft at the end of 1991, and after being delivered there, the mighty machine made its debut at the North Weald Fighter Meet in 1992. Registered to the UK on 10 May 1993 as G-RAID, it went on to spend a decade on

LEFT 126922 pictured on the grass at Duxford in June 1992 when she was registered F-AZED. The Fighter Collection had just purchased 922 from the Amicale Jean-Baptiste Salis, and she remained on the French register until 1993. *(Tony Clarke)*

RIGHT The Fighter Collection repainted 922 as an aircraft of VA-176 flying off USS *Intrepid*, captured here at Duxford in July 2009. *(Peter Arnold)*

the TFC strength, its most notable moment in that time was its use as a cameraship for the making of the film *Pearl Harbor* in 2001. It transferred to Orion Enterprises in October 2003. It now appears painted as per its original colours worn in the Korean War, and carries the names of its pilots who flew it at this time.

Korean War

The Skyraider was produced too late to take part in the Second World War, however, it proved its lethal competency by becoming the backbone of United States Navy (USN) aircraft carrier and United States Marine Corps (USMC) strike sorties in the Korean War (1950–53). The first ADs went into action from USS *Valley Forge* with VA-55 on 3 July 1950 carrying out a planned strike against an airfield near the North Korean capital of Pyongyang. The 'Able-Dog' was chosen for this precision mission as its weapons load and 10-hour flying time far surpassed the military jets that were available at the time. As more AD units arrived on station to bolster the carrier task force, the type quickly began to earn a reputation as the best all-round attack aircraft in the combat zone. In daytime operations, ADs typically carried an 8,000lb mixed load of ordnance, which was four times greater than that carried by either the F4U-4 or the USAF's P/F-51D. ADs were the only planes capable of delivering 2,000lb bombs with dive-bomber precision against hard targets like mountain bridges and hydroelectric dams. By 1951 two AD-equipped Marine squadrons, VMA-121 and VMA-251, joined the battle from

land bases in Korea. To continue the war around the clock, night attack sorties were flown by AD-3N and -4N aircraft carrying bombs and flares, while ECM and radar-equipped ADs carried out radar-jamming and early-warning missions from carriers and land bases. On 2 May 1951, another USAF first was carried out when Skyraiders made the only aerial torpedo attack of the war, hitting the Hwacheon Dam, then controlled by North Korea.

The only documented Skyraider air victory of the war occurred on 16 June 1953, when an USMC AD-4 from VMC-1, piloted by Major George H. Linnemeier with CWO Vernon S. Kramer, shot down an antiquated Soviet-built Polikarpov Po-2 biplane.

BELOW War in Korea: AD-2 Skyraider 'Betty Lou' from VF-54 'Hell's Angels' embarked on USS *Essex* (CVA-9), pictured in January 1952.

ABOVE Mike Stanton (left), and Dan Daniels in Yokuska, Japan, 1953. *(Mike Stanton)*

RIGHT Mike Stanton in 2014. *(Tim Manna)*

BELOW G-RADR on board the USS *Princeton* during deployment in Korea. *(Mike Stanton)*

Mike Stanton – a pilot's experience

Checking my logbook, the first time I flew G-RADR, or as we knew it then – BuNo 126922 – was on 6th February 1953 during a Close Air Support (CAS) mission whilst I was attached to VA-728/155 aboard USS Princeton *(CV-37). Originally VA-728, which was re-designated VA-155 during the deployment, was based at NAS Moffett Field, California. Our squadron had 16 AD-4NAs and 24 pilots. We had six aircraft shot down by flak during our deployment, but we were lucky and recovered all the pilots. Each of us flew 48 missions before the ceasefire on 27th July, so BuNo 126922 saw lots of action. During those years, all fleet Navy airplanes were the standard glossy sea blue – in other words quite non-descript.*

Our airplanes wore the letter 'H' on their tails, as this was the designator for Carrier Air Group [CVG] 15, to which we belonged. VA-728 was originally a reserve attack squadron from NAS Glenview, Illinois, that had been called up for active service in Korea. On February 4th 1953, whilst aboard Princeton, *all four reserve squadrons in the air group were converted to regular Navy units, hence the change to VA-155. I reported to VA-728 at NAS Moffett Field for flying duty as an ensign in October 1952. We departed NAS Alameda, California, embarked on* Princeton *on 24th January 1953 and good old BuNo 126922 was aboard the vessel with us.*

We joined Task Force 77 in the Sea of Japan in February and began combat operations immediately. By the end of the deployment we had completed 1,152 missions as a squadron. That figure divided by our complement of 16 aeroplanes works out to be 72 missions per Skyraider. Each mission averaged three hours, so that means each AD-4 completed around 216 hours of combat time over Korea. Our missions were always around three hours in duration. The airplane could have flown longer sorties, but we had to cycle around the jet launch and recovery schedules. The F9F Panther jets could only stay airborne for 90 minutes because of fuel limitations. The deck crew would catapult the jets – armed with just one

250lb bomb apiece – off first, and then we would make our deck runs. After 90 minutes the carrier would recover the jet divisions and launch a new group. Right after the second group's return, they would recover the ADs and F4Us. That would give us three to three-and-a-half hours 'chock to chock'. Any other schedule would have badly clogged up the deck re-spotting time.

Our missions once in the Sea of Japan were three fold – strikes on specific targets such as railway bridges and factories; Close Air Support (CAS) for the Army; and terribly boring anti-submarine warfare (ASW) patrols. My logbook shows that our total mission split was 70 per cent CAS, 25 per cent pre-planned strikes and 5 per cent ASW. The Navy flew in support of the Army in the eastern half of Korea, while the Marines, also flying Skyraiders, supported their own troops in the western half of the country.

The ordnance we carried on these sorties varied depending on the mission requested by Army HQ. The North Koreans were dug into caves, so on many of our missions we had a 2,000lb bomb on the centre station and single 1,000lb on the wing stubs. These weapons effectively killed by concussion. On other occasions the tactical staff would ask for Napalm, and this was always carried on the centre station. We also carried five-inch high velocity airplane rockets from time to time, but the forward air controllers on the ground really liked the big bombs.

The Skyraiders took off without catapult assistance with all weapon loads except when performing an ASW mission, as we carried no external stores for these sorties. The folks running the flight deck were always concerned that Newton's Laws would come into play if the Skyraider was catapulted into the sky when carrying bombs – in other words the airplane leaving its weaponry behind when it was launched! Our deck roll was typically about 625 feet from brakes off to take-off.

We never loaded more than 4,500lb of ordnance onto the airplane. The gross weight for the AD-4NA was 17,400lb, so with bombs aboard we were up to 21,900lb. This was considered to be the optimum weight for the Skyraider when the limited deck run

on Princeton was taken into account. The only time I took off in an AD-4 that exceeded this weight was during training, when I flew an airplane with a gross weight of 25,000lb for the sole purpose of familiarising myself with the Skyraider's handling characteristics when heavily laden.

The ceasefire for the Korean conflict was high noon on 27 July 1953. We were informed of this the day before and the Air Wing thought that there wouldn't be a flight schedule established for the 27th. WRONG! The operations officer for Task Force 77 published a schedule to display a show of air power with all of our carriers in the Sea of Japan launching all of their available airplanes through to midday. These included BuNo 126922, which launched on the morning of the 27th although I don't know who had the honour of flying the airplane, but it wasn't me!

BELOW The USS *Princeton* (CV-37) photographed during the Korean War. One of 24 Essex Class aircraft carriers built during the Second World War, she was launched in July 1945. Serving throughout the Korean and Vietnam wars, she was finally sold for scrap in 1971. One of her last missions was to serve as the prime recovery ship for the Apollo 10 space mission, the penultimate space flight prior to the moon landings. *(Mike Stanton)*

During the Korean War, AD Skyraiders were flown only by the US Navy and US Marine Corps, and were normally painted in dark navy blue. Marine Corps Skyraiders suffered heavy losses when used in low-level close-support missions. A necessary part of ground troop support, in order to allow low-level operations to continue without unacceptable losses, a package of additional armour was fitted consisting of 0.25–0.5in (6.4–12.7mm) thick external aluminium armour plates fitted to the underside and sides of the aircraft's fuselage. The armour package weighed a total of 618lb (280kg) and thanks mainly to the enormous power generated by the 3350 engine these additions had little effect on either the performance or handling. This enormous power came at a sad cost on occasions. A total of 128 Navy and Marine AD Skyraiders were lost in the Korean War – 101 in combat and 27 to operational causes. Most operational losses were during training or when ADs that were 'waved-off' during carrier recovery operations would suffer a fatal torque roll into the sea or the deck of the aircraft carrier if the pilot mistakenly advanced the throttle too quickly. So mighty was the engine's torque, and so large was the propeller, that rapid changes in propeller rpm would overcome the effectiveness of the rudder and ailerons, resulting in a rapid departure from flight at low level. Although

holding a reputation for its ease of handling, the Skyraider commanded respect at all times.

Cliff Johns – Skyraider torque roll

In relating how the Skyraider could often kill its pilots during training due to torque roll, Cliff Johns underlines the need to train pilots to expect this situation, which claimed the lives of more AD pilots in Korea than combat.

As I turned left off the highway onto the base access road at NAS Cabanas Field, Texas, in July 1957 with my wife in the right seat, a student pilot, trying to recover from an overshoot on the approach, stalled and went into the field some 200 yards to our left. He crashed and burnt. My wife said 'And that is the plane you will be flying?' All I could reply was 'Yes, but I am not going to do that.' This was the first time I had seen an AD Skyraider.

I had come from the T-34 and T-28, the second all nosewheel aircraft class. Previous students had the SNJ [a US Navy military trainer] tailwheel experience, which helps when you climb into a big 2,700hp tail-dragger like the Spad [the A-1]. The torque was something to fear at first. Also, the visibility forward was not good until you got up some speed and were able to lift the tail off the runway. Once airborne it was a great bird.

Nothing could prepare you for the torque roll though, experienced in training at 8,000 feet on your first flight. Slow flight, feet on the deck, jam on full power – then you found out what a torque roll was all about. Once was enough for me – nothing like I'd ever experienced previously or since – except maybe a snap roll!

Not that my non-operational flying went smoothly. When I was in VA-115 in 1960 we were home at NAS Jax; I was flying a routine training mission, practice bombing with MK-76s, and upon returning my starboard main landing gear would not come down. I climbed out of my approach and called squadron common frequency for advice. I tried pulling Gs while lowering the handle, all to no avail. I ended up putting it down intentionally wheels-up on a foamed runway, taking the short field arresting gear. At the

RIGHT **Lt Cdr Cliff Johns USN deployed on USS Kitty Hawk, 1965-6 and USS Hancock 1966-7.** (Cliff Johns)

cut by the LSO [landing signal officer], I pulled the mixture to idle cut off and landed – trying to save the engine. The prop cut into the concrete and the belly started smoking as I slid to a halt. Upon egress I failed to disconnect my head set, hit the wing covered with oil, got jerked back a little, and slid some six feet or so off the wing onto my back. I still have many problems with my back today (only got 10% disability from our great VA), but didn't even think of getting grounded in those days. Ah, youth!

Turns out the mechanic had installed the wrong size hex nut on the telescoping rod and the oleo expanded in the wheel well when I raised the gear on take-off. It would have never come down no matter what. My wife had watched it live on TV!

Dick Hall – force-landing G-RADR in Japan

I will always remember the 1st September 1953 – the day I put my Skyraider down in the rice paddies in Japan. For some reason unknown to me the Navy didn't want us to return with aircraft on the carrier USS Princeton (CV-37), instead they wanted all the planes to be left in Japan and the carrier to return home empty. Our mission brief that day was for our squadron of 16 Skyraiders to depart to NAS Atsugi, however Aerology had told us there was a stationary front southwest of Japan but luck wasn't with us. Unfortunately the front began moving just about the time we launched and it was a wicked front. We could not maintain a 16-plane formation, so the skipper separated us into four divisions of four aircraft to be separated by altitude. He put four planes each at 16,000, 12,000, 8,000 and 4,000 feet, I was in the lowest division at 4,000 feet. It was no problem for the pilots in the upper three divisions to penetrate clouds because they were safely above the terrain, but at our level we had to maintain visual contact with the ground. The rain was so fierce and the clouds so thick and low that we were gradually forced down to about 300–400 feet. Staying in formation in all that teeming rain was almost impossible. We had been flying 4.5 hours on what was originally supposed to be

a 40-minute flight. Visibility was so bad that during a turn I had become separated from the rest of my formation. During that whole flight I had just missed two mid-air collisions and now flying on my own, I estimated I had at most 15 minutes of gas left.

It was as I was contemplating my situation that I spotted a group of buildings that had painted their roofs in bright yellow paint indicating that there was located an US Army Tank battalion. I called the other planes of my formation on the radio telling them that I was going to put my plane down and they should start climbing (we were all at about 300–500 feet at the time) and hopefully on the ground I could contact NAS Atsugi, and they could find them on radar and lead them to the field.

I knew they were all as low on gas as I was and that if I didn't do something quick we would all crash. The Skyraider is a strong brute, but so as to minimize the damage to the engine I shut it down straight away. I had my flaps down and put my hook down to hopefully give the ground guys a signal that I was about to touch down. The Skyraider carried a lot of momentum so I bounced on and on through the rice paddies. It felt like I was never going to stop.

The Japanese use human manure as fertilizer and store it in 'honey pots' scattered throughout the rice paddies. I destroyed dozens of honey pots. The plane itself suffered very little damage, the worst being

ABOVE Dick Hall reunited in 2014 at North Weald airfield with the Skyraider he crashed 51 years previously. *(Tim Manna)*

to the flaps which, of course, I had down for the landing. I recall that I could see what I thought was mud flying about me, but it must have been more fertilizer-based as the men on the ground were quite anxious to get me into a shower once I got inside! When I ditched my plane I found that although it was still an army base, the tank battalion was long gone. They were surprised to learn of the painting on the roofs, but helpfully realizing that I was about to ditch my plane they had called the field to alert them and were holding the line open for me to make my report.

Atsugi did locate the other planes and led them to the field where all four landed safely. Two planes had enough gas left to taxi to the flight line and park. One plane ran out of gas while taxiing in, and the other one ran out of gas immediately upon landing, before he could leave the runway – a close call.

I am fully convinced that through my ditching I was able to save four other planes and probably the lives of their pilots. However, about two years later the Accident Review Board, sitting in their 'shining castle' in Norfolk, VA, and without interviewing anyone, ruled that my ditching was 100% pilot error. I have been bitter about that now for all these years. Subsequently I was passed over for my promotion to commander and I am positive it was completely due to the ruling that my ditching was all my fault; for my entire career I continually had very high grades on all my fitness reports so there could be no other reason. Of course no-one could ever be proud of being passed over, but a further result is that it has caused me the loss of many thousands of dollars in both active duty and retirement pay. For that one action I am being punished for all of my life.

BELOW A fine study of AD-4NA, 126965, in Vietnam conflict markings, photographed in 2012.
(Clemens Vasters)

LEFT VA-115 in the Tonkin Gulf, Vietnam on board USS *Kitty Hawk* in 1965. Cliff Johns is standing third from right. *(Cliff Johns)*

BELOW USS *Kitty Hawk* showing ADs parked on the stern around 1965. *(Cliff Johns)*

Vietnam War

As American involvement in the Vietnam War began, the A-1 Skyraider was still the medium attack aircraft in many carrier Air Wings, although it was planned to be replaced by the A-6A Intruder as part of the general switch to jet aircraft. On 5 August 1964, from carriers USS *Constellation* and USS *Ticonderoga* stationed near Vietnam, A-1Hs attached to VA-52 and VA-145 participated in the first naval airstrikes against North Vietnamese patrol boats in the Tonkin Gulf. In the new conflict, at a time when many regarded prop-driven aircraft as throwbacks to a bygone era, the A-1s became affectionately known as 'Spads' and their pilots 'Spad-drivers'. Over the next 4 years, Navy A-1s flew hundreds of combat sorties over Vietnam in close air support of American troops, rescue combat air patrol (RESCAP), bombing of Viet Cong and North Vietnamese army targets and ECM as part of the ongoing naval task force stationed off the coast. Owing to their slower speed and excellent loiter time, A-1s were judged the best planes in South-east Asia for escorting troop-laden helicopters or for ground fire suppression in RESCAP operations.

RIGHT A-1E-5 52-135177 1st SOS, December 1970. This aircraft was part of Operation Tropic Moon, a research programme using low-light television in 1966. *(Gary Schaffer)*

Cliff Johns

VA-115 (The Ayrabs) were on Yankee Station aboard USS *Hancock* on 17 March 1967.

Six Skyraiders were assigned to interdict some Wiblicks (Waterborne Logistics Craft) resupplying the Viet Cong at night. They were divided into three sections of two planes each: the CO, Commander Hank Bailey and his wingman, Lieutenant, Junior Grade Gene Gaeden; Lieutenant Arnold Henderson and his wingman, Lieutenant Robert 'Brev' Moore; Lieutenant Commmander Clifford Johns and his wingman.

Henderson's aircraft was working along the coast just off a river mouth not far from a North Vietnamese army base when he was hit by 23mm anti-aircraft fire. Weather was rain showers, low overcast and it was night. His outboard fuel tank was on fire and control surfaces were damaged; he was forced to ditch.

The same ground fire hit Moore's plane and he lost electrical power. He attempted to stay on station and circle his leader holding a small flashlight with his teeth, but in a dark cockpit it was hopeless and he headed for the carrier with no way of finding it. Commander Bailey and his wingman headed for the downed plane and found the site just as a destroyer and its helicopter arrived there. Commander Bailey and

wingman Gene Gaeden came down through the overcast and broke out at 500ft with the helo right at their 12 o'clock. Bailey avoided the helo but Gene, in trying to avoid it, ran into Bailey's plane and cut it in half. The next thing Bailey knew he was in the water, then underwater. He evacuated the cockpit and clawed his way to the surface. Gene Gaeden was never found.

Commander Bailey inflated his survival vest, lit a flare, and got out his radio. Lieutenant Commander Cliff Johns, who had earlier been a VAW-12 pilot, came down to the scene at 500ft, in and out of the bottom of the overcast and found him. Relief Skyraiders under Commander Whitey Gooding, XO of VA-52, another former VAW-12 pilot, led a relief group of Skyraiders with more flares to drop. The destroyer's helo couldn't find any pilots, but two helos from the *Hancock* did as Cliff Johns led them to the locations. He did a wonderful job of finding and maintaining contact. They got Henderson first and eventually found Bailey. Brev Moore never found the *Hancock* and ditched out of gas. He was found in his raft the next day by a lookout on the USS *Ponchatoula*, a fleet oiler.

That's the occasion Cliff Johns got his Silver Star.

BELOW ADs are readied for launch from USS *Midway* in 1965. *(US Navy)*

During the war, US Navy Skyraiders shot down two North Vietnamese Air Force (NVAF) Mikoyan-Gurevich MiG-17 jet fighters: one on 20 June 1965, a victory shared by Lieutenant Clinton B. Johnson and Lieutenant, Junior Grade, Charles W. Hartman III of VA-25; and one on 9 October 1966 by Lieutenant, Junior Grade, William T. Patton of VA-176. Using their cannon, this was the first gun kill of Vietnam. While on his very first mission, US Navy pilot Lieutenant, Junior Grade, Dieter Dengler took damage to his A-1H over Vietnam on 1 February 1966, and crash-landed in Laos.

Cliff Johns again:

The Skyraider was mighty sturdy – I got hit four times over North Vietnam and was able to land back aboard ship each time. Once was a 57mm hit outboard of the wing fold area on the port side; the hole was big enough for me to stand up in but no control cables or hydraulic lines were hit. Lucky for me of course was that there is no fuel out there. Before attempting to land the aircraft I decided to practice slow flight handling and even with the huge hole in the wing, there was not one knot of difference in the stall speed! The ship wanted me to divert to Danang at first, but I insisted and brought it aboard without incident.

On the next deployment on the USS Hancock, 1966, I led the first two napalm raids in North Vietnam and I will never forget it. Our good guys were across the canal, which went due east; they were crouched behind the only brick building in the area, a church. The targets that day were barges (which the RA5C had found) in a canal covered with canvas and heavily defended. The VC [Viet Cong] had taken over a village across the canal and had our guys pinned down. Following the FAC's directions, I rolled in from 8,500 feet to the west and immediately took fire, but it was behind me.

ABOVE AD landing back on USS *Hancock*. (*Cliff Johns*)

BELOW A-1J 52-142076 of 1st SOS, Nakhon Phanom, Thailand, written off following combat damage and crash-landing, March 1972. (*Gary Schaffer*)

At 450kts I levelled out amid tracers and flak, down to 200 feet and released eight napalm bombs on the barges. I pulled up to the right and watched my wingman do the same, he took 32 bullet holes in his airplane but survived. The use of napalm was top secret at that time. We burned the barges, but my wingman was a rookie and didn't allow for our excess airspeed since we rolled in high. His last four napalms walked through a village to the north where the canal turned west. VC came running out, some burning, and I strafed them with my four 20mm cannon. I

killed a lot of people that day. I can't forget it. I did what I had to do and I was good at it. But it haunts me until this day. I regret and sweat this action. We egressed down on the deck at full power, jinking to the coast, but this day will never leave me and my thoughts return to my actions that day, every night. This is real and one of my dreams. This one makes me sweat.

Operations in Vietnam gave rise to probably one of the Skyraider's most famous roles: the 'Sandy' helicopter escort on combat rescues. USAF Major Bernard F. Fisher piloted an A-1E on a 10 March 1966 mission for which he was awarded the Medal of Honour for rescuing Major 'Jump' Myers at A Shau Special Forces Camp. USAF Colonel William A. Jones III piloted an A-1H on 1 September 1968 mission for which he too was awarded the Medal of Honour. In that mission, despite damage to his aircraft and suffering serious burns, he returned to his base and reported the position of a downed US airman.

Rescue of Falcon 84 – Gary Schaffer

On March 22, 1971 at about 1600 hours local time, while flying an F4-D Phantom on an escort mission for 2 RF4-Cs over North Vietnam, Falcon 84 was hit by hostile fire from Surface-to-Air missiles near Dong Hoi, North Vietnam. After avoiding at least one missile, another detonated above and slightly behind the aircraft. The rear portion of the airplane caught fire, and pieces of the tail were blown off. When the pilot realized the airplane was not recoverable, he successfully ejected himself and his back-seater. Because they were shot down so late in the day, it was not possible to effect a rescue until the next morning. The first Sandy flight arrived on scene shortly after the shoot down and advised the crew to sit tight for the night and be ready for a rescue attempt at sunrise. The crewmembers spent a long time on the ground. The North Vietnamese ground troops were near, so it made for a stressful and tense night.

The next morning at sunrise Sandy 1 & 2 arrived over the survivors. After confirming

RIGHT Gary Schaffer.
(Gary Schaffer)

BELOW Skyraider over Laos, 1971.
(Gary Schaffer)

both Falcon 84 pilots were safe and ready for the rescue attempt the two Sandy pilots started trolling for ground fire to determine the level of resistance in the immediate area of the survivors. The Sandys did find a small concentration of enemy troops about 4 miles to the west of the survivors. Sandy 1 directed a flight of F-4s on the target and eliminated the threat very quickly. There appeared to be no enemy troops near the survivors, although during the previous night the back-seater was stalked by a small squad of North Vietnamese regulars that passed within a few yards of him. With no imminent threat, Sandy 1 & 2 set about developing a plan for the ingress and egress of the Jolly Green rescue helicopter.

While Sandy 1 & 2 were working above the survivor, Alan Young and I (Sandy 3 & 4) took off from Da Nang AFB and rendezvoused with Jolly Green 70 & 72 just off shore near the Demilitarized Zone (DMZ). Our job was to escort and protect the helicopters during the mission. We headed north until we reached a point where we made a hard turn to the west and headed toward the survivors. Jolly 70 was to be the 'Low Bird' and make the actual pickup of the survivors. Jolly 72 was the 'High Bird' and was to remain clear of the area and at a safe altitude. Sandy 1 briefed us on his plan as we thundered toward the survivors at tree-top level. We stayed low to avoid

North Vietnamese AAA guns and Surface to Air Missiles (SAMs) known to be in the heavily fortified artillery emplacements at Bat Lake, just north of our ingress route. The low level over the thick jungle canopy also limited the time any enemy ground troops could have us in sight and take shots with small arms like the AK-47. As we neared the area, Sandy 1 launched a series of smoke rockets that marked the ingress route directly to the downed pilot. The downed pilot activated a coloured smoke signal which Jolly 70 saw immediately. As Jolly 70 went into a hover over the survivors, the four Sandy pilots formed the well-rehearsed 'daisy chain' around the survivors and Jolly Green 70. At tree-top level, we laid down cluster bombs and strafed with our 20mm cannon expecting at any moment we would face a withering assault of ground fire from the level nine gunners known to be in that area. The Jolly Green crew lowered a rescue device known as a jungle penetrator through the thick tree canopy toward the survivors. I clearly remembered seeing the pilot and then the back-seater clear the jungle canopy as they were reeled toward the safety of the Jolly Green helicopter. With both survivors safely inside the Jolly, we headed east to get 'feet wet' over the South China Sea as soon as possible. Crossing the coastline brought that extra margin of safety back to our mission and we began to relax and

BELOW A-1H 52-139608, 1st Special Operations Squadron. This photo was taken in Da Nang, South Vietnam, in January 1971. The aircraft has a Sandy Load and was standing search and rescue alert. *(Gary Schaffer)*

realize that we had flown into the jaws of a fire dragon that fortunately had been asleep. The 'North' was very stingy about giving back pilots that had been shot down and for us to get out of this mission unscathed was like sticking one's head into the jaws of a 24-foot crocodile and being able to talk about it later. This was a textbook search and rescue mission. It was planned, flown and executed in accordance with the best of existing procedures and techniques. As with any military plan, it is only good until the first shot is fired. Every effort was made to avoid enemy fire and with just enough luck on our side this mission had a happy ending. As we turned south and headed for Da Nang AFB, we each celebrated or gave thanks in our own way. I'm quite certain there was one North Vietnamese sampan fisherman that had to put on a clean pair of black pyjama pants after we passed his boat!

After November 1972, all A-1s in US service in South-east Asia were transferred to the South Vietnamese Air Force (VNAF) and their roles taken over by the subsonic LTV A-7 Corsair II. The Skyraider in Vietnam pioneered the concept of tough, survivable aircraft with long loiter times and large ordnance loads. The Skyraider suffered heavy losses in Vietnam, mostly from ground fire as only three were shot down in air-to-air combat; two of those by North Vietnamese MiG-17s.

RIGHT Gary Schaffer today. *(Gary Schaffer)*

ABOVE G-RADR banks over the English Channel and shows how effective the USN Korean Blue scheme against the Pacific would have been. *(Lee Howard)*

SKYRAIDER PAINT SCHEMES

From manufacture and throughout the Korean War, the Navy AD series Skyraiders were all painted in ANA 623 Glossy Sea Blue as standard. After the Korean War the colour scheme was changed to light gull grey (FS26440) and white (FS27875). The USAF initially used the same grey and white naval pattern, but by 1967 they began to paint their Skyraiders in a camouflaged pattern using two shades of green and one of tan.

In contrast to the Korean War, fought a decade earlier, the US Air Force used the much updated A-1 Skyraider series for the first time in Vietnam. As the Vietnam War progressed, USAF A-1s were painted in camouflage, while USN A-1 Skyraiders were grey/white in colour; again, in contrast to the Korean War, when A-1s were painted dark blue.

LEFT Skyraider Grey – a Skyraider of VA-115 on USS *Kitty Hawk* in 1966. The aircraft is armed with 6 M117 bombs for a mission over Vietnam. This plane went on to serve with 1st SOS, 56th SOW. It was shot down by flak at Ban Karai Pass, Quang Binh Province on 28 July 1970. The pilot bailed out and was rescued. *(Cliff Johns)*

RIGHT Skyraider early camouflage – an interesting study of another of VA-115's aircraft on USS *Kitty Hawk* in 1966. Hostilities in Southeast Asia saw the USAF revert to aircraft camouflage; the Navy tried it as well but decided against adopting. *(Cliff Johns)*

BELOW The widely known 'Sandy' camouflage scheme of the late 1960s is seen here on A1-H 'TT 517' of the 602nd SOS, 56th SOW, in South East Asia. *(G. Merrit)*

Algerian War of Independence

The Algerian War of Independence began to get hostile in 1954 when the Front de Libération Nationale (FLN) began a guerrilla war against France and sought diplomatic recognition at the UN to establish a sovereign Algerian state. It was, however, far deeper-rooted, with its origins back in the First World War, which were further stirred by broken promises from the French government following the Second World War. Although Algerian fighters operated in the countryside – particularly along the country's borders – the most serious fighting took place in and around Algiers, where FLN fighters launched a series of violent urban attacks that came to be known as the Battle of Algiers (1956–57). The French forces responded with a mass deployment of 500,000 troops who managed to regain control but only through harsh measures. Torture was rife on both sides, and so brutal were the hostilities over so many years that it sapped the political will of the French to continue the conflict. In 1959 Charles de Gaulle declared that the Algerians had the right to determine their own future, and effectively the French presence was as a peacekeeping force to oversee the transition of power. Originally fought using aged P-47 Thunderbolt aircraft, the arrival of the Skyraider in 1960 brought more modern technology to form the air defence of the country. Despite many terrorist acts by French Algerians opposed to independence and an attempted coup in France by elements of the French Army, an agreement was signed in 1962, with Algeria becoming fully independent by 1963. The independence also saw the withdrawal of the French fighting forces from the country.

Chad conflict

By January 1962, politician François Tombalbaye had banned all political parties except his own, the Chadian Progressive Party (PPT), and started immediately concentrating all power into his own hands. His treatment of opponents, real or imagined, was extremely harsh, filling the prisons with thousands of political prisoners. What was even worse was his constant discrimination against the central and northern regions of Chad, where the southern Chadian administrators came to be perceived as arrogant and incompetent.

This resentment at last exploded in a revolt on 1 November 1965, in the Guéra Prefecture, causing 500 deaths. The year after saw the birth in Sudan of the National Liberation Front of Chad (FROLINAT), created to militarily oust Tombalbaye and end southern dominance. It was the start of a bloody civil war. Tombalbaye then, to try to pacify the people, granted limited autonomy to northern Muslim leaders and released several political prisoners. These changes only added more leaders and rebels to the growing movement.

Tombalbaye resorted to calling in French troops; while moderately successful, they were not fully able to quell the insurgency. Tombalbaye eventually broke his partnership with the French and instead sought friendly ties with Libyan leader Muammar al-Qaddafi, taking away the rebels' principal source of supplies.

Chad had formed an air force in 1961 but all it consisted of was approximately 100 men, one DC-3 cargo aircraft, three light observation aircraft and two helicopters. By 1973, when its strength was increased to 200 men, the air force possessed three C-47 medium transport aircraft (increased to 13 in the mid-1970s), three light transport planes and one helicopter, all serviced at the local French air base in N'Djamena.

In 1976, the Chadian Air Force obtained

BELOW French Armée de l'Air Skyraider AD-4s flying from Djibouti.
(Armée de l'Air)

seven Douglas AD Skyraiders from France, which were used in anti-guerrilla campaigns in the north until 1985 when they were deemed inoperable. It was these Skyraiders that were flown by French mercenaries.

Jacques Borne – AD fighter pilot and mercenary

Jacques Borne was an engineer, air gunner, fighter pilot and instructor who fought with the French Armée de L'Air and as a mercenary with the Presidential Flight of Gabon and flew many missions in G-RADR. Awarded the Médaille Militaire and the War Cross with Bronze Star for Operation Koro, Jacques flew numerous types and accumulated over 1,000 combat hours on the Skyraider. He lives in Toulouse, France.

Jacques Borne was born on 28 May 1938 in Nîmes, France. Orphaned at the age of 7, he was brought up by his aunt and his uncle, a painter, which then gave Jacques his first job – painting number plates and advertising boards at the local Peugeot garage. At 19, he left this vocation to join the Air Force in order to become an engineer – a role he was advised was the best road to become a pilot – it was a long road and not straightforward. . . .Initially Jacques began repairing H-34 helicopters as a volunteer in Algeria, but he was soon asked by an officer to become a gunner on the H-34 and in 1960 was posted back to Algeria to go to war. After 2 years and 144 missions of gunner operations, having studied many engineering and flight manuals, Jacques applied to transfer to be a pilot. He passed all the tests, but the last step which he feared the most was the medical. Jacques was very tall and very much on the thin side – so much so that on the day of his medical, in order to balance his size and weight, Jacques drank 3 litres of water just before he went in! The subterfuge worked as he passed the medical with a profile of '1.1.1.1', that is to say, 'suitable for fighter pilot'!

Pilot training began in earnest in 1963 from Cognac in France, and progress was rapid through the training programme. As a sergeant he was keen, sometimes too keen; stories of getting lost at night in the training T-6, and pulling too hard on dive-bombing of practice targets abound. After time on the Fouga and T-33, Jacques got his fighter pilot wings in

ABOVE Jacques Borne. *(Jacques Borne)*

1965. Qualifying operationally on the Mystère IV, then F-84F, before moving on to the Mirage III, Jacques became a fighter pilot instructor on the T-33 – but not for long.

The opportunity of a trip overseas with a transfer to a new type arose. Jacques had been offered the chance to fly what pilots had nicknamed 'The Beast' – the Douglas AD-4N Skyraider. With 2,800hp, and a 4m-diameter propeller, rumour had it that it was not easy to keep on the runway for take-off and landing. Jacques' propeller experience was only on the T-6, and, determined to master it, he therefore set out to familiarise himself with the problem at the airbase at Tours, where he spent about 10 hours flying the Broussard.

This is how Jacques came to arrive in Madagascar in May 1973 for his training course on 'The Beast'. As he recalls:

The pilots had conditioned me so much on how to handle the throttle with extreme caution and because of this I began to appreciate more and more this particular aircraft. I carried out seven training flights totalling nearly 8 hours with 13 landings. Of these, five flights were carried out on Skyraider 54 and two flights on Skyraider 42. It turns out Skyraider 42 survives to this day as G-RADR in England.

In fact, I have always respected this

ABOVE Jacques
Borne in Skyraider
42, extant to this day
in the UK flying as
G-RADR.
(Jacques Borne)

*aircraft so much, the huge beast is so
impressive, the engine noisy and its handling
so special, for me it always has been the
best plane. I feel so lucky to have passed
my course and to have experienced my
thousand hours of flying in its exciting
company!*

In June 1973 Jacques was transferred to the
EALA 1/22 in N'Djamena, Chad, for a 2-year
stay and then quickly deployed to Faya-
Largeau, an oasis in the north of the country.
The missions consisted essentially of numerous
RAVs (reconnaissance) on the side of Bar-Dai
and Zouar. Faya airfield had the characteristic of
being very powdery, sometimes the planes sank
to their wheel hubs. Often the aircraft took off in
a tight formation to prevent the crew from being
hampered by the dust raised by the leader.
Jacques flew many missions one after the other,
although not without the occasional interesting
event, as he recalls:

*On February 26, 1974, I was patrol leader
for the take-off from N'Djamena on a routine
night flight. All was not right, however, as I
felt some sort of blockage in the controls.
The take-off continued but it seemed I
couldn't get full control of movement. I
tried and tried to rectify the situation, but
I couldn't. Checking my wings from the
cockpit with my torch, I could see the
familiar shape of the red control locks on
the ailerons! On our particular frequency, I
informed my number 2 who confirmed to me
the presence of the locks. I decided against*

*abandoning the aircraft and instead returned
to base. I informed the tower of a 'slight
technical incident' and returned to thankfully
make a perfectly normal but slightly messy
landing. Upon return to the apron area
under the bewildered eye of the mechanics,
I indicated to them to remove the control
locks so I could then take off again to rejoin
my team-mate waiting for me above the
aerodrome. The moral of the story: a good
pre-flight inspection and a good read of the
departure checks are not to be neglected!*

At the end of 1974, the unit participated in
Operation Koro, in Tibesti, against rebel forces
surrounded by Libyan mercenaries. The crews
have pictures of the objectives of the mission
which are dealt with using bombs, then rockets
and lastly cannon. The Skyraiders involved all
picked up holes of some sort, but Jacques'
major incident occurred flying Skyraider 42,
some months later:

*February 5, 1975: I am the leader of a patrol
to make a bombing assault in the north. I
have always enjoyed a cigarette and so, on
the low-level transit out from bombing the
target, I treat myself to a light up. Almost
straight away I have a big shock as a large
shudder passes through the aircraft. I quickly
change frequency to analyse the damage
with my wingman who indicates a large
impact on the leading edge of the left wing
with a tear of 60cm on the outer and another
of around 50cm on the inner wing. We climb
for height and I carry out a handling and
stall test. Everything seems well but I need
an extra 5 knots airspeed on normal speeds
to keep things comfortable. We decide to
land on a small open area of bushland near
a village to assess the aircraft. I have to
declare the incident as a birdstrike to my
superiors and as such the aircraft is visited
by the officials, photographed and reports
are made. The aircraft will be repaired, but
in the meantime, I travel to the local village
to purchase some chickens for the aircrew
mess dinner table and return to base. The
next day I am summoned to the boss's
office where there was an enormous piece
of wood and a few feathers on his desk. 'Are*

you sure it's a collision with a bird?' he asks. I had to come up with an answer quickly, 'My Commandant, I think that this bird was perched!' Luckily my humour was taken well and the repaired aircraft returned some time later to the unit.

Jacques quietly finishes his 2 years in Chad without further incident, but he is asked to carry out a third year, which is granted to him but with one change in circumstances. One of his friends, who had left Gabon the previous month, contacted him: 'I have a job for you, come join me.' Together they formed a squadron of the Gabonese Presidential Guard. It consisted of just three fighter pilots to fly six T-6s (from South Africa), a Navajo VIP and a Grumman seaplane! Later three Fouga jets join them as a gift from France! Of course, Jacques decided this was the life for him and much to the annoyance of his superiors, he decided to take retirement from the French Air Force. At the time he was 36 years old – and officially retired!

He arrived in the Presidential Guard aboard a C-130 of the Gabonese Air Force. The main mission of the Presidential Guard squadron, as the name suggests, was the security of the President and thus consisted essentially of reconnaissance flights along the borders. They worked closely with the Gabonese Air Force but also the squadron worked in close collaboration with all the Gabonese armed forces, policemen,

police, paras and also with the French Air Force on hand. Most of the flying was carried out in the faithful T-6 which allowed Jacques to hone his skills further.

Then at the end of 1975, good news arrived at the squadron: France gave Gabon four Skyraider AD-4s. The three pilots travelled to Châteaudun where they took delivery of the machines after a few test flights. Jacques recalls the trip back:

Then began an epic journey for 4 days from 9–13 February 1976. In total 28 hours flying from Châteaudun to Libreville through Istres, Agadir, Dakar, Ouagadougou, Lomé and Douala. We had borrowed a French pilot to fly the last Skyraider with us, but I chose Skyraider No. 126956 No. 45 to be my main machine and carried red colours. I also made acquaintance again with Skyraider 42 which I had damaged the year before, and which now carried blue colours. When we arrived in Libreville we carried out flypasts over the port, seaside and the Presidential apartments. Upon landing, we taxied in and folded our wings in front of everyone – they were amazed!

The Skyraiders would take part in the Renaissance and Independence Day parades, but only having three pilots, they could be seen landing the Fouga and jumping immediately into

BELOW Gabonese Skyraiders on the apron – G-RADR to the extreme right with its wings folded.
(Jacques Borne)

the Skyraiders to return over the troops at low altitude!

In June 1977, the Gaullist President sent two Skyraiders (19 and 42) to assist the Chadian forces fighting rebels in northern Chad. Jacques and his colleague René departed on 25 June for N'Djamena. The next day, they took another positioning flight to Faya-Largeau where they were joined by two more Skyraiders flown by French mercenaries paid for by the Chadians. The Skyraiders were armed with four bombs of 500lb, ten 5in rockets and 400 shells of 20mm per cannon.

The weaponry and mechanical support was provided by the Armée de l'Air, but there were still problems:

We quickly realised that when the mission was led by a contractual colleague, we were picking up too many holes in the planes. So we decided that René and I would be the leaders for all missions. The mercenaries flew too high and therefore made the whole flight more vulnerable. We felt that it was necessary to arrive at very low altitudes, of the order of 200ft (60m) and at maximum speed, that is to say, 240kts, with the loads we carried. We certainly put some spice in the missions! The only holes we had were on top of the aircraft; for my part I had two impacts in the canopy but nothing serious. This way we held the element of surprise, and it helped perfect the placement of my bombs. Often I flew through the hot fallout of my bomb burst, but I achieved good results and flying like this was much less risky than being shot.

But it did not work every time:

On 3 July René announced to me over the radio that his engine was failing, he had fluctuating oil pressure and a strong release of smoke in the cabin. We left the patrol to the other two planes and set course immediately for the airfield at Zouar, 20 minutes away. This airfield had only just been evacuated by the Chadian troops and therefore posed some considerable risk. René and I landed safely and I loaded him up in the rear radio compartment, leaving Skyraider 19 alone on the tarmac of Zouar. We flew back to Faya-Largeau, where following debriefing we created a plan to go back and get the Skyraider! So the next day, the group took off in three Skyraiders plus a Chadian Dakota which carried the mechanics, some spares and René, who was determined to bring his camera! While the mechanics worked, the three Skyraiders flew air support, ready to take out any opposition forces that entered the airport. It was soon discovered that the problem was in fact of an impact sustained on a rocker push rod tube. The mechanics repaired it using the sheet metal of a box of beer and copious amounts of wire. Filling the tank full of oil, we returned to Faya with five planes, happy to have recovered our good old 19 when we believed it almost impossible!

Three days later, the four Skyraiders would return to Zouar but this time would destroy this land and anything that could fall into the hands of the rebels. At the end of the intervention in Chad, the two Presidential Guard aircraft had dropped 64,500lb of bombs, fired 480 rockets and 24,000 20mm shells. Jacques and René considered the return to Libreville quite a rest after their deployment. First, though, Skyraider 42 would throw Jacques another challenge on the return by consuming 130 litres of oil out of the 140 that the tank could hold! It was to be expected, however, as Skyraider 42 was known to be greedy, regularly using 26 litres an hour.

On 20 February 1978, Jacques was called by the President, who asked him to return to Chad with two pilots to help the mercenaries again. The aircraft would be provided on site by

BELOW Jacques Borne sitting aside Skyraider 42 in Chad; note the empty bomb racks indicating a recent return from a mission.
(Jacques Borne)

the Chadians. Jacques and René went, but they only carried out two missions, returning on 10 March. The Presidential Guard was expanded further in July 1978, when France gave the Gabonese four additional Skyraiders, and one of these gave Jacques his next surprise.

On 1 February 1980, I was the patrol leader of four Skyraiders, this time flying No. 68. Taking off, all was well, so I retracted the undercarriage but then noticed the oil particle lamp had illuminated. Suddenly, passing around 500ft, the engine decided to stop! I announced 'engine failure', and decided to turn back to land on the runway in the opposite direction. I called again to clear the runway quickly – my numbers 2 and 3 had taken off, but upon turning back I found I was facing the number 4 which was accelerating in its take-off roll. I lowered the landing gear as the number 4 took off and immediately turned to the right. The runway was clear, the engine had stopped, but I secured a safe landing. Had the emergency occurred 30 seconds later, I would have not have made it back to the runway and I would have been faced with ditching at sea. To this day I have retained the piece of the connecting rod that caused the failure.

This wasn't to be the last time the Skyraider would create some excitement for Jacques:

On 17 March 1981, I was the leader of a patrol of four Skyraiders carrying out a flypast at low altitude above the squadron. The number four in the box – that is, in the position directly behind me – made contact with my rudder, his propeller shredding the majority of it. I instinctively put on full throttle, but with the loss of rudder control I rolled towards my wingman who thankfully managed to avoid me. I got the Skyraider back on the runway, but burst a tyre on the rollout as I lost some control. I was more scared than hurt from the experience, but metal damage is just metal and not a human life so it ended happily.

Not long afterwards came heartbreak for Jacques: the end of the Skyraiders! The problems of maintenance, parts acquisition and the price of fuel saw the end of the service life of 'The Beast'! On 3 November 1982, Jacques made his last flight in his good old No. 45, but happily it wasn't the last time he was to see the plane! It is preserved to this day at the National Museum of Naval Aviation, Pensacola, Florida.

Chapter Three

Anatomy of the Skyraider

The first thing most people are surprised by when they encounter the Skyraider is its size: for a single-engine, single-seat aircraft it really is huge. However, the robustness of the airframe is immediately apparent and the level of thought that went into its design made it a most excellent platform for multi-role carrier operations.

OPPOSITE Combined oil temperature and oil and fuel pressure gauge on G-RADR. The all-important cylinder head temperature is close by. *(Author)*

Structurally, the Skyraider was fairly typical of the time, with pretty much all parts interchangeable from one aircraft to another. Unlike most other single-engine aircraft of American design, however, it was not possible to separate the centre section from the fuselage, which today in particular, rules out the ability to road transfer the aircraft at all. It must be remembered that, all in all, this is a carrier-borne aircraft, and it needs to survive months at sea in all weathers. Reliability in these conditions was key and, as with other aircraft of the period, mechanical linkages and redundancy takes precedence over electronic control reliance.

Obviously with fuel prices being one of the most significant costs of operating a Skyraider, many flying examples are stripped of most of their unnecessary equipment to reduce weight and therefore fuel burn. Equally in the UK, we don't use full combat power or the autopilot system, so these standard items have been removed from the aircraft. This chapter gives a general overview of the various standard systems as found in the Skyraider, although to fully describe them all in depth would run to many thousands of pages!

Airframe

Fuselage

The fuselage is of all-metal semi-monocoque construction consisting of stressed skins, longitudinal engine upper mount stiffeners, engine lower mount stiffeners, lower longitudinal stiffeners, vertical stiffeners, frames, bulkheads and interior structure. The two engine upper mount stiffeners, the two engine lower mount stiffeners and the two lower longitudinal stiffeners are the main structural components of the fuselage. Frames, stiffeners and bulkheads strengthen the fuselage and take loads from the wing, spars and arresting hook. The tailwheel retracts forwards into a well and the arresting hook folds against the fuselage aft of the wheel well.

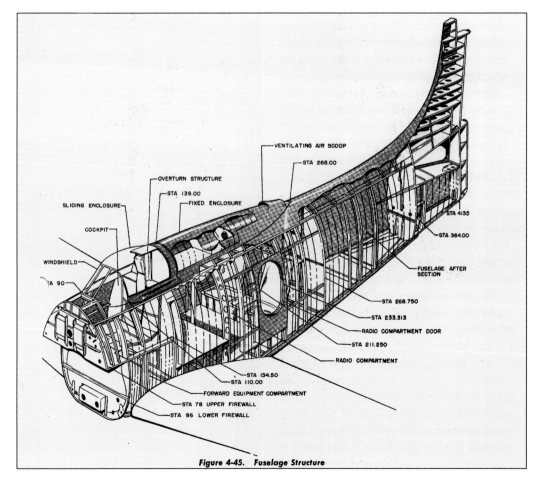

Figure 4-45. Fuselage Structure

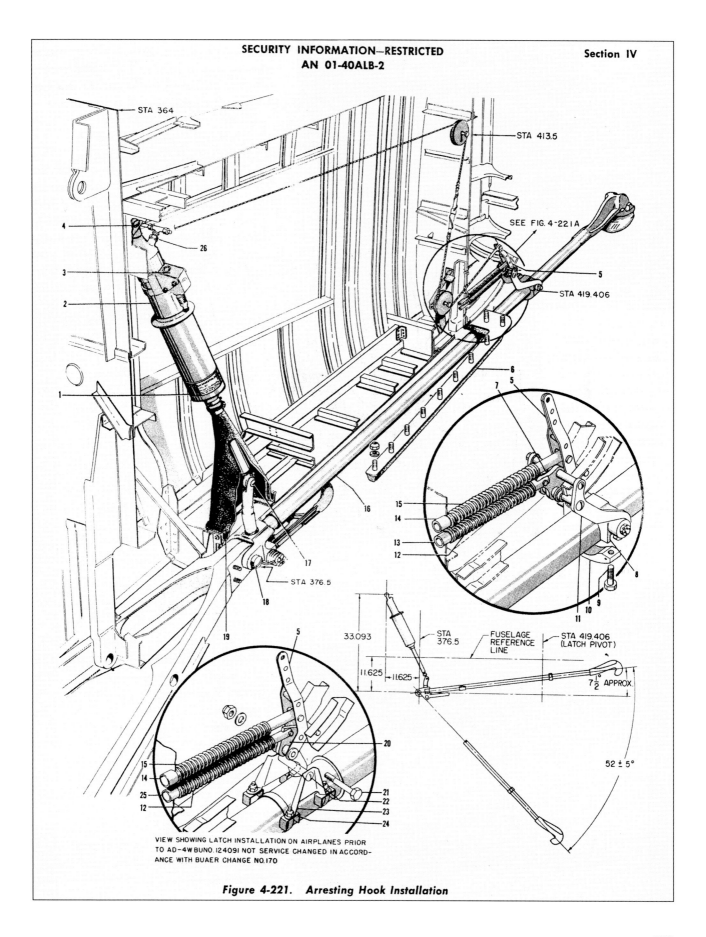

STA 364

STA 413.5

SEE FIG. 4-221A

STA 419.406

STA 376.5

STA 413.5

33.093

STA
376.5

FUSELAGE
REFERENCE
LINE

STA 419.406
(LATCH PIVOT)

11.625

11.625

7½° APPROX.

52 ± 5°

VIEW SHOWING LATCH INSTALLATION ON AIRPLANES PRIOR
TO AD-4W BUNO.124091 NOT SERVICE CHANGED IN ACCORD-
ANCE WITH BUAER CHANGE NO.170

Figure 4-221.   Arresting Hook Installation

Douglas A-1 Skyraider.

(Mike Badrocke)

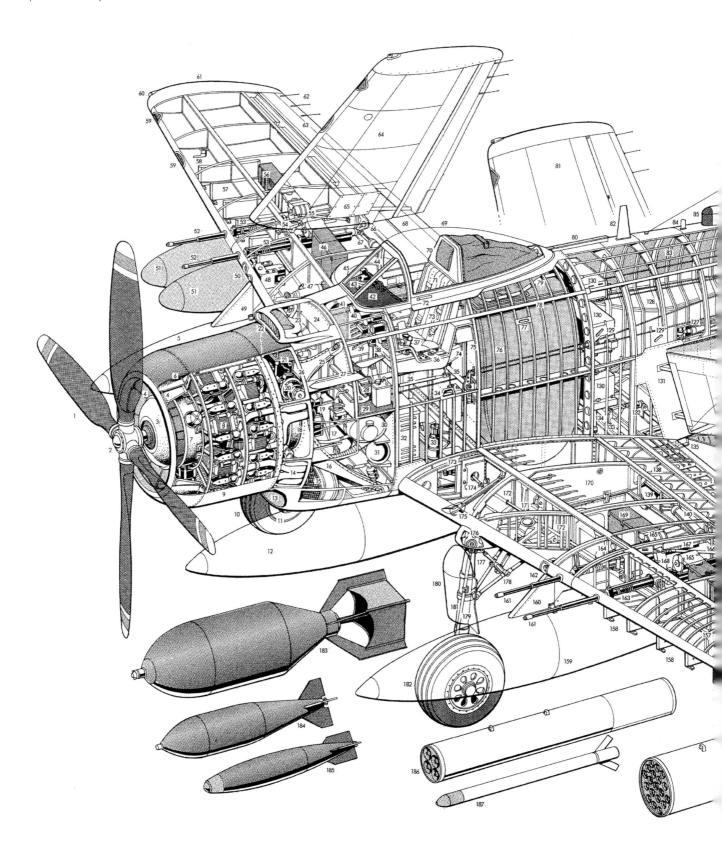

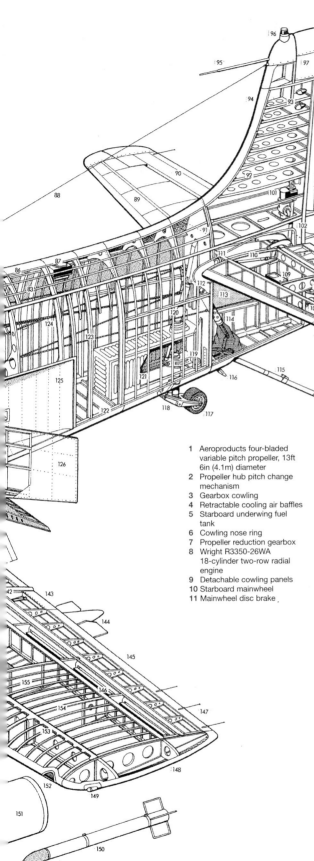

1 Aeroproducts four-bladed variable pitch propeller, 13ft 6in (4.1m) diameter
2 Propeller hub pitch change mechanism
3 Gearbox cowling
4 Retractable cooling air baffles
5 Starboard underwing fuel tank
6 Cowling nose ring
7 Propeller reduction gearbox
8 Wright R3350-26WA 18-cylinder two-row radial engine
9 Detachable cowling panels
10 Starboard mainwheel
11 Mainwheel disc brake

12 Centreline auxiliary fuel tank, capacity 300 US gal (1,136 litres)
13 Oil cooler intake
14 Exhaust stubs
15 Oil cooler
16 Engine bearer lower segment
17 Oil tank, capacity 38.5 US gal (146 litres)
18 Engine mounting ring
19 Engine accessory equipment
20 Port magneto
21 Carburettor
22 Carburettor air intake
23 Cockpit air ducting
24 Armoured front bulkhead
25 Engine bearer upper segment
26 Cowling air exit flaps
27 Exhaust shields
28 Rudder pedals
29 Cockpit floor level
30 Hydraulic reservoir
31 Oxygen bottle
32 Electrical system distribution box
33 Autopilot controller
34 Boarding step
35 Control linkages
36 Port side console panel
37 Engine throttle and propeller control levers
38 Control column
39 Circuit breaker panel
40 Instrument panel
41 Windscreen de-misting air duct
42 Instrument panel shroud
43 Reflector gunsight
44 Armoured glass windscreen
45 Starboard mainwheel, retracted position
46 Ammunition tank, 200 rounds
47 Main undercarriage retraction jack
48 Gun camera
49 Starboard inboard pylon
50 Approach light

51 BLU-11B 500lb (227kg) napalm tanks
52 Cannon barrels
53 M3 20mm cannon
54 Front spar hinge joint
55 Ammunition feed drums
56 Outboard ammunition tank, 200 rounds
57 Starboard outer underwing pylons (six)
58 Ventral pitot tube
59 Radar warning antennae
60 Starboard navigation light
61 Wing tip fairing
62 Static dischargers
63 Starboard aileron
64 Starboard wing, folded position
65 Cannon bay access panels
66 Rear spar hinge joint
67 Wing fold hydraulic jack
68 Starboard Fowler-type flap
69 Sliding cockpit canopy cover
70 Armoured headrest
71 Pilot's seat
72 Canopy external handle
73 Safety harness
74 Adjustable seat mountings
75 Armoured cockpit rear bulkhead
76 Main fuel tank; internal fuel capacity 378 US gal (1,431 litres)
77 Handgrip
78 Fuselage top longeron
79 Fuel vent pipe
80 Sliding canopy rail
81 Port wing, folded position
82 VHF aerial
83 Dorsal section frame and stringer construction
84 IFF aerial
85 ADF antenna
86 Fuselage dorsal skin panelling
87 Remote compass transmitter
88 HF aerial
89 Starboard variable incidence tailplane
90 Starboard elevator
91 Tailplane/fuselage joint frame
92 Tailfin construction, offset 3 deg to port
93 Tail navigation and formation lights
94 Fin leading edge
95 Static head
96 Anti-collision light
97 Rudder horn balance
98 Static dischargers
99 Rudder tabs
100 Rudder construction
101 Tailplane incidence control jack
102 Sternpost
103 Fixed elevator tab
104 Port elevator construction
105 Elevator horn balance
106 Port tailplane construction
107 Rudder tab jack
108 Rudder hinge control
109 Radar altimeter transmitter/receiver
110 Elevator control rod
111 Variable incidence tailplane pivot fixing
112 Tailplane sealing plate
113 Starboard side access panel
114 Arrestor hook jack/damper
115 Deck arresting hook, down position
116 Catapult hold back link
117 Tailwheel solid tyre
118 Castoring tailwheel forks
119 Tailwheel pivot fixing
120 Hydraulic retraction jack
121 Tailwheel housing
122 Rear fuselage box section lower longeron

123 Fuselage side panel frame construction
124 Tail control cables
125 Airbrake housing
126 Port lateral airbrake, open
127 Airbrake hydraulic actuators
128 Starboard lateral airbrake housing
129 Handgrips
130 Radio and electronics equipment racks
131 Airbrake reinforced hinge panel
132 Central flap hydraulic jack
133 Flap torque shaft
134 Battery
135 Boarding step
136 Ventral airbrake, open
137 Port Fowler-type flap construction
138 Flap shroud ribs
139 Flap external hinge
140 Wing fold hydraulic jack
141 Rear spar hinge joint
142 Trailing edge fence
143 Aileron tab
144 Auxiliary fuel tank tail fins
145 Port aileron construction
146 Aileron balance weights
147 Static dischargers
148 Wing tip fairing
149 Port navigation light
150 5in (12.7cm) HVAR air-to-ground rocket
151 Rocket pack, 19 x 2.75in (6.99cm) folding fin rockets
152 Radar warning antenna
153 Main spar
154 Port wing rib construction
155 Inter-rib stiffeners
156 Outboard ammunition tank, 200 rounds
157 Leading edge rib construction
158 Port outboard wing pylons (six)
159 Auxiliary fuel tank, capacity 300 US gal (1,136 litres)
160 Inboard pylon
161 Cannon barrels
162 Approach light
163 Recoil spring
164 Front spar hinge joint
165 Ammunition feed drums
166 Aileron control rod
167 M3 20mm cannon
168 Cartridge case ejector chute
169 Inboard ammunition tank, 200 rounds
170 Main undercarriage wheel bay
171 Hydraulic retraction jack
172 Main undercarriage mounting diagonal ribs
173 Wing spar/fuselage attachment joint
174 Aileron push-pull control rod
175 Catapult strop attachment link
176 Main undercarriage pivot fixing
177 Retraction linkage
178 Folding rear struts
179 Main undercarriage leg strut
180 Leg strut fairing
181 Wheel rotation push-rod, wheel rotated 90 deg to lie flat in wing bay
182 Port mainwheel
183 AN-M66A2 2,000lb (907kg) HE bomb
184 Mk 82 500lb (227kg) bomb
185 Mk 81 250lb (113.5kg) low drag bomb
186 SUU-11A rocket launcher, 4 x 5in (12.7cm) folding fin rockets
187 5in (12.7cm) folding fin air-to-ground rocket

ABOVE The position
of the cockpit relative
to the wings is clearly
seen here and it is
this combination of
forward positioning
and height that gives
the pilot an excellent
field of view while on
the ground. Note the
area forward of the
firewall that is covered
by the main and
accessory cowlings.
(Author)

The fuselage itself is divided into several compartments, these being a cockpit, forward equipment bay, a fuel tank bay and a radio – or rear fuselage bay depending on the variant of Skyraider in question.

The cockpit is located in the upper part of the fuselage, immediately aft of the firewall. It contains all of the instruments and controls necessary for flight, is adequately insulated and is sealed to protect the crew from carbon monoxide. A section of the cockpit floor is attached to the fuselage structure with screws and can be easily removed for access to equipment in the upper part of the forward equipment bay. The windshield is mounted in front of the cockpit and consists of a flak-resistant laminated plate glass centre panel and two laminated plate glass side panels mounted on a sheet metal supporting structure. These three panels can be removed individually for replacement should the need arise. Although not used on G-RADR, a rain-repellent compound can be flowed on to the forward windscreen for flights in rain conditions and is stored as part of a 'rain repellent kit' that would accompany the aircraft on deployments. Access

to the rear of the instrument panel is only via removing the glare shield immediately under the windscreen and directly above the instrument panel. The cockpit enclosure is finished with a sliding formed acrylic plastic 'bubble' canopy mounted in an aluminium frame. The enclosure frame is attached to two forward roller trucks which fasten to two tracks either side of the cockpit, and the rear of the enclosure rides on a roller which in turn rides on a single track aft of the enclosure. The enclosure operating mechanism consists of a cable-controlled hydraulic actuating cylinder which is attached to the enclosure. The cables are operated by handles inside and outside attached to a common shaft that extends through the port side of the fuselage just below the cockpit rail. The enclosure control handle operates a cable and pulley system which, in turn, actuates a hydraulic valve and cylinder to open and close the canopy. Part of the canopy operating system is the overturn structure. This comprises the cockpit rear armour plate and a steel strut which extends from the armour plate aft along the fuel cell compartment cover. As well as adding strength to the overturn structure, the

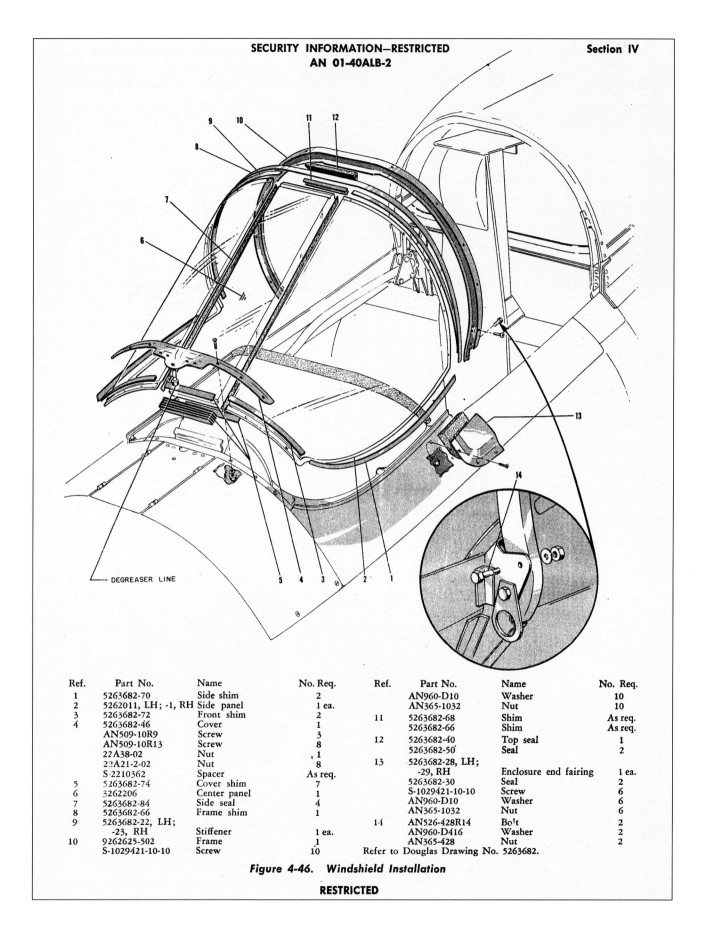

DEGREASER LINE

Ref.	Part No.	Name	No. Req.		Ref.	Part No.	Name	No. Req.
1	5263682-70	Side shim	2			AN960-D10	Washer	10
2	5262011, LH; -1, RH	Side panel	1 ea.			AN365-1032	Nut	10
3	5263682-72	Front shim	2		11	5263682-68	Shim	As req.
4	5263682-46	Cover	1			5263682-66	Shim	As req.
	AN509-10R9	Screw	3		12	5263682-40	Top seal	1
	AN509-10R13	Screw	8			5263682-50	Seal	2
	22A38-02	Nut	1		13	5263682-28, LH;		
	22A21-2-02	Nut	8			-29, RH	Enclosure end fairing	1 ea.
	S-2210362	Spacer	As req.			5263682-30	Seal	2
5	5263682-74	Cover shim	7			S-1029421-10-10	Screw	6
6	3262206	Center panel	1			AN960-D10	Washer	6
7	5263682-84	Side seal	4			AN365-1032	Nut	6
8	5263682-66	Frame shim	1		14	AN526-428R14	Bolt	2
9	5263682-22, LH;					AN960-D416	Washer	2
	-23, RH	Stiffener	1 ea.			AN365-428	Nut	2
10	9262625-502	Frame	1		Refer to Douglas Drawing No. 5263682.			
	S-1029421-10-10	Screw	10					

Figure 4-46.   Windshield Installation

RESTRICTED

LEFT External canopy enclosure control on the port side of the fuselage. The white strip guides the crew's foot to the external footstep for dismounting. *(Author)*

strut serves as an air-to-oil transfer cylinder for the emergency canopy opening system. The structure is designed to protect the pilot if the aeroplane overturns on contact with a crash barrier during deck landing. The strut and its forward-attaching fittings are removable.

The emergency canopy opening system is powered by compressed air. The air supply cylinder for this is located on the forward face of the centre wing spar in the port side of the forward equipment bay. The cylinder has a minimum capacity of 125cc and should be charged with compressed air to 1,980psi via the charging valve at the rear of the cockpit. When the enclosure handle is moved to the 'EMER'

LEFT Overturn structure aft of the headrest. The red handle is the bail-out bell used by the pilot to alert crew in the rear cabin as to the immediate requirement to abandon the aircraft. *(Author)*

BELOW Emergency canopy bottle located on the port side aft wall of the forward equipment compartment *(Author)*

BELOW Both forward equipment bay access hatches open in the belly of the Skyraider. Visible top left is the open panel for the external ground power unit. *(Author)*

position, the cable-operated control valve opens, directing air pressure to the oil transfer cylinder, and fluid pressure is furnished to the cylinder head to open the canopy. Later models of AD-4 Skyraider have spring-loaded positive stops installed on the enclosure control handle to prevent accidental activation of the emergency canopy opening system on the ground.

The forward equipment compartment is directly below the cockpit and contains most of the electrical and hydraulic system units. It is reached through the two access doors in the bottom of the fuselage. Either door can be opened by holding it down at the hand-hold door latch, unlocking the cam-lock fasteners,

and then pushing it up into the compartment and off its hinges.

The fuel tank compartment is located immediately aft of the cockpit. The fuel cell is suspended in the compartment from structures attached to the engine upper mount stiffeners. The cell is accessible through upper and lower access doors for inspection and can be removed through the top of the fuselage.

The rear equipment or radio compartment and aft fuselage is located immediately aft of the fuel tank compartment. Depending on the aircraft fit, it can contain crew, radio equipment, radar equipment, target towing equipment or the dive brake mechanisms. In all but the

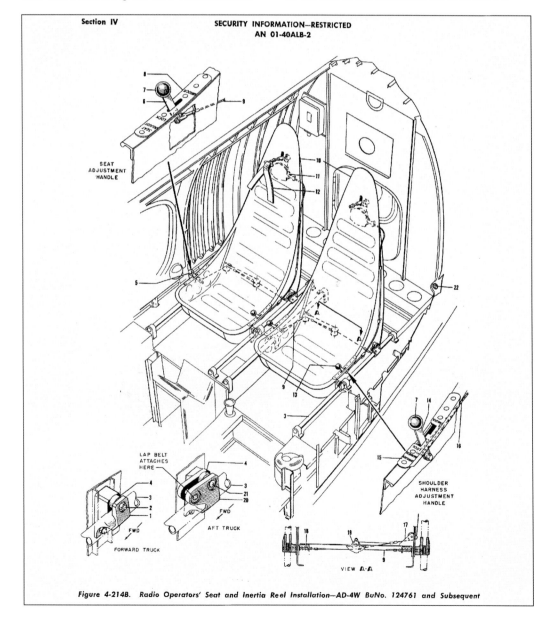

Section IV

Figure 4-214B. Radio Operators' Seat and Inertia Reel Installation—AD-4W BuNo. 124761 and Subsequent

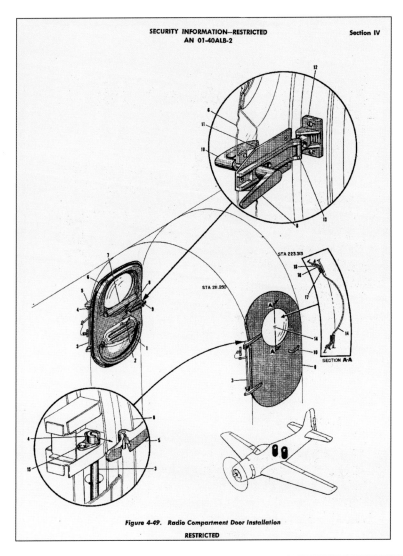

Figure 4-49. *Radio Compartment Door Installation*

RESTRICTED

ABOVE Inside rear fuselage with the wheel box for the tailwheel clearly visible in the lower portion of the fuselage. Above it can be seen the control run cables and just in view above those – the first of the vertical stabiliser formers. *(Author)*

RIGHT Rear cabin doors on the AD-4NA. Operation is quite simplistic and these doors are jettisoned by the withdrawal of the hinge pins upon pulling the emergency handle in the cabin. For general use the doors are held open with a strap clipped to the fuselage, but in this condition does restrict access to the cockpit via the wing walkway. *(Author)*

dive brake configuration, access to the rear equipment or radio compartment is via doors either side of the fuselage. For aircraft carrying crew in the radio compartment, these doors can be jettisoned by pulling on a handle at each door that releases the hinge pins. The fuselage aft section extends from the aft end of the radio compartment to the vertical stabiliser, and is divided by a bulkhead which is the support point for the tailgear and arresting hook. Rigging points are located forward of this bulkhead which is reached through the radio compartment through an access door. In dive brake-equipped aircraft, this door is situated in the starboard dive brake well.

Tail unit

The horizontal stabiliser is constructed of a front spar, a rear shear web, chord-wise ribs and hat section stiffeners with stressed skin plating. The spar and shear web are continuous throughout the span. The aeroplane tail hoist fitting is attached to the forward face of the horizontal stabiliser spar just outboard of the port side of the fuselage. The horizontal stabiliser is installed in a slot in the fuselage aft section. It hinges at two fittings on the front spar and can be adjusted in flight to obtain optimum trim. The fairings which seal the gap in the fuselage at the slot for the horizontal stabiliser are spring loaded against the side of the fuselage to keep the gap sealed at all angles of incidence. The fairings are attached to the horizontal stabiliser with screws and are easily removable. The vertical stabiliser is constructed of a single spar, chord-wise ribs and stressed skin. This stabiliser is built integrally with the fuselage and is not removable. The horizontal stabiliser operating mechanism is installed on the forward side of the vertical stabiliser spar and is serviced

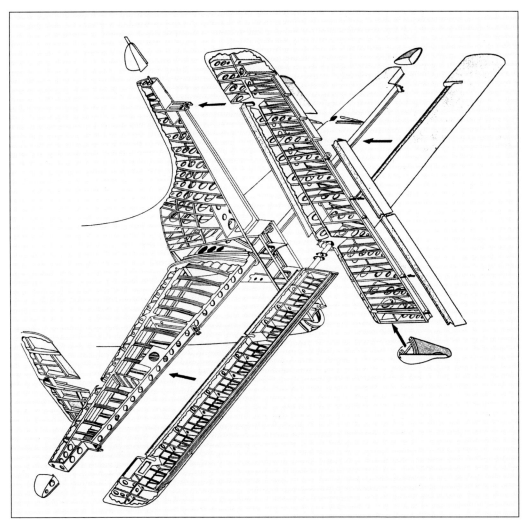

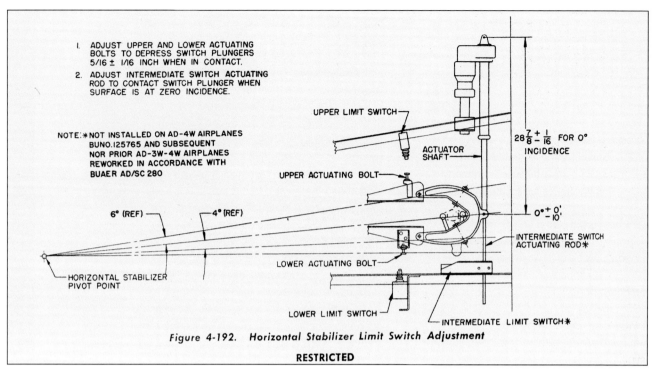

1. ADJUST UPPER AND LOWER ACTUATING BOLTS TO DEPRESS SWITCH PLUNGERS 5/16 ± 1/16 INCH WHEN IN CONTACT.
2. ADJUST INTERMEDIATE SWITCH ACTUATING ROD TO CONTACT SWITCH PLUNGER WHEN SURFACE IS AT ZERO INCIDENCE.

NOTE:✳ NOT INSTALLED ON AD-4W AIRPLANES BUNO.125765 AND SUBSEQUENT NOR PRIOR AD-3W-4W AIRPLANES REWORKED IN ACCORDANCE WITH BUAER AD/SC 280

UPPER LIMIT SWITCH
ACTUATOR SHAFT
UPPER ACTUATING BOLT
6° (REF)
4° (REF)
$28\frac{7}{8}+\frac{1}{16}$ FOR 0° INCIDENCE
$0°\,{+\,0' \atop -\,10'}$
INTERMEDIATE SWITCH ACTUATING ROD✳
HORIZONTAL STABILIZER PIVOT POINT
LOWER ACTUATING BOLT
LOWER LIMIT SWITCH
INTERMEDIATE LIMIT SWITCH✳

Figure 4-192. Horizontal Stabilizer Limit Switch Adjustment

RESTRICTED

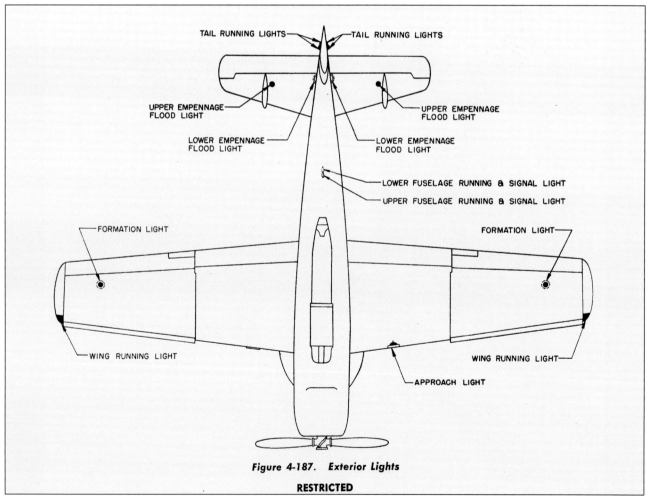

TAIL RUNNING LIGHTS
TAIL RUNNING LIGHTS
UPPER EMPENNAGE FLOOD LIGHT
UPPER EMPENNAGE FLOOD LIGHT
LOWER EMPENNAGE FLOOD LIGHT
LOWER EMPENNAGE FLOOD LIGHT
LOWER FUSELAGE RUNNING & SIGNAL LIGHT
UPPER FUSELAGE RUNNING & SIGNAL LIGHT
FORMATION LIGHT
FORMATION LIGHT
WING RUNNING LIGHT
WING RUNNING LIGHT
APPROACH LIGHT

Figure 4-187. Exterior Lights

RESTRICTED

RIGHT Stabiliser trim jack, with the access panel off for lubrication and maintenance. Located on the port side of the tail fin, here we see the aircraft with the rudder removed. *(Author)*

through a large access door on the port side of the vertical stabiliser. Two tail running lights are mounted in each side of the stabiliser, just below the tip.

Main planes

The wing of the Skyraider has a 50ft span, a 6° dihedral, and a 6° sweepback. It is designed to fold at the junction of the centre panel and the outboard panels. The outboard wing panels fold 125°, and, since the hinge line is not parallel to the wing reference plane, they fold slightly aft. Each wing folding joint is provided with synthetic rubber seals to prevent air seepage

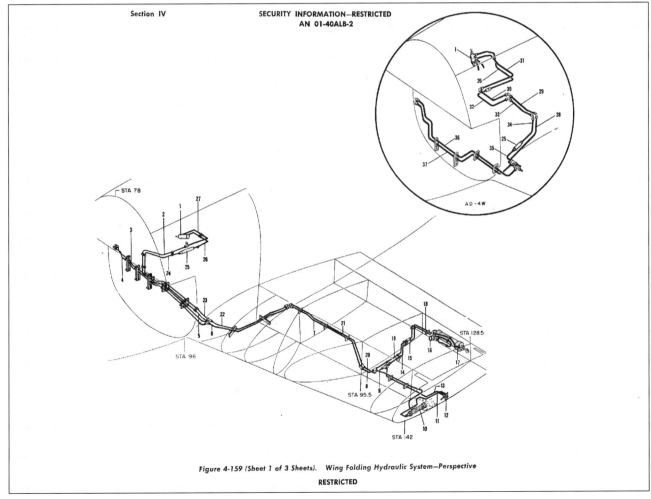

Figure 4-159 (Sheet 1 of 3 Sheets). Wing Folding Hydraulic System—Perspective

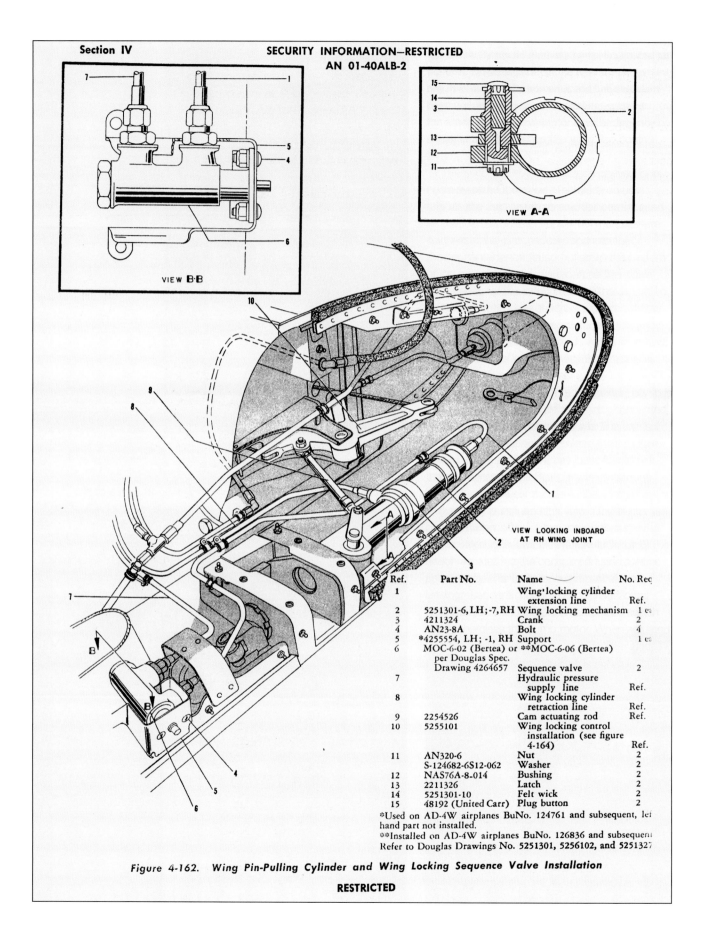

VIEW B-B

VIEW A-A

VIEW LOOKING INBOARD
AT RH WING JOINT

Ref.	Part No.	Name	No. Req
1		Wing locking cylinder extension line	Ref.
2	5251301-6, LH; -7, RH	Wing locking mechanism	1 ea
3	4211324	Crank	2
4	AN23-8A	Bolt	4
5	*4255554, LH; -1, RH	Support	1 ea
6	MOC-6-02 (Bertea) or **MOC-6-06 (Bertea) per Douglas Spec. Drawing 4264657	Sequence valve	2
7		Hydraulic pressure supply line	Ref.
8		Wing locking cylinder retraction line	Ref.
9	2254526	Cam actuating rod	Ref.
10	5255101	Wing locking control installation (see figure 4-164)	Ref.
11	AN320-6	Nut	2
	S-124682-6S12-062	Washer	2
12	NAS76A-8-014	Bushing	2
13	2211326	Latch	2
14	5251301-10	Felt wick	2
15	48192 (United Carr)	Plug button	2

*Used on AD-4W airplanes BuNo. 124761 and subsequent, left hand part not installed.
**Installed on AD-4W airplanes BuNo. 126836 and subsequent. Refer to Douglas Drawings No. 5251301, 5256102, and 5251327

Figure 4-162. Wing Pin-Pulling Cylinder and Wing Locking Sequence Valve Installation

RESTRICTED

through the joint during flight. The seals are held in place by an aluminium alloy strip riveted to the centre wing section. The wing consists of the following principal components: centre wing panel, outboard wing panels, wingtips, wing flaps and ailerons. All components except the centre wing panel, which is built as an integral part of the fuselage, are readily removable from the aeroplane.

The span-wise structure of the centre wing panel comprises a front spar and a rear shear web, both of which are continuous through the fuselage from wing joint to wing joint. Chord-wise structure includes eight main bulkheads, four in each section of the centre wing outboard of the fuselage, and contour is maintained by hat section stiffeners spaced approximately 5in apart. The wing

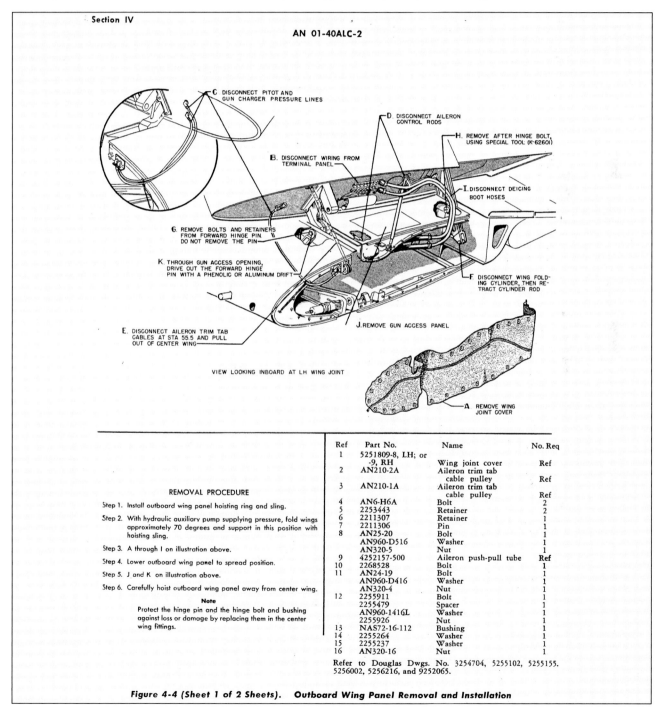

REMOVAL PROCEDURE

Step 1. Install outboard wing panel hoisting ring and sling.

Step 2. With hydraulic auxiliary pump supplying pressure, fold wings approximately 70 degrees and support in this position with hoisting sling.

Step 3. A through I on illustration above.

Step 4. Lower outboard wing panel to spread position.

Step 5. J and K on illustration above.

Step 6. Carefully hoist outboard wing panel away from center wing.

Note
Protect the hinge pin and the hinge bolt and bushing against loss or damage by replacing them in the center wing fittings.

Ref	Part No.	Name	No. Req
1	5251809-8, LH; or	Wing joint cover	
	-9, RH	Wing joint cover	Ref
2	AN210-2A	Aileron trim tab cable pulley	Ref
3	AN210-1A	Aileron trim tab cable pulley	Ref
4	AN6-H6A	Bolt	2
5	2253443	Retainer	2
6	2211307	Retainer	1
7	2211306	Pin	1
8	AN25-20	Bolt	1
	AN960-D516	Washer	1
	AN320-5	Nut	1
9	4252157-500	Aileron push-pull tube	Ref
10	2268528	Bolt	1
11	AN24-19	Bolt	1
	AN960-D416	Washer	1
	AN320-4	Nut	1
12	2255911	Bolt	1
	2255479	Spacer	1
	AN960-1416L	Washer	1
	2255926	Nut	1
13	NAS72-16-112	Bushing	1
14	2255264	Washer	1
15	2255237	Washer	1
16	AN320-16	Nut	1

Refer to Douglas Dwgs. No. 3254704, 5255102, 5255155. 5256002, 5256216, and 9252065.

Figure 4-4 (Sheet 1 of 2 Sheets). Outboard Wing Panel Removal and Installation

ABOVE Proof of the extreme ruggedness of the Skyraiders structure. Skyraider AD-4N F-AZDP is seen rolling out on 10 July 2011 at the Flying Legends Air Show, Duxford having lost the majority of the outboard starboard wing panel. The aircraft had been flying in the display finale and during the formation break at the end of the flypast, the Skyraider's starboard wing contacted the tail of the formation lead Mustang. The Mustang pilot had to abandon the aircraft but the Skyraider pilot managed to regain control and made a safe landing back on the airfield. The Mustang pilot suffered minor injuries, but the Skyraider pilot was unhurt. *(Peter Arnold)*

BELOW LEFT A clear view looking aft in the port wheel bay. The main mounting points are to the top right of the picture and the arms here can be seen extending back to the rear shear web. The red device in the middle is a ground safety lock on the retract actuator arm. Note also the electronic switches that indicate gear lock condition. *(Author)*

BELOW The port side catapult spool located between the fuselage and wing fold. *(Author)*

skin is stressed and flush riveted; the upper skins are faired into the fuselage using fillets, the lower skin is continuous and forms the bottom contour of the fuselage from the lower firewall to aft of the rear wing shear web.

The main landing gear is mounted in the centre wing nose sections and each is supported by a truss between the central bulkheads. The main landing gear wheels retract into the wing, between the spar and the shear web. When retracted, the gear is enclosed by fairings and doors. A bumper mounted on the rear shear web is provided to protect the wing structure in the event of failure of the main landing gear telescoping mechanism. Catapult hooks are installed in the left and right nose sections of the centre wing, just outboard of the fuselage.

Similarly, the span-wise structure of the outboard wing sections also consists of a front main spar and a rear shear web. Chord-wise structure between the spar and the shear web includes five main bulkheads spaced approximately 36in apart and contour is maintained by hat section stiffeners at approximately 5in intervals. The trailing edge is supported by a large span-wise hat section and by chord-wise alternating ribs and stiffeners. The skin structure contains fittings for installing a jury strut, hoisting sling, formation lights and rocket launchers. When outboard guns are installed, access to the guns and ammunition boxes is provided by means of access doors in the wing upper skin.

Systems

Fuel system

The function of the fuel system is to supply fuel to the carburettor in amounts adequate for all conditions of engine operation. The system consists of a fuselage fuel cell, three optional external auxiliary fuel tanks, a fuel tank selector valve, a fuel strainer, an auxiliary fuel pump, an engine driven fuel pump, an engine primer valve and the necessary lines, fittings and controls. A fuel pressure gauge and a fuel quantity gauge on the instrument panel provide an accurate indication of fuel pressure and fuel quantity.

LEFT The main fuel cell removed to allow maintenance. Fuel lines have a finite life for UK operations; the increasing ethanol content of aviation fuel causes degradation over time. Note the drain and feed housing at the bottom of the tank. To this attaches the brace cables that hold the tank steady in the fuselage. *(Author)*

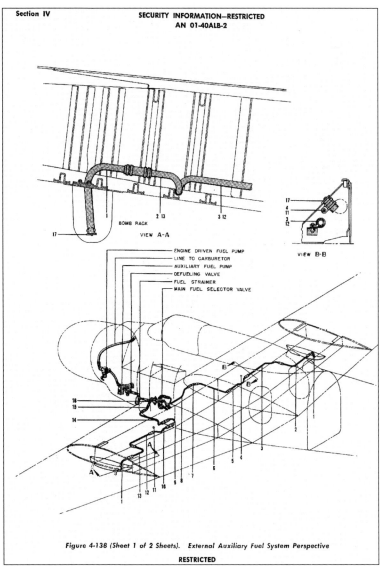

Section IV

SECURITY INFORMATION—RESTRICTED
AN 01-40ALB-2

BOMB RACK
VIEW A-A

VIEW B-B

ENGINE DRIVEN FUEL PUMP
LINE TO CARBURETOR
AUXILIARY FUEL PUMP
DEFUELING VALVE
FUEL STRAINER
MAIN FUEL SELECTOR VALVE

Figure 4-138 (Sheet 1 of 2 Sheets). External Auxiliary Fuel System Perspective
RESTRICTED

A hammock-type fuel cell which has a service capacity of 380 US gallons is installed in the fuselage directly behind the cockpit. The cell consists essentially of a self-sealing container supported by a hammock, of which the container can be removed from the hammock to facilitate repair or inspection. A cap, constructed of four plies of heavy-gauge rayon fabric is installed between the self-sealing container and the hammock. The self-sealing container embodies three main elements: the fuel-resistant inner liner, which is a sheet of Buna stock treated with three coats of nylon cement on the outer side to form a barrier between the liner and the sealant; two layers of sealant, separated by one ply of rayon cord; and two plies of rayon cord which form the outer retainer and give strength to the cell. All the elements of the container are cemented together to form an integral unit.

The fuel cell is filled through a well on the top of the cell which is accessible through a door in the starboard side of the fuselage just aft of the cockpit enclosure. A catch basin above the cell prevents stray fuel or tools from falling between the cell and the hammock; a drain line from the basin diverts spilled fuel from the area and exhausts it overboard. A metal access door on the top of the cell can be removed to permit access to the interior for cleaning and repairing the cell. The access door incorporates a fitting for the attachment of the cell vent line, the fuel quantity tank unit and an inspection door. There is an inspection window in the compartment cover directly above the access door which facilitates inspection of the fuel cell fittings and for leakage without having to remove the compartment cover. The carburettor vent line is attached to the fuel cell vent line at a point adjacent to the fitting on the cell access door. As a result, vaporised fuel returning from the carburettor is directed into the fuel cell. An anti-siphon vent line is attached at the same point as the carburettor vent line. This line is routed aft to an outlet in the port side of the fuselage to prevent fuel from siphoning out via the fuel vent line.

The fuel outlet fitting is in the bottom of the tank, which incorporates a screen that strains the fuel before it enters the supply line. There is a defuel valve installed in the boss aft of the outlet fitting, access to which is through a

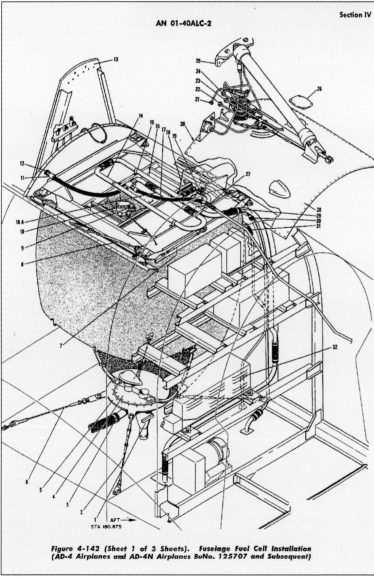

Figure 4-142 (Sheet 1 of 3 Sheets). Fuselage Fuel Cell Installation (AD-4 Airplanes and AD-4N Airplanes BuNo. 125707 and Subsequent)

RIGHT The top of the fuel tank showing tank vent lines, fill lines, anti-siphon lines and carburettor vent line. Also visible here are the tank brace rods that hold the tank securely within the tank bay.
(Author)

door in the bottom of the fuselage. To defuel the cell, a hose is connected to the defuelling valve and the valve handle is rotated 180° anti-clockwise from the closed position. To drain condensed moisture from the cell, the defuelling valve should be rotated approximately 30°. If sediment accumulates at the defuelling valve, the valve should be fully opened until about 2 gallons of fuel have drained out, and then quickly closed. The hammock which bears the self-sealing container is in turn supported at the top by a shock-mounted structure bolted to the upper surface of the engine mount stiffeners. Possible sagging of the cell is prevented by clips bolted to intermediate channels. Fore-and-aft and sidewise movements are prevented at the top of the cell by rods which extend between the cell-supporting structure and the engine mount stiffeners and by a rod which extends between the cell-supporting structure and the fuselage frame aft of the cell. Movement at the bottom of the cell is prevented by a circular brace assembly and four adjustable cables; the brace assembly is bolted to the cell; two of the four cables extend forward to the spar, the other two cables extend aft to the rear shear web.

Provision is made for installation of either the Mk 5 or the Mk 12 external auxiliary fuel tank on each wing bomb rack and on the fuselage bomb rack; however, an external auxiliary fuel tank can be carried on the fuselage bomb rack only when the bomb ejector rack is installed. Both the Mk 5 and the Mk 12 auxiliary tanks have a capacity of 150 US gallons. A sump fitting is installed on the bottom of the tank in the area which is lowest when the aeroplane

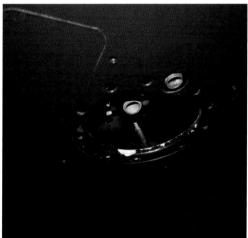

LEFT Centre fuel tank defuel valve with the cover plate removed. A manually operated handle next to the valve allows fuel to be drained for either tank maintenance purposes or for the removal of condensed water when the aircraft has been left standing.
(Author)

RIGHT Wing tank mounts are fitted to the inboard wing sections just outboard of the landing gear. Lacking suitable original external tanks, these fittings are currently not used on G-RADR.
(Author)

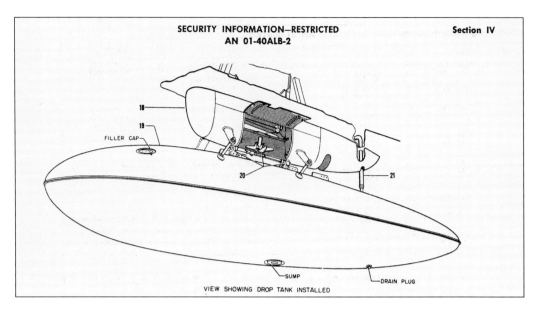

18

19

FILLER CAP

20

21

SUMP

DRAIN PLUG

VIEW SHOWING DROP TANK INSTALLED

BELOW Fuel tank selector. *(Author)*

BELOW RIGHT Firewall fuel strainer mounted on the lower port side of the firewall. Behind the fuel strainer can clearly be seen the hydraulic pressure accumulator and next to it, the accumulator system pressure gauge and charging valve. *(Author)*

is in normal level-flight attitude. The tank sump is connected with a fuel outlet fitting on top of the tank, directly aft of the aft portion of the suspension beam. A filter screen, which is part of the sump fitting, prevents foreign particles from entering the supply line. A vent fitting is located on the top of the tank near the forward end. A filler opening is provided on the top of the tank, also near the forward end. A drain plug, located on the bottom of the tank, approximately midway between the sump fitting and the aft end, should be removed periodically to drain condensed moisture from the tank. The external auxiliary fuel tanks can be released

from the aeroplane by operating either the bomb electric or the manual release controls.

The tank selector valve is controlled by a handle on the port side control panel in the cockpit. The handle is connected with the valve by a control rod. Valve positions are designated in clockwise order as follows: OFF, LH DROP, MAIN, CENT DROP, RH DROP.

Another fuel strainer is installed on the port side of the forward face of the firewall. The strainer prevents foreign particles from entering the fuel pumps and the carburettor. Its inlet port, on the aft side of the strainer, is connected to the line of the main fuel supply from the fuel

RIGHT Engine-driven fuel pump mounted on the lower port side of the supercharger. Fuel is drawn in from the right, passed through the pump, and out the left side of the pump up to the carburettor fuel intake. *(Author)*

tank selector valve; its outlet port, on the top of the strainer, is connected to the line to the auxiliary fuel pump. A short section of tubing at the outlet port facilitates engine removal. The strainer is equipped with an easily removable screen and with a drain valve for draining condensed moisture from the system.

An engine-driven fuel pump is installed on the lower port side of the engine accessory case. It is a positive displacement vane type pump which is coupled directly to the engine pump drive by a splined shaft which has a reduced diameter shear section to protect the engine and the pump against excessive loads. The pump contains a bypass valve which allows fuel to flow around the engine-driven fuel pump when it is inoperative and the auxiliary pump is operating. The bypass valve also serves as a safety valve if backfiring should reverse the direction of rotation of the engine.

An electrically driven auxiliary fuel pump is installed directly forward of the fuel strainer, on the lower port leg of the engine mount. This positive displacement pump furnishes fuel pressure for starting the engine and should be used for take-off, high altitude, diving and landing operations. The auxiliary pump aids the engine-driven fuel pump in maintaining sufficient operating pressures at high altitudes and minimises the possibility of fuel system failure as a result of vapour lock. It incorporates an adjustable pressure relief valve which is similar to the one on the engine-driven pump and is adjusted in a like manner. The diaphragm of the auxiliary pump is vented to the atmosphere; consequently the pressure at which fuel is discharged from the pump is equal to the force exerted upon the relief valve by a combination of spring and atmospheric pressure. A pressure increase of 2.5psi maximum whenever the auxiliary pump is being operated in conjunction with the engine-driven pump is satisfactory. The switch for the auxiliary fuel pump is on the port cockpit control panel and is marked 'FUEL

BOOSTER'. If the engine-driven fuel pump fails to function, the switch should be turned on in order to maintain sufficient pressure to keep the engine operating. When the auxiliary pump is inoperative, fuel is drawn through the engine-driven pump bypass valve. The location of the auxiliary pump between the tank selector valve and the engine enables it to supply fuel under

BELOW Auxiliary fuel pump mounted on the lower port engine frame forward of the hydraulic accumulator. The auxiliary fuel pump is used for starting, take-off and landing and in the event of engine-driven pump failure. The red blanking cap is covering the electrical connector terminal. *(Author)*

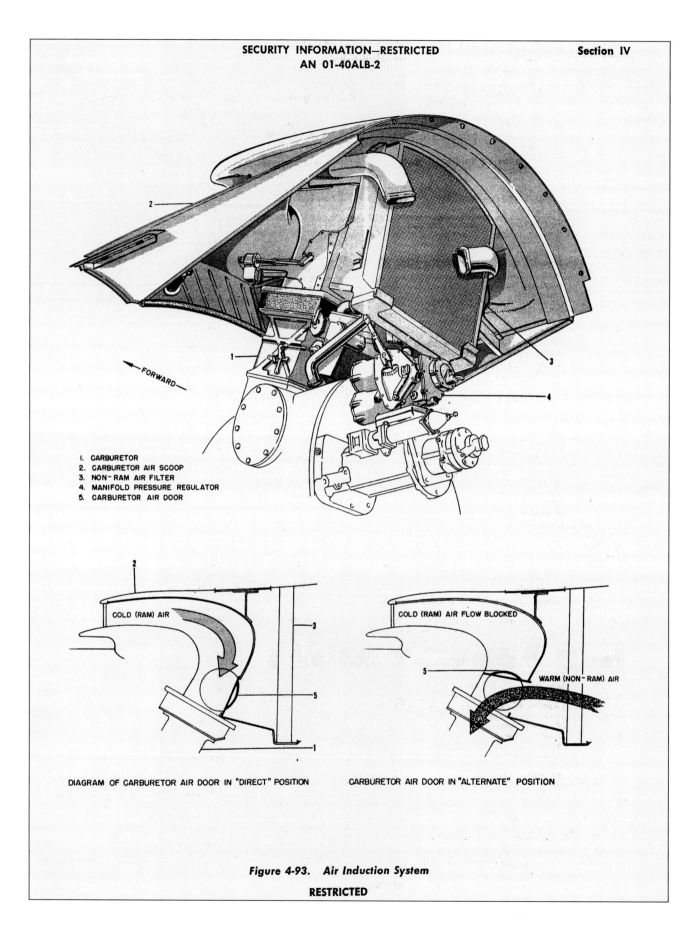

1. CARBURETOR
2. CARBURETOR AIR SCOOP
3. NON-RAM AIR FILTER
4. MANIFOLD PRESSURE REGULATOR
5. CARBURETOR AIR DOOR

←FORWARD←

COLD (RAM) AIR

COLD (RAM) AIR FLOW BLOCKED

WARM (NON-RAM) AIR

DIAGRAM OF CARBURETOR AIR DOOR IN "DIRECT" POSITION

CARBURETOR AIR DOOR IN "ALTERNATE" POSITION

Figure 4-93.   Air Induction System

RESTRICTED

OPPOSITE **Air is taken into the carburettor via a scoop forward of the cockpit. It is filtered with an electrically controlled door and can be removed as a complete unit for servicing and inspection.** *(US Navy)*

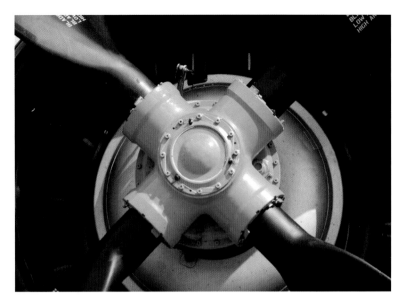

pressure to the engine, regardless of which tank is being used.

An engine priming valve is attached to the aft side of the carburettor; fuel flows directly from the pressure side of the carburettor into the priming valve, and then through two lines to the blower case of the engine. The engine is primed by building up pressure with the auxiliary fuel pump and holding the primer switch on the starboard cockpit pedestal. When the primer switch is ON the plunger in the solenoid valve is lifted from the valve seat and fuel flows through the unit to the blower case.

Propeller

The Skyraider is fitted with the Aeroproducts model A642-G8 series propeller which interestingly incorporates a fully automatic rpm control regulator, a separate propeller oil supply and four huge hollow propeller blades.

The blades are of hollow steel construction

incorporating a longitudinal strengthening rib. The blade is composed of the thrust member and the camber sheet which are brazed together to create the blade shape. The thrust member is a machine steel forging which forms the thrust face, blade shank, longitudinal rib and the leading and trailing edge reinforcements. This member is completely ground and polished as is the steel camber sheet which is formed, polished and attached to the thrust member by brazing. On the root of the blade is machined a

ABOVE The Aeroproducts propeller fitted to G-RADR. *(Phil Glover)*

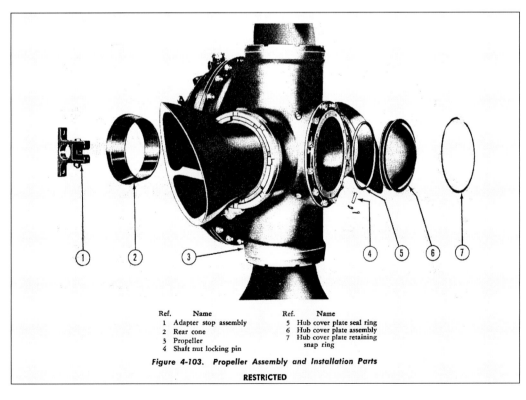

Ref.   Name
1   Adapter stop assembly
2   Rear cone
3   Propeller
4   Shaft nut locking pin

Ref.   Name
5   Hub cover plate seal ring
6   Hub cover plate assembly
7   Hub cover plate retaining snap ring

Figure 4-103. Propeller Assembly and Installation Parts

RESTRICTED

ABOVE Propeller blades fresh from the paint shop. Blades are routinely paint stripped and examined for corrosion through both visual and non-destructive testing methods. The bare blades are then specially treated before etching, priming and painting. *(Author)*

ABOVE Blade seals and nuts fitted to blade roots prior to fitting to the hub. The pins on the bottom of the blades engage with the blade gear plate within the hub. *(Author)*

BELOW Propeller hub assembly on its support stand. The rear of the hub passes through the centre of the regulator and is secured with a large regulator nut. *(Author)*

special buttress-type thread which is designed to absorb the centrifugal load adequately, yet retain the self-centring load distributing characteristics of a normal 'V' thread. A relief plug is incorporated in the blade butt. By relieving pressure, the plug will prevent grease and hydraulic fluid from being forced past the balance cup into the blade cavity. This is a non-metallic plug compound to resist deterioration from the propeller fluids. Each blade has a balance cup in the shank which has lead added in the appropriate location to give uniform

vertical and horizontal balance. To allow for final balance and adjustment of the blades and hub in the field, a stud is provided in the centre of the blade balance cup on to which may be added balance washers. The blade is held in the hub by a blade retaining nut, a stack of ball bearings and a blade nut. The bearings are assembled in matched sets to distribute the centrifugal load evenly. The blade nut holds the blade bearings on the blade shank, while the blade retaining nut faces against the bearings and screws into the hub socket, holding the entire assembly in place.

The propeller hub assembly is a machined alloy steel forging. Torque units are mounted in each blade socket and transfer passages permit the transfer of hydraulic fluid under pressure from the regulator to the torque units. A torque unit is incorporated in each hub socket. These units use hydraulic force to change blade angle. The torque units consist of a steel fixed spline, a bronze piston and a steel torque cylinder. The fixed spline is attached to the hub by a fixed spline bolt containing a tube which extends outward through the piston head, to a fluid passage to the outboard side of the torque piston. An offset hole at the base of the fixed spline permits passage of the fluid to the inboard side of the piston. The exterior surfaces

RIGHT The first blade installed in the hub unit. The blade cylinders can be seen clearly protruding from each blade socket; the cylinders slide in and out of the hub over the fixed spline units. *(Author)*

of the hub are treated to provide a corrosion-resistant finish. Splines in the inner diameter of the hub mate on installation with the splines of the propeller shaft. At both ends of the splines in the hub, cone seats provide proper alignment of the propeller on the shaft. So that all blades will change angle to exactly the same degree, it is necessary to use a synchronising device. Therefore, a master gear in the hub meshes with the blade gears that are dowelled to the root of each blade. The blade gears and master gear function only as synchronising units.

The propeller regulator assembly is a doughnut-shaped unit which serves as a reservoir for the hydraulic fluid and contains a pump, pressure control valve, governor, filter screen and a manual rpm control mechanism. The unit is composed of a cover and a regulator housing. The housing is a machined, lightweight alloy casting on which are mounted the gear type hydraulic fluid pump, pressure control valve, governor and filter screen. A removable plug is threaded into the cover to permit the addition and removal of fluid and to permit access to the governor adjusting screw. The regulator assembly is mounted to the rear of the hub by means of a regulator nut having a left-handed thread. The unit provides controlled hydraulic pressure to the torque units located in each hub socket controlled by the governor. The regulator reservoir should be kept half-filled at all times when in operation.

The governor assembly mounted on the regulator housing automatically distributes hydraulic fluid to the torque units as required by the operating conditions. A cylinder is mounted in synthetic seals within the governor body, a piston moves within the cylinder. Since the

LEFT Propeller regulator unit seen from the rear. The regulator is essentially a reservoir with internal pumps to supply oil to the propeller gears and spline units to move the blades. The reservoir is entirely independent from the other fluid systems on the aircraft. *(Author)*

governor revolves at propeller rpm, the piston is thrown outward by centrifugal force. The extent of its outward movement depends upon a spring and the position of a governor fulcrum roller. Centrifugal force acting on the piston is

RIGHT Fitting the blades to the hub is a two-person job; once located on the blade gear, the blade nut is tightened by hand and then torqued. *(Author)*

PROPELLER TECHNICAL SPECIFICATIONS

Overall diameter – 13ft 6in
Blade angle range – 40°
Low pitch angle – 28°
High pitch angle – 68°
The model designation is arrived at as follows:
    A – Aeroproducts
    6 – no. 60 shaft size
    4 – Number of blades
    2 – Blade shank size
    G – Major design specification
    8 – Minor design specification

ABOVE Rick Herndon (left) and Barry Rowland carrying out their version of a propeller balance on an A-1 Spad in 1970.
(Barry Rowland)

opposed by spring force which acts directly on a lever. One end of the lever engages on one end of the governor piston. The other end of the lever is supported by a moveable fulcrum. The fulcrum roller is mounted on a carriage which may be moved forward or aft on the carriageways. If the fulcrum is moved towards the piston, correspondingly less and less centrifugal force is required to move the piston outward. At a given position of the fulcrum, an increase or decrease in engine rpm causes the governor piston to move outward or inward, thereby opening or closing hydraulic ports to the torque units. A curved steel shoe extends

from the underside of the carriage and rides in a stationary groove of the control mechanism to provide rpm control from the cockpit.

Hydraulics

The function of the supply, pressure and return system is to furnish power for the various sub-systems. The pressurised hydraulic reservoir is the source of the supply and fluid flows from it to the engine-driven pumps which deliver the fluid under pressure to the control valves through a pressure regulator and a pressure accumulator. Return lines carry the fluid from the control valves back to the reservoir. The

RIGHT Hydraulic reservoir tank fitted on the port side of the fuselage firewall.
(Author)

SECURITY INFORMATION—RESTRICTED
AN 01-40ALB-2

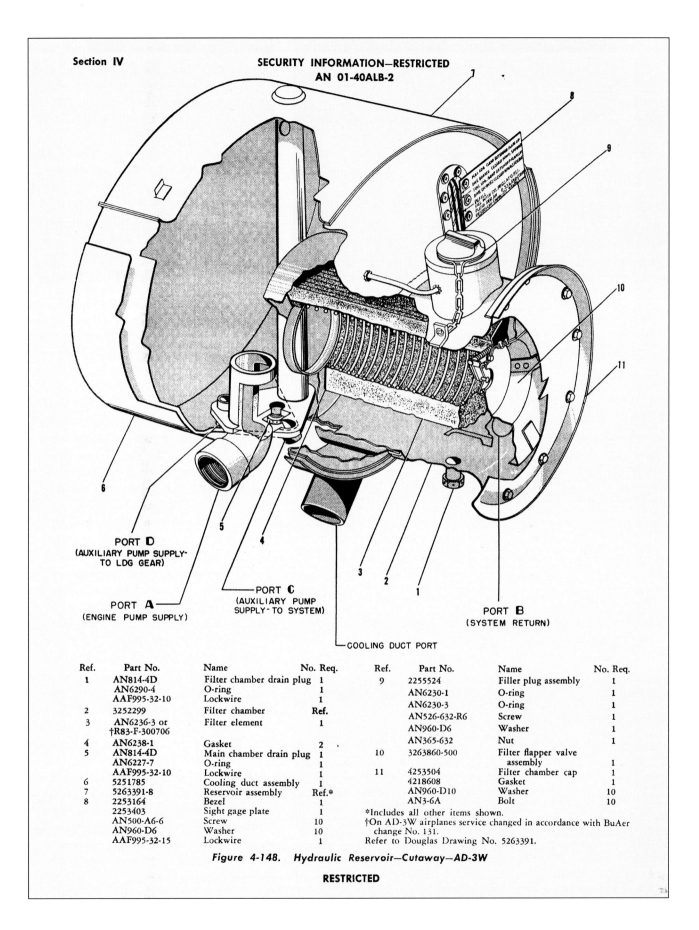

PORT **D**
(AUXILIARY PUMP SUPPLY-
TO LDG GEAR)

PORT **A**
(ENGINE PUMP SUPPLY)

PORT **C**
(AUXILIARY PUMP
SUPPLY-TO SYSTEM)

PORT **B**
(SYSTEM RETURN)

COOLING DUCT PORT

Ref.	Part No.	Name	No. Req.
1	AN814-4D	Filter chamber drain plug	1
	AN6290-4	O-ring	1
	AAF995-32-10	Lockwire	1
2	3252299	Filter chamber	Ref.
3	AN6236-3 or	Filter element	1
	†R83-F-300706		
4	AN6238-1	Gasket	2
5	AN814-4D	Main chamber drain plug	1
	AN6227-7	O-ring	1
	AAF995-32-10	Lockwire	1
6	5251785	Cooling duct assembly	1
7	5263391-8	Reservoir assembly	Ref.*
8	2253164	Bezel	1
	2253403	Sight gage plate	1
	AN500-A6-6	Screw	10
	AN960-D6	Washer	10
	AAF995-32-15	Lockwire	1

Ref.	Part No.	Name	No. Req.
9	2255524	Filler plug assembly	1
	AN6230-1	O-ring	1
	AN6230-3	O-ring	1
	AN526-632-R6	Screw	1
	AN960-D6	Washer	1
	AN365-632	Nut	1
10	3263860-500	Filter flapper valve assembly	1
11	4253504	Filter chamber cap	1
	4218608	Gasket	1
	AN960-D10	Washer	10
	AN3-6A	Bolt	10

*Includes all other items shown.
†On AD-3W airplanes service changed in accordance with BuAer change No. 131.
Refer to Douglas Drawing No. 5263391.

Figure 4-148. Hydraulic Reservoir—Cutaway—AD-3W

RESTRICTED

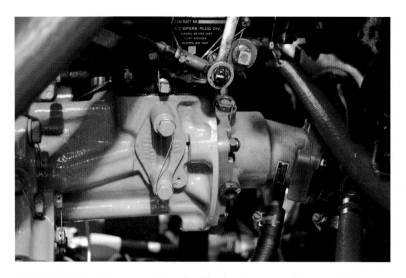

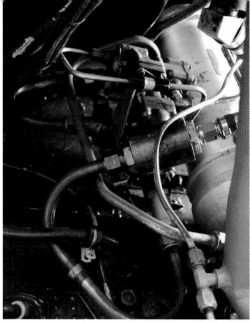

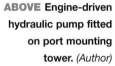

ABOVE Engine-driven hydraulic pump fitted on port mounting tower. *(Author)*

ABOVE RIGHT Hydraulic system pressure regulator situated inboard of the hydraulic pressure accumulator. *(Author)*

pressurised hydraulic reservoir is a welded aluminium alloy container held in a support shroud attached to brackets mounted on the horizontal firewall. The capacity is approximately 5.8 US gallons. A sight gauge and filling instruction plate are located on the outboard end of the reservoir adjacent to the filler plug. Two standpipes in the bottom of the reservoir provide ports for the supply lines; these lines are then connected to the engine-driven pumps, the aileron pump and the emergency and auxiliary pump selector valve for ground or emergency operation of any portion of the hydraulic system. The second standpipe reserves 0.4 US gallons of fluid to supply the auxiliary pump selector valve for emergency

lowering of the main landing gear. A common return line carries fluid back from the system to the return port in the reservoir. A filter chamber in the forward end of the reservoir contains a replaceable micronic filter. The filler and return ports are both located in the filter chamber; consequently, new fluid added to and fluid returning from the system are filtered before being routed to the pumps. Should the element become clogged, a flapper valve in the filter chamber opens and allows the fluid to bypass the filter. There are two drains in the bottom of the reservoir: one in the main chamber and one in the filter chamber. A cooling duct of moulded synthetic rubber and sheet aluminium encases the lower part of the reservoir and circulates the cooling air to keep fluid temperatures below 71°C. The reservoir is pressurised by a venturi installation in the aileron boost return line. Air is added to the reservoir through the venturi from a vent line that terminates at the lower firewall. A relief valve and filter relieves excess pressure from the reservoir. When the internal pressure of the reservoir reaches 14psi, excess air is allowed to pass through the filter, restrictor and the relief valve to the engine drain manifold. The valve closes when the pressure is reduced to approximately 10psi. The engine-driven hydraulic pump is a piston and cylinder type pump mounted on the left side of the engine accessory section. The ratio of the pump speed to engine speed is 1.4:1 and the direction of rotation is marked on the pump. The pump displaces 0.5cu in of fluid on each rotation and at 2,000 engine rpm, delivers approximately 12 US gallons of fluid per minute.

BELOW Engine-driven aileron boost hydraulic pump. Although linked to the main hydraulic system feed, the output feeds directly the aileron boost unit and is commonly situated on the starboard accessory mounting pad. The same unit can also be mounted on the lower mounting pad. *(Author)*

The hydraulic main system pressure regulator is installed on a manifold on the forward side of the lower firewall just below the hydraulic reservoir. The function of the regulator is to maintain adequate pressure in the system by cutting in when the pressure drops below 2,650psi and it continues to operate until the pressure has been restored to approximately 3,100psi. When not operating, the regulator bypasses fluid directly from the pumps back to the reservoir, thus preventing overheating of the fluid and possible damage to the system. In the event of malfunctioning of the regulator, the hydraulic main system relief valve opens at

3,400psi or the pilot may manually open the hydraulic emergency bypass valve to relieve excess system pressure.

The hydraulic system pressure accumulator is mounted on brackets on the lower firewall outboard of the hydraulic reservoir. It is a cylindrical steel shell containing a piston. A port in the top of the shell is connected with the pressure line from the manifold on which the pressure regulator is mounted. At zero system pressure the piston is fully depressed by compressed air (1,500–1,900psi). As system pressure is increased, the piston is forced upwards and the air content is further

SECURITY INFORMATION—RESTRICTED
AN 01-40ALB-2

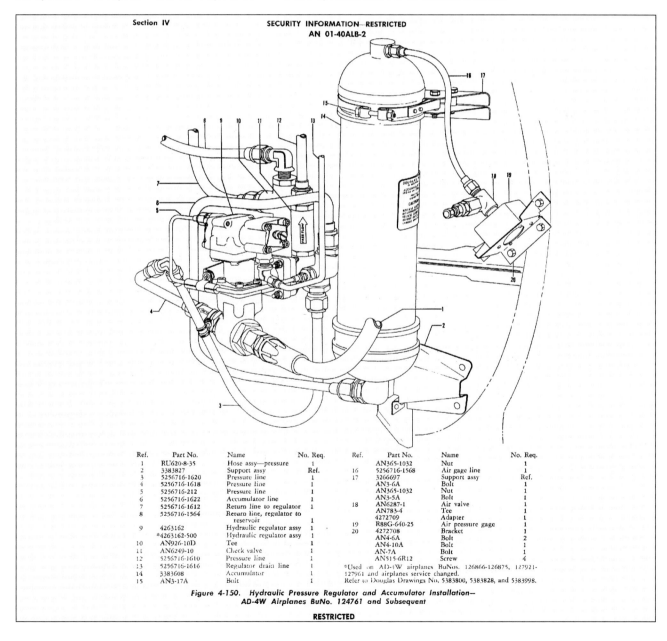

Ref.	Part No.	Name	No. Req.	Ref.	Part No.	Name	No. Req.
1	RU620-8-35	Hose assy—pressure	1		AN365-1032	Nut	1
2	3383827	Support assy	Ref.	16	5256716-1568	Air gage line	1
3	5256716-1620	Pressure line	1	17	3266697	Support assy	Ref.
4	5256716-1618	Pressure line	1		AN3-6A	Bolt	1
5	5256716-212	Pressure line	1		AN365-1032	Nut	1
6	5256716-1622	Accumulator line	1		AN3-5A	Bolt	1
7	5256716-1612	Return line to regulator	1	18	AN6287-1	Air valve	1
8	5256716-1564	Return line, regulator to reservoir	1		AN783-4	Tee	1
9	4263162	Hydraulic regulator assy	1		4272709	Adapter	1
	*4263162-500	Hydraulic regulator assy	1	19	R88G-640-25	Air pressure gage	1
10	AN926-10D	Tee	1	20	4272708	Bracket	1
11	AN6249-10	Check valve	1		AN4-6A	Bolt	2
12	5256716-1610	Pressure line	1		AN4-10A	Bolt	1
13	5256716-1616	Regulator drain line	1		AN-7A	Bolt	1
14	3383608	Accumulator	1		AN515-6R12	Screw	4
15	AN3-17A	Bolt	1				

*Used on AD-4W airplanes BuNos. 126866-126875, 127921-127961 and airplanes service changed.
Refer to Douglas Drawings No. 5383800, 5383828, and 5383998.

*Figure 4-150. Hydraulic Pressure Regulator and Accumulator Installation—
AD-4W Airplanes BuNo. 124761 and Subsequent*

RESTRICTED

compressed. Operation of a hydraulic unit relieves the fluid pressure and the compressed air then forces a fresh supply of high-pressure fluid out of the accumulator and into the system. An adapter fitting bolted to the bottom of the accumulator contains an air filler valve and a boss for the attachment of the air pressure gauge. The gauge is mounted below the accumulator and faces outboard for ready reference. Air should be added at the filler valve when the gauge indicates less than 1,500psi pressure in the accumulator.

The emergency and hydraulic auxiliary pump is operated by an integral electric motor connected with the aircraft DC power system. The unit is mounted on supports attached to the structure in the forward equipment bay just outboard of the port access door. Pump minimum output is 0.4 US gallons per minute to the emergency and auxiliary pump selector valve. The pump can be actuated in either of two ways: electrically by turning on the 'EMER HYDRAULIC PUMP' switch, located on the cockpit port side control panel, or mechanically by over travel of the landing gear control handle and linkage into 'EMERGENCY' to operate an automatic switch which energises the pump motor. When actuated by the cockpit switch, the pump can be used in place of a test stand to provide pressure for ground operation of aeroplane equipment or to operate hydraulic units in case of main system failure in flight. When the pump is actuated by the landing gear control, it furnishes pressure only to lower the main gear; the tailwheel would remain retracted in this situation.

Electrics

The electrical system on the AD-4 series aeroplane consists of power supply, instrument lighting, warning, radio and radar circuits, which operate on direct current and/or alternating current. As power sources, the system utilises a 24V battery and two engine-driven generators.

Section IV

SECURITY INFORMATION—RESTRICTED
AN 01-40ALB-2

LH CONTROL PANEL

EMERGENCY AND AUXILIARY PUMP CONTROL SWITCH

FORWARD

FORWARD EQUIPMENT COMPARTMENT LH ACCESS

LANDING GEAR CONTROL LINKAGE

FORWARD

Ref.	Part No.	Name	No. Req.
1	4261469	Emergency hydraulic selector valve	1
2	4262006	Landing gear selector valve	1
3	3268925-8	Lever assembly	1
4	AN3210-1 9-10851 (Micro-Switch Corp.)	Switch	1
5		Actuator	1
		Forward equipment compartment structure	Ref.
6	AN23-8A	Bolt	5
	AN960-D10f.	Washer	5
	AN365-1032	Nut	5
7	5261577-2	Angle	1
8	AN4-7A	Bolt	4
	AN960-D416L	Washer	4
	AN365-428	Nut	4
9	3262211	Pump and motor assembly	1
10	4265901	Vent guard	1
11	°5256716-1450	Supply line	1
	°°5256716-946	Supply line	1
12	5256716-944 or -926	Auxiliary pressure line	1

°Used on AD-4W airplanes only.
°°Used on AD-3W airplanes only.
Refer to Douglas Drawings No. 3262211 and 5261577.

Figure 4-151. Hydraulic Auxiliary Pump Installation
RESTRICTED

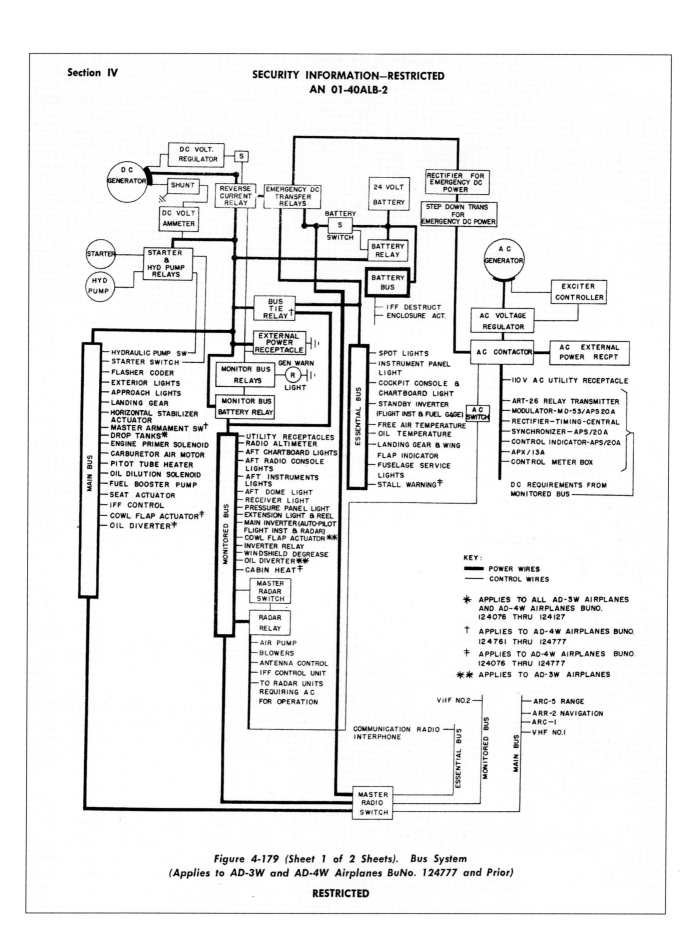

Figure 4-179 (Sheet 1 of 2 Sheets). Bus System
(Applies to AD-3W and AD-4W Airplanes BuNo. 124777 and Prior)

RESTRICTED

Sources of three-phase alternating current are two inverters, which are included in the automatic pilot system. The wiring of the system is generally of the open wire type, although conduit is used forward of the firewall and through the fuel tank bay. Power is distributed from the power supply circuits to the various other circuits of the aeroplane by means of power buses.

The electrical direct current circuits of the electrical system require a nominal 24V power supply and are of single wire, ground return type. Allowable voltage drop for continuous circuits (ie lights, radio, etc.) is 1V; and for intermittent circuits (ie actuators, pump motors, etc.) 2V. The electrical circuits using alternating current require either 115V, three-phase, 400-cycle supply distributed by two wires with the third phase at ground return, or a nominal single phase, 800-cycle supply distributed by a single wire with neutral at ground potential and ground return. Depending on build number, electrical generation on the aircraft is in one of two forms. For those AD-4s built prior to BuNo 127844, the starboard generator produces both alternating and direct current. The port generator only generates direct current. Additional alternating current is supplied by the main inverter. For aircraft built later than 127844, the power derived from both generators is direct current, with the alternating current requirement being supplied only from the main inverter.

The pilot's controls for electrical equipment are installed in positions adjacent to other controls for related equipment (ie engine and surface controls in the port cockpit panel; armament controls in the armament panel; lighting, electronic and miscellaneous controls in the starboard control panel). Controls for related electrical or electronic equipment are grouped together on consoles such as the exterior light console, the interior light control console, master radio control console, IFF radio control console and so on. These consoles with all controls can be removed as separate units from the control panels by removing the attaching screws.

A cockpit circuit breaker panel is mounted in the forward, inboard face of the starboard control panel, and contains button-type circuit breakers which are identified by the name of the circuit they protect.

The DC power supply circuit consists primarily of a 24V battery installation and two engine-driven generators which supply direct current through voltage regulators and reverse current relays to three buses: the main DC bus, the monitor bus and the armament bus. The battery is a standard 24V, 34Ah unit. The generators are identified as 'normal' (starboard engine pad) and 'alternate' (port engine pad). Power from each generator is controlled by an on–off switch located in either the cockpit or in the rear compartment. Generator power is regulated by a separate voltage regulator and reverse-current relay system for each generator. A generator warning light for each generator is mounted on the instrument panel.

The AC power circuit consists primarily of the AC section of each of the two engine-driven AC/DC generators. The AC power is controlled by the AC power transfer switch in the cockpit. The output of each generator is single phase and is regulated by separate voltage regulators and compensating condensers.

Starting

The starting system consists primarily of a direct cranking electric starter and a starting vibrator. The system is remotely controlled from the starboard cockpit panel using the switch marked 'STARTER'. The starter control circuit is protected against current overloads by a 10amp reset-type circuit breaker. When the starter

BELOW Port DC generator viewed with the port-side armoured panels removed. Access to the generator is very awkward and replacement is only made slightly easier by removing the oil cooler. (Author)

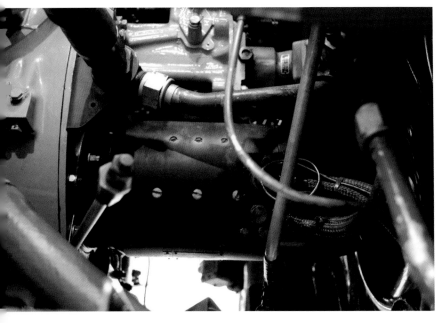

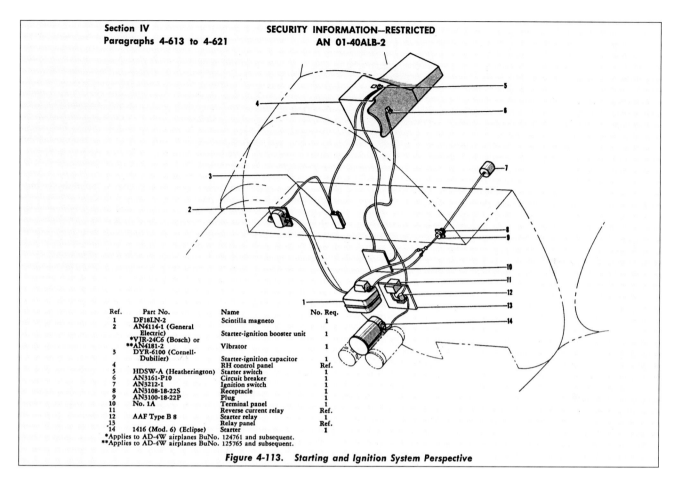

Ref.	Part No.	Name	No. Req.
1	DF18LN-2	Scintilla magneto	1
2	AN4114-1 (General Electric)	Starter-ignition booster unit	1
	*VJR-24C6 (Bosch) or **AN4181-2	Vibrator	1
3	DYR-6100 (Cornell-Dubilier)	Starter-ignition capacitor	1
4		RH control panel	Ref.
5	HDSW-A (Heatherington)	Starter switch	1
6	AN3161-P10	Circuit breaker	1
7	AN3212-1	Ignition switch	1
8	AN3108-18-22S	Receptacle	1
9	AN3100-18-22P	Plug	1
10	No. 1A	Terminal panel	1
11		Reverse current relay	Ref.
12	AAF Type B 8	Starter relay	1
13		Relay panel	Ref.
14	1416 (Mod. 6) (Eclipse)	Starter	1

*Applies to AD-4W airplanes BuNo. 124761 and subsequent.
**Applies to AD-4W airplanes BuNo. 125765 and subsequent.

Figure 4-113. Starting and Ignition System Perspective

switch is depressed into the 'ON' position, the starter relay closes and permits 24V DC power from either the aeroplane battery or from an external power source to energise the starting motor. Placing the starter in the 'ON' position also energises the starting vibrator. A capacitor in the starting system protects the radio circuits from ignition interferences.

The starter is essentially a heavy-duty electric motor containing three planetary gear trains in series, having a total reduction of 133:1, a friction disc clutch pre-set to a torque of 800ft/lb and an automatic jaw engaging and disengaging mechanism. The starter is mounted in the centre of the supercharger rear housing cover directly in line with the engine crankshaft. It is secured to a mounting pad by six studs and nuts. A grounding link, electrically grounded to the firewall structure through a cable, is fastened under one of the mounting studs.

The starter relay is located in the forward starboard section of the forward equipment bay. The relay is a solenoid type, the switch contacts of which are rated to handle

BELOW Starter mounted centrally in the accessory section. From this position it can directly turn the crankshaft from the rear. It is clutched so if there is any restriction in the engine cylinders due to hydraulic locking, the clutch will automatically disengage the starter to prevent engine damage. *(Author)*

RIGHT Starter relay and vibrator. *(Author)*

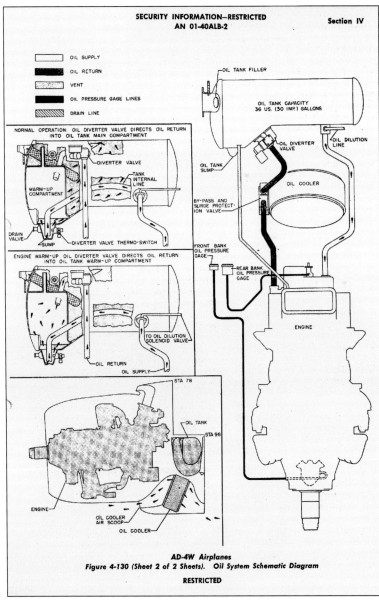

OIL SUPPLY

OIL RETURN

VENT

OIL PRESSURE GAGE LINES

DRAIN LINE

NORMAL OPERATION: OIL DIVERTER VALVE DIRECTS OIL RETURN INTO OIL TANK MAIN COMPARTMENT

DIVERTER VALVE

TANK INTERNAL LINE

WARM-UP COMPARTMENT

DRAIN VALVE

SUMP

DIVERTER VALVE THERMO-SWITCH

ENGINE WARM-UP OIL DIVERTER VALVE DIRECTS OIL RETURN INTO OIL TANK WARM-UP COMPARTMENT

TO OIL DILUTION SOLENOID VALVE

OIL RETURN

OIL SUPPLY

OIL TANK FILLER

OIL TANK CAPACITY
36 US. (30 IMP.) GALLONS

OIL DIVERTER VALVE

OIL DILUTION LINE

OIL TANK SUMP

OIL COOLER

BY-PASS AND SURGE PROTECTION VALVE

FRONT BANK OIL PRESSURE GAGE

REAR BANK OIL PRESSURE GAGE

ENGINE

STA 78

OIL TANK

STA 96

ENGINE

OIL COOLER AIR SCOOP

OIL COOLER

AD-4W Airplanes
Figure 4-130 (Sheet 2 of 2 Sheets). Oil System Schematic Diagram
RESTRICTED

200amps of continuous current. Primarily, the relay serves as a remotely operated high-current capacity switch to connect the battery with the starter. Next to the starter relay is the starting vibrator. The vibrator unit operates on 24V DC which it transforms into interrupted DC. This interrupted DC voltage is conducted to the right-hand primary coil in the magneto, and permits high-tension current to be created by the secondary coil when the magneto is turning at engine-cranking speed. This high-tension current is transmitted to the right-hand distributor, and thence to the forward spark plug in each cylinder.

Oil

The function of the oil system is to cool the engine internally and to provide the lubrication necessary for proper engine operation. The principal units of the oil system include a supply tank, a bypass and surge protection valve, an oil cooler, an oil diverter valve, a thermos switch, an oil cooler door actuator, an oil cooler door control unit, a thermostat and an oil dilution valve. An engine gauge unit on the starboard side of the instrument panel contains an engine oil temperature gauge and a gauge which indicates rear bank oil pressure. A second gauge mounted above the engine gauge unit indicates front bank pressure.

The flow of the oil through the system is as follows: the oil flows from the outlet fitting at the bottom of the tank to the 'OIL IN' connection on the port side of the engine rear sump.

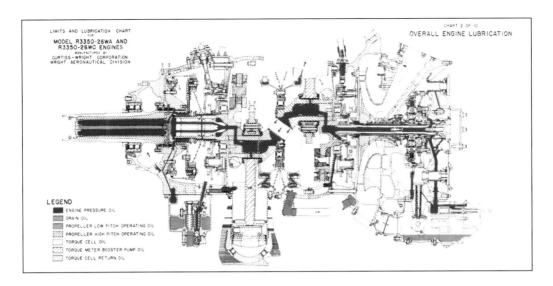

CHART 2 OF 10

LIMITS AND LUBRICATION CHART
for
MODEL R3350-26WA AND
R3350-26WC ENGINES
MANUFACTURED BY
CURTISS-WRIGHT CORPORATION
WRIGHT AERONAUTICAL DIVISION

OVERALL ENGINE LUBRICATION

LEGEND
ENGINE PRESSURE OIL
DRAIN OIL
PROPELLER LOW PITCH OPERATING OIL
PROPELLER HIGH PITCH OPERATING OIL
TORQUE CELL OIL
TORQUE METER BOOSTER PUMP OIL
TORQUE CELL RETURN OIL

LEFT Oil tank fitted to the fuselage firewall. The impressions in the tank give some limited working access to the rear of the port and starboard generators and the starter motor. *(Author)*

Just below the 'OIL IN' connection is a fitting to which an external oil line is attached, the purpose of which is to route some of the oil from the rear sump through to the front sump.

RIGHT Rear oil sump and pump. Shown here during engine installation; the rear sump would take oil directly from the tank and pump it up through the main oil passageways of the engine and forward to the forward oil sump. The rear pump also contains filters and magnetic chip detectors for engine health monitoring. *(Author)*

Two pressure pumps in the rear sump force the oil to the various parts of the engine that require lubrication. As the oil drains from the engine, it is scavenged by four gear-type pumps: two sets of scavenging gears are in the front sump, while the other two sets are in the rear sump. The scavenged oil in the front sump is discharged into an external line which attaches to the 'OIL OUT' fitting on the starboard side of the rear sump. The oil output of all four scavenge pumps is discharged through the 'OIL OUT' connection into a return line which leads to the inlet port of the bypass and surge protection valve on the starboard side of the oil cooler. At the valve assembly, the oil follows one of three routes. Under normal temperatures and pressures, the oil passes through the core of the cooler and into the return line which leads to the tank. When the oil temperature is below normal, flow pressure is high because of high oil viscosity, and the path of flow is primarily through the cooler muff and into the return line. Under extremely low temperatures (very high pressures), the oil bypasses the core and muff of the cooler entirely and flows directly into the return line which leads to the tank. At the diverter valve the oil is directed to either the tank warm-up compartment or to the main tank compartment.

A bypass and surge protection valve is installed on the valve mounting flange of the oil cooler. This valve directs the flow of oil through or around the cooler, and, to that extent, controls the oil temperature. The action of the valve is automatic and depends upon the pressure and the temperature of the oil reaching the valve and cooler assembly. The bypass and surge protection valve consists of a cast machined aluminium alloy housing which contains ports for three valves: a surge protection valve, a bypass jacket and core relief valve and a core check valve. The housing is partitioned adjacent to the inlet port so that the oil can flow either into the cooler or can bypass the cooler by flowing from the inlet port directly to the outlet port of the valve assembly. The direction of flow is determined by the pressure of incoming oil on the two-way actuating surge protection valve. The valve assembly contains four valve seats: one is a hardened, machined valve seat, while the other three are integral

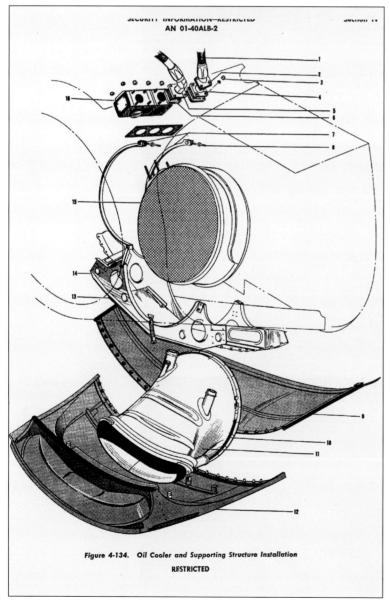

Figure 4-134. *Oil Cooler and Supporting Structure Installation*
RESTRICTED

parts of the valve housing. Two of the seats are used for the two-way surge protection valve. The core check valve is seated by a small spring pressing against it; the bypass jacket and core relief valve by a larger spring; and the surge protection valve by a flat steel spring of greater force than the springs of the bypass jacket, core relief valve and core check valve.

Hot oil coming from the engine is cooled by a 'free flow' 22in-diameter cylindrical oil cooler before the oil is returned to the tank. The cooler is supported by an assembly which is bolted to the lower legs of the engine mount. The air intake duct for the oil cooler is located directly forward of the oil cooler and joins the oil cooler front fairing assembly. The exit duct is directly aft of the cooler and vents the air into the atmosphere at the lower firewall. A door in the exit duct controls the amount of air allowed to flow through the oil cooler, this door being opened or closed by an electrically operated actuator, and can be controlled either automatically or manually as desired.

The all-aluminium construction of the oil cooler offers two advantages: the cooler is lighter in weight than one of the same size which incorporates copper tubes and a brass shell, and brazing the core tubes, rather than soldering them, results in greater strength.

Undercarriage

The main landing gear is located in the centre wing panel, approximately 3½ft outboard of the fuselage. It is fully retractable and hydraulically operated. The main gear operates in conjunction with the tailgear, both being controlled by the landing gear control handle and valve. The principal components of each main gear include a pneumatic/hydraulic shock strut, a high-pressure 32 × 8.8in mainwheel, a hydraulic brake unit and an actuating linkage which raises and lowers the gear. This linkage also causes the strut to pivot so that the wheel is stowed flush with and in the same plane as the wing lower surface, and mechanically locks the gear in the full-up and fully down positions. A telescoping mechanism supplements the actuating linkage by partially retracting the strut for stowage in the wheel well. On some aeroplanes a combination lock-up and lock-

LEFT Oil cooler mounted. (*Author*)

BELOW Undercarriage assembly complete. Part of the success of the Skyraider as a carrier aircraft was the strength of its landing gear; its simple ruggedness is clearly shown here.
(*Neil Hutchinson*)

RIGHT Undercarriage lever in the cockpit – the red safety lock prevents the lever being removed to the retracted position accidentally on the ground. *(Author)*

down indicating switch is mounted on the lock linkage of each gear, while others only have the lock-down indicating switch. The switches are actuated by the linkage through a transfer switch on the gear-supporting truss, to indicate the locked positions of the gear on the landing gear and flap position indicator in the cockpit. A retraction release switch, clamped to the barrel of the port shock strut telescoping mechanism, is actuated by compression of the shock strut

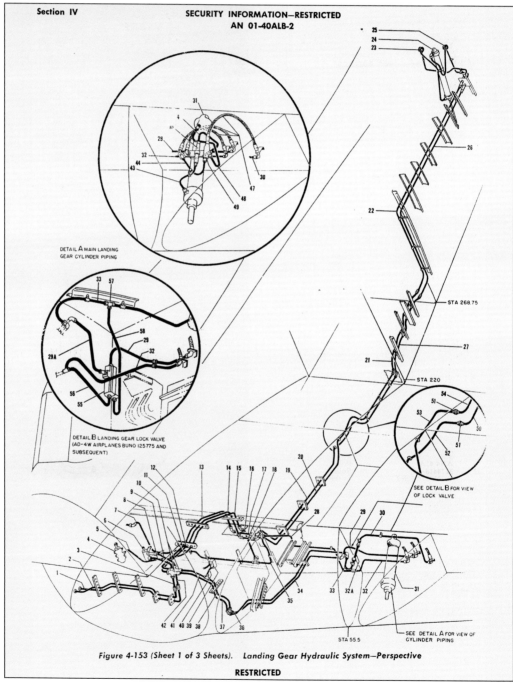

DETAIL A MAIN LANDING GEAR CYLINDER PIPING

DETAIL B LANDING GEAR LOCK VALVE (AD-4W AIRPLANES BUNO 125775 AND SUBSEQUENT)

SEE DETAIL B FOR VIEW OF LOCK VALVE

SEE DETAIL A FOR VIEW OF CYLINDER PIPING

STA 268.75

STA 220

STA 55.5

Figure 4-153 (Sheet 1 of 3 Sheets).   Landing Gear Hydraulic System—Perspective

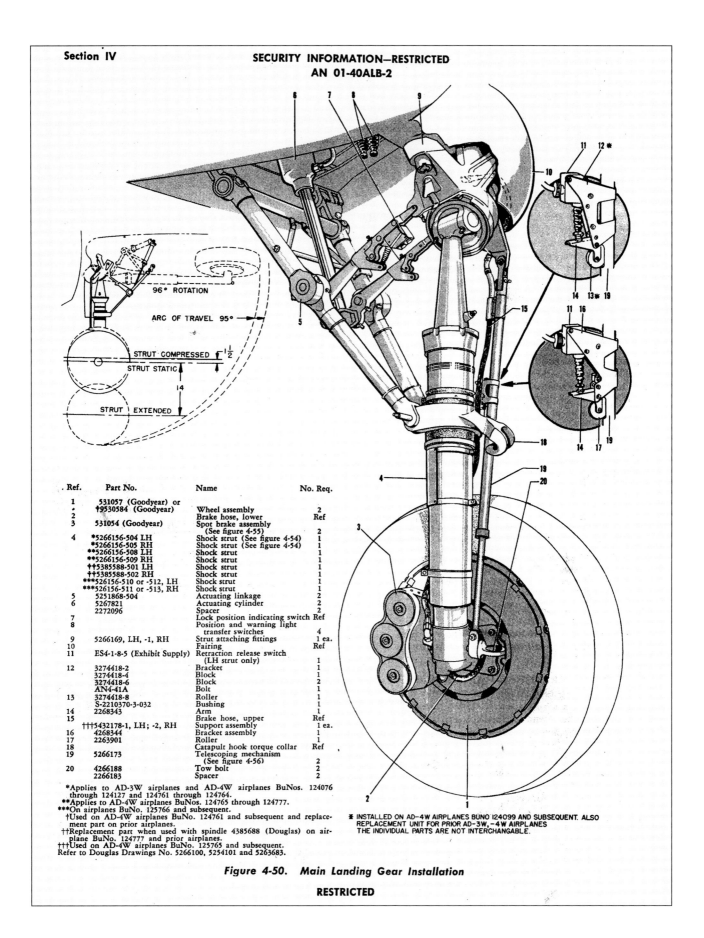

Ref.	Part No.	Name	No. Req.
1	531057 (Goodyear) or	Wheel assembly	2
	†9530584 (Goodyear)		
2		Brake hose, lower	Ref
3	531054 (Goodyear)	Spot brake assembly	2
		(See figure 4-55)	
4	*5266156-504 LH	Shock strut (See figure 4-54)	1
	*5266156-505 RH	Shock strut (See figure 4-54)	1
	**5266156-508 LH	Shock strut	1
	**5266156-509 RH	Shock strut	1
	††5385588-501 LH	Shock strut	1
	††5385588-502 RH	Shock strut	1
	***526156-510 or -512, LH	Shock strut	1
	***526156-511 or -513, RH	Shock strut	1
5	5251868-504	Actuating linkage	2
6	5267821	Actuating cylinder	2
	2272096	Spacer	2
7		Lock position indicating switch	Ref
8		Position and warning light	4
		transfer switches	
9	5266169, LH, -1, RH	Strut attaching fittings	1 ea.
10		Fairing	Ref
11	ES4-1-8-5 (Exhibit Supply)	Retraction release switch	1
		(LH strut only)	
12	3274418-2	Bracket	1
	3274418-4	Block	1
	3274418-6	Block	2
	AN4-41A	Bolt	1
13	3274418-8	Roller	1
	S-2210370-3-032	Bushing	1
14	2268343	Arm	1
15		Brake hose, upper	Ref
	†††5432178-1, LH; -2, RH	Support assembly	1 ea.
16	4268344	Bracket assembly	1
17	2263901	Roller	1
18		Catapult hook torque collar	Ref
19	5266173	Telescoping mechanism	2
		(See figure 4-56)	
20	4266188	Tow bolt	2
	2266183	Spacer	2

*Applies to AD-3W airplanes and AD-4W airplanes BuNos. 124076
through 124127 and 124761 through 124764.
**Applies to AD-4W airplanes BuNos. 124765 through 124777.
***On airplanes BuNo. 125766 and subsequent.
†Used on AD-4W airplanes BuNo. 124761 and subsequent and replace-
ment part on prior airplanes.
††Replacement part when used with spindle 4385688 (Douglas) on air-
plane BuNo. 124777 and prior airplanes.
†††Used on AD-4W airplanes BuNo. 125765 and subsequent.
Refer to Douglas Drawings No. 5266100, 5254101 and 5263683.

✱ INSTALLED ON AD-4W AIRPLANES BUNO 124099 AND SUBSEQUENT. ALSO
REPLACEMENT UNIT FOR PRIOR AD-3W, -4W AIRPLANES
THE INDIVIDUAL PARTS ARE NOT INTERCHANGABLE.

Figure 4-50. Main Landing Gear Installation

RESTRICTED

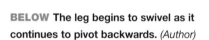

ABOVE Main gear retraction sequence starting with the gear down and locked. *(Author)*

ABOVE The down locks disengage with the movement of the retraction jack, the leg is now travelled aft to a vertical position. *(Author)*

BELOW The leg begins to swivel as it continues to pivot backwards. *(Author)*

BELOW It continues to rotate as it travels aft. *(Author)*

BELOW The wheel is now completely aligned to fit in the wing wheel bay – once the retract sequence is complete, the doors will close to streamline the wheel bay. *(Author)*

to de-energise a safety solenoid which prevents inadvertent movement of the landing gear control handle to the 'wheels up' position when the aeroplane is resting upon its gear. When retracted, the gear is enclosed by a contoured fairing and hydraulically operated doors.

The landing gear control handle is connected to the landing gear control valve and the emergency and auxiliary pump selector valve by control rod, bellcrank and lever linkage. Placing the handle in the 'wheels up' or 'wheels down' position operates the landing gear control valve to raise or lower the gear by pressure from the main hydraulic system; placing the handle in the 'EMER' position causes the linkage to over travel and operate a lever and limit switch to cut in the auxiliary valve and pump to supply sufficient pressure to lower the main gear only.

The tailgear is retractable, non-steerable, but fully castoring through 360°. It is actuated hydraulically and operates simultaneously with the main landing gear. The tailgear is housed in the fuselage forward of the rear bulkhead below the vertical stabiliser. Principal components of the tailgear include an actuating cylinder, a pneumatic/hydraulic shock strut, a yoke, a solid tyre wheel, a retraction shaft, a wheel centring and a separate wheel locking mechanism which operates to hold the wheel in a straight forward– and aft–position for retraction and extension. A position indicating switch is mounted on the supporting structure and is actuated by a special bolt through the port side of the retracting shaft to register the full up or down position of the gear on the landing gear and flap position indicator in the cockpit.

Wheels and brakes

The aircraft is equipped with 32 × 8.8in mainwheels and Goodyear single disc 'spot' brakes. The mainwheel is a drop-centre type aluminium-alloy casting with a removable outer rim with the axle bore containing inboard and outboard roller bearings. The wheel itself weighs 29.5lb and is statically balanced. The steel drive ring bolted to the inboard flange of the wheel engages with the rotor disc of the spot brake. The wheel carries a 12-ply tyre with regular tubes and inflating valve.

The spot brake consists of an aluminium alloy housing which contains three

LEFT Tailwheel unit with weight off and therefore oleo strut fully extended. *(Author)*

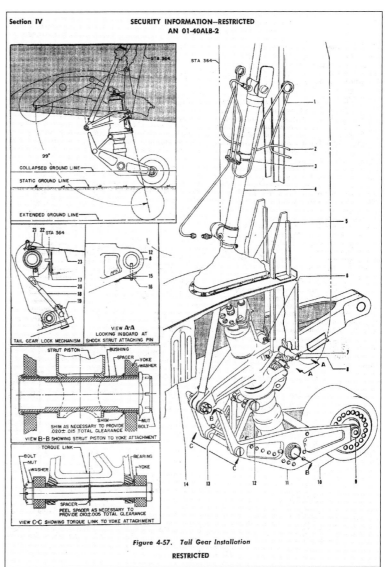

Figure 4-57. Tail Gear Installation

VIEW A
AD-4W AIRPLANES
BUNO 124761 & SUBSEQUENT

Figure 4-157 (Sheet 1 of 2 Sheets). Brake Hydraulic System—Perspective

RESTRICTED

ABOVE LEFT Mainwheels. Clearly visible here are the three brake cylinders which apply braking pressure to the disc, and, forward of the leg, the red towing ring for ground towing of the aircraft. *(Author)*

ABOVE The single brake disc and axle stub of the port gear leg. *(Author)*

interconnected, magnesium alloy 'spots' or pistons, and a single chrome-plated steel rotor disc held between two raybestos linings housed in each piston cavity. The disc contains 12 keyways which engage the keys on the drive ring of the wheel so that the disc revolves with the wheel. The pistons are held in the housing cavities by individual cylinder heads sealed with O-rings. The fluid supply port is located between the middle and lowest cavities and the bleeders are in the lowest cavity. The operation of the spot brake is substantially as follows: when hydraulic pressure is applied it acts against the cylinder heads and the pistons. The increased volume presses the pistons against the inboard linings, the inboard linings against the rotor disc and the disc against the outboard linings so that equal pressure is exerted on both sides of the disc to retard the speed of the disc and the wheel. When braking pressure is released, two washer-type springs, held in each piston by a lock ring, assist in releasing the brake. As the linings wear, brake clearance is automatically

RIGHT The Skyraider's large and powerful aileron surfaces. Seen here is the cockpit adjustable trim tab – the same tab on the other side is ground adjustable only. *(Author)*

adjusted by the action of the springs to maintain the correct return distance of the piston, although the complete piston unit gradually pulls the adjustment pin through its packing nut and moves closer to the disc to absorb the amount of lining wear.

Flying controls

The ailerons are metal-covered moveable surfaces installed at the trailing edges of the outboard wing panels. Each aileron incorporates a main spar, an auxiliary channel in the nose and a trailing edge channel, together with chord-wise ribs. The aileron is hinged to the outboard wing panel at three points and is actuated by a push-pull tube at the inboard end. A fabric gap seal is riveted to the aileron nose and is attached by Dzus fasteners to a channel along the shear web. Each aileron incorporates one tab: a moveable trim tab on the port aileron and a fixed ground adjustable only tab on the starboard aileron. Cables extend from the aileron trim tab control drum in the port side cockpit through the centre wing nose section to a lead screw mechanism in the outboard wing panel. The lead screw shaft is connected to a push-pull tube which operates the trim tab. A cable take-up mechanism consisting of a pair of spring-loaded pulley arms, is provided in the centre wing section to maintain the proper tension in the cables when the wing is folded. The trailing edges of the ailerons incorporate static wick dischargers, the number depending on the

RIGHT Aileron access panels for servicing the aileron hinge points. There is a fabric seal between the aileron leading edge and the rear spar to reduce the volume of air leaking from the lower wing surface up and over the top of the control surface, which would reduce the aileron's effectiveness. *(Author)*

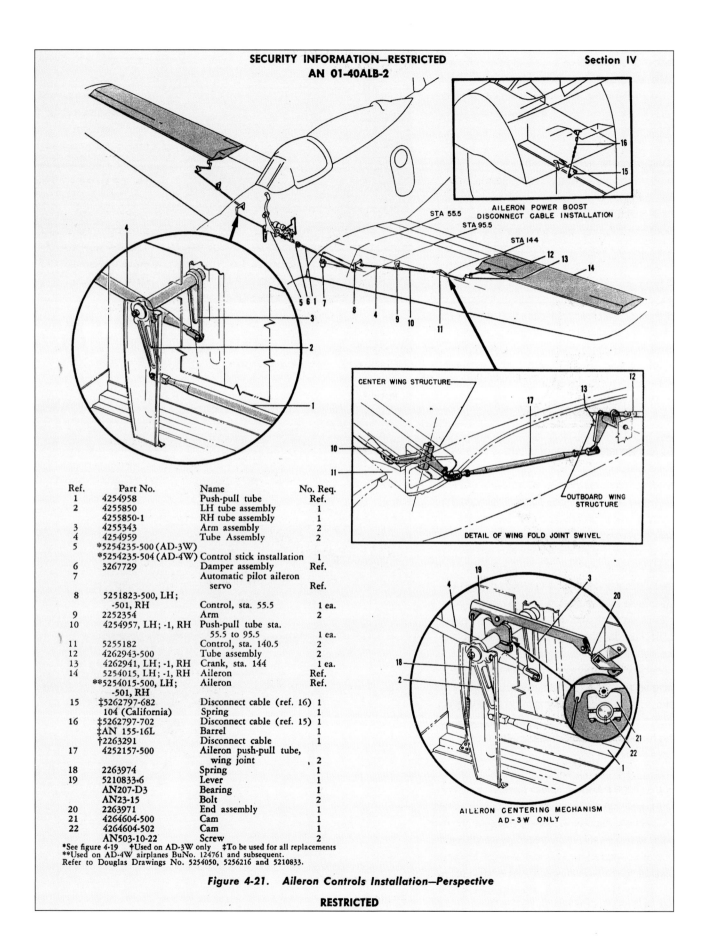

AILERON POWER BOOST
DISCONNECT CABLE INSTALLATION

STA 55.5
STA 95.5
STA 144

CENTER WING STRUCTURE

OUTBOARD WING
STRUCTURE

DETAIL OF WING FOLD JOINT SWIVEL

AILERON CENTERING MECHANISM
AD-3W ONLY

Ref.	Part No.	Name	No. Req.
1	4254958	Push-pull tube	Ref.
2	4255850	LH tube assembly	1
	4255850-1	RH tube assembly	1
3	4255343	Arm assembly	2
4	4254959	Tube Assembly	2
5	*5254235-500 (AD-3W)		
	*5254235-504 (AD-4W)	Control stick installation	1
6	3267729	Damper assembly	Ref.
7		Automatic pilot aileron servo	Ref.
8	5251823-500, LH; -501, RH	Control, sta. 55.5	1 ea.
9	2252354	Arm	2
10	4254957, LH; -1, RH	Push-pull tube sta. 55.5 to 95.5	1 ea.
11	5255182	Control, sta. 140.5	2
12	4262943-500	Tube assembly	2
13	4262941, LH; -1, RH	Crank, sta. 144	1 ea.
14	5254015, LH; -1, RH	Aileron	Ref.
	**5254015-500, LH; -501, RH	Aileron	Ref.
15	‡5262797-682	Disconnect cable (ref. 16)	1
	104 (California)	Spring	1
16	‡5262797-702	Disconnect cable (ref. 15)	1
	‡AN 155-16L	Barrel	1
	†2263291	Disconnect cable	1
17	4252157-500	Aileron push-pull tube, wing joint	2
18	2263974	Spring	1
19	5210833-6	Lever	1
	AN207-D3	Bearing	1
	AN23-15	Bolt	2
20	2263971	End assembly	1
21	4264604-500	Cam	1
22	4264604-502	Cam	1
	AN503-10-22	Screw	2

*See figure 4-19   †Used on AD-3W only   ‡To be used for all replacements
**Used on AD-4W airplanes BuNo. 124761 and subsequent.
Refer to Douglas Drawings No. 5254050, 5256216 and 5210833.

Figure 4-21. Aileron Controls Installation—Perspective

RESTRICTED

model of Skyraider (early models having two fitted, later models three).

Aileron power boost system

The ailerons are normally operated by stick-controlled linkages augmented by hydraulically boosted power to reduce stick forces. The hydraulic booster system includes an engine-driven pump, an actuating cylinder, a relief valve, a line filter and a check valve. It is a closed system with fluid supplied by and returning to the main system reservoir, and operates under a pressure of 500–650psi. The return line passes through a venturi assembly and introduces air for pressurising the reservoir. The hydraulic system is connected with the aileron mechanical linkage by the actuating cylinder and can be disconnected in flight or on the ground by operating the release handle installed in the port control panel in the cockpit.

The elevators are of all-metal construction. Each incorporates a formed spar, a trailing edge channel, formed chord-wise ribs, chord-wise angle stiffeners and stressed skin. The tip of the elevator includes a balance horn in which steel weights are mounted to statically balance the elevator. A fabric gap seal is attached to the nose section of the elevator and to the trailing edge of the horizontal stabiliser. The elevators are interchangeable and can be installed on either the port or starboard side of the horizontal stabiliser. A metal tab which is adjustable by hand bending is riveted on to the trailing edge of each elevator.

The rudder is of all-metal construction; it incorporates a formed spar, a trailing edge closing channel, formed chord-wise ribs, chord-wise angle stiffeners and stressed skin. The top of the rudder includes a balance horn in which lead weights are mounted to statically balance the rudder. A fabric gap seal is attached to the nose section of the rudder and to the trailing edge of the vertical stabiliser, between the two upper hinge points. A spring tab and a trim tab form a portion of the trailing edge of the rudder.

The wing flaps at the trailing edge of the centre wing panel are hydraulically controlled and are operated through mechanical linkage originating in the fuselage and extending to the inboard hinge of each flap. The hydraulic actuating cylinder in the bottom of the radio

compartment is linked to torque tubes which extend from their connection with the cylinder to links fastened to the flap hinges. Co-ordination of port to starboard flap movement is achieved by the connection of both torque tubes to the single drive link attached to the actuating cylinder piston rod and by an idler link connecting the piston rod with the flap mechanism support. Extension of the piston rod

LEFT Aileron hydraulic boost control unit in the forward equipment bay seen here behind the aileron control cables. The hydraulic circuit is completed by the two yellow collared lines leading into the back of the unit. Also seen at the top of this image is the silver-painted hydraulic filter element. *(Author)*

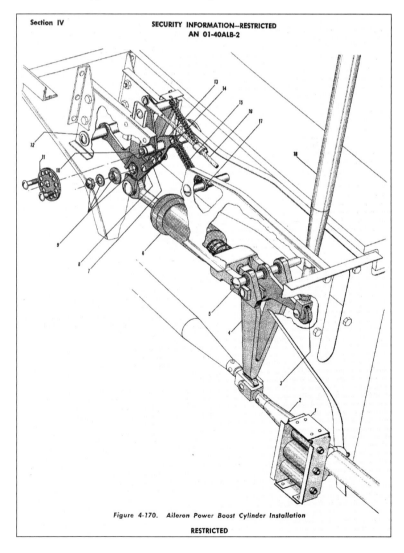

Section IV

SECURITY INFORMATION—RESTRICTED
AN 01-40ALB-2

Figure 4-170. Aileron Power Boost Cylinder Installation

RESTRICTED

RIGHT Elevator balance horn on the starboard elevator. *(Author)*

RIGHT The rudder on the Skyraider is tall but not particularly wide. Given the offset fin and rear fuselage that helps counteract the torque from the propeller, it doesn't need to be. However, it does carry both pilot-controllable and sprung trim tabs (seen here) to help ease the loads on the pilot's thigh muscles for long flights. *(Neil Hutchinson)*

BELOW Flaps lowered. *(Author)*

BELOW RIGHT Flap control lever situated outboard and below the throttle quadrant. *(Author)*

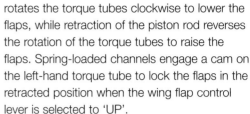

rotates the torque tubes clockwise to lower the flaps, while retraction of the piston rod reverses the rotation of the torque tubes to raise the flaps. Spring-loaded channels engage a cam on the left-hand torque tube to lock the flaps in the retracted position when the wing flap control lever is selected to 'UP'.

These control surfaces include conventional cable systems to operate the elevators, the rudder and the aileron and rudder trim tabs; a hydraulically boosted push-pull tube system to operate the ailerons; electrical control of the horizontal stabiliser and hydraulic control of the wing flaps and, if fitted, fuselage dive brakes. The ailerons and elevators are operated by the control stick in the cockpit, the rudder by foot pedals. For the elevators, a push-pull tube connects the horn of the control stick with a differential cable drum, the cables of which actuate sectors bolted to the left- and right-hand torque tubes in the aft end of the forward equipment bay. Movement of the stick rotates the torque tubes and pulls dual sets of cables connected to bellcranks riveted to the outboard end of the torque tubes. A load-feel bungee spring mechanism is attached to the right-hand bellcrank. A bob weight is fixed to the torque tube to reduce high forces in the elevator control system. Cables are routed through the fuselage to bellcranks on the forward side of the major rear bulkhead. A push-pull tube extends from one bellcrank through the bulkhead to an operating arm mounted on the horizontal stabiliser yoke and attached to the elevator

torque tubes. The rudder is operated by cables, firstly from the rudder pedals to a bellcrank and then aft of that bellcrank to a push-pull tube to a spring mechanism secured to the rudder spar. Forward movement of the rod deflects the rudder to starboard, therefore aft movement of the rod deflects the rudder to port. A spring tab in the rudder operates automatically to decrease pedal forces.

Cockpit and instrumentation

The majority of the instruments installed in this aeroplane are located on the instrument panel. These are classified according to purpose, including flight instruments, engine instruments, hydraulic instruments and warning light indicators. The pilot's instrument panel is installed immediately aft of the firewall and is shock mounted. It is held in a vertical position by two rods, which are affixed through grommets at two points on the upper portion of the panel and shock mounted to brackets on the gun sight support. For indirect lighting of the instruments, a mask assembly is fastened over the face of the panel. A shock-mounted panel located at the lower port corner of the instrument panel contains the wheels and flaps position indicator and the ignition switch.

Automatic pilot system

The automatic pilot system is essentially a gyroscopically controlled, electrically actuated system automatically operating flight controls to maintain the desired magnetic heading and simultaneously retain stabilised pitch and bank attitudes of the aeroplane. Operation of the system is dependent upon electrical signals emanating from three sources (1) the direction signal originating in the remote compass, (2) the rate-of-turn signal originating in the bank and turn indicator and (3) the pitch and bank signal originating in the gyro horizon indicator. These signals control the direction of rotation of servo units that are connected to the flight controls, thereby converting electrical impulses into mechanical motion. To prevent over-control of the aeroplane a follow-up signal originating in the servo unit opposes the control signal. By proper combination of control and opposing

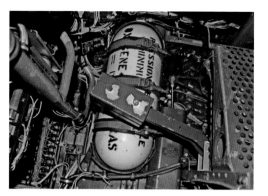

LEFT Elevator bob weight in the forward equipment bay. Behind, mounted on the starboard wall of the fuselage, is the crew's oxygen supply bottle. *(Author)*

follow-up signals, the aeroplane is returned to the proper attitude or heading without a tendency to 'hunt' about a straight and level flight condition.

The automatic pilot system is disabled on G-RADR due to permit to fly restrictions for operation in the United Kingdom.

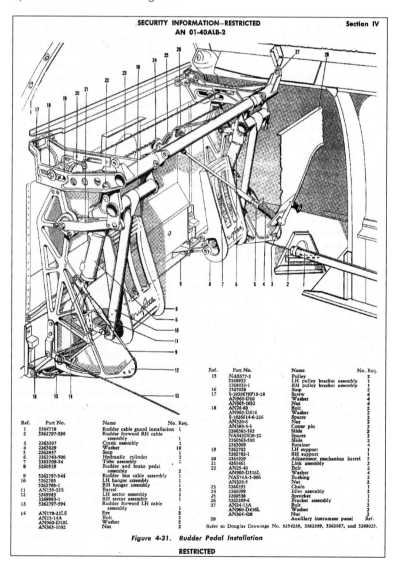

Figure 4-31. Rudder Pedal Installation

RIGHT Instrument panel as fitted to G-RADR. Of special note is the yellow and black striped handle on the starboard side of the cockpit – this is actually a short blade knife, used by the pilot in case of the need to cut his straps or deflate an accidentally inflated life vest. *(Author)*

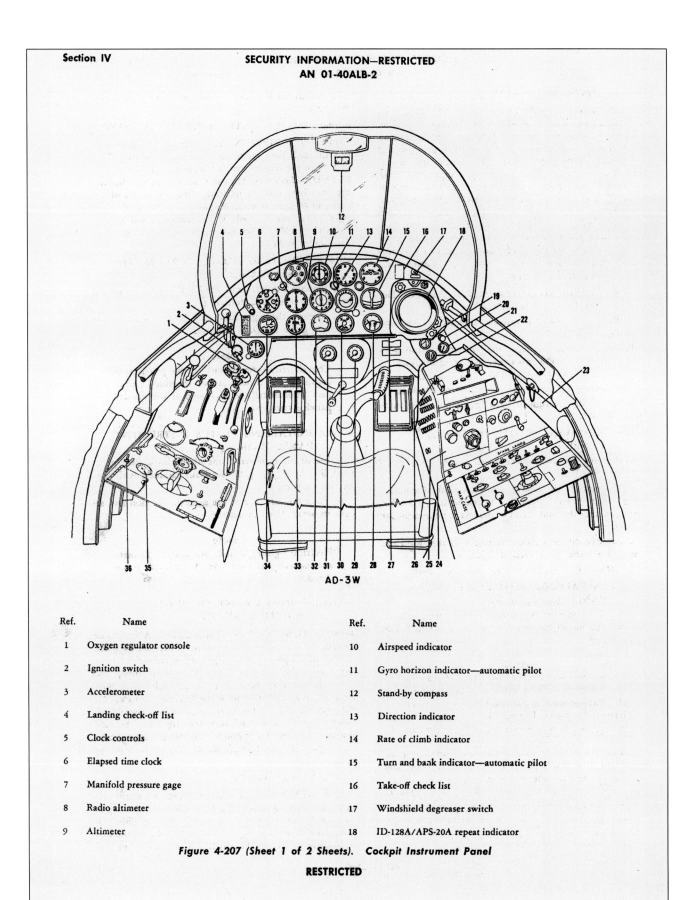

AD-3W

Ref.	Name	Ref.	Name
1	Oxygen regulator console	10	Airspeed indicator
2	Ignition switch	11	Gyro horizon indicator—automatic pilot
3	Accelerometer	12	Stand-by compass
4	Landing check-off list	13	Direction indicator
5	Clock controls	14	Rate of climb indicator
6	Elapsed time clock	15	Turn and bank indicator—automatic pilot
7	Manifold pressure gage	16	Take-off check list
8	Radio altimeter	17	Windshield degreaser switch
9	Altimeter	18	ID-128A/APS-20A repeat indicator

Figure 4-207 (Sheet 1 of 2 Sheets). Cockpit Instrument Panel

RESTRICTED

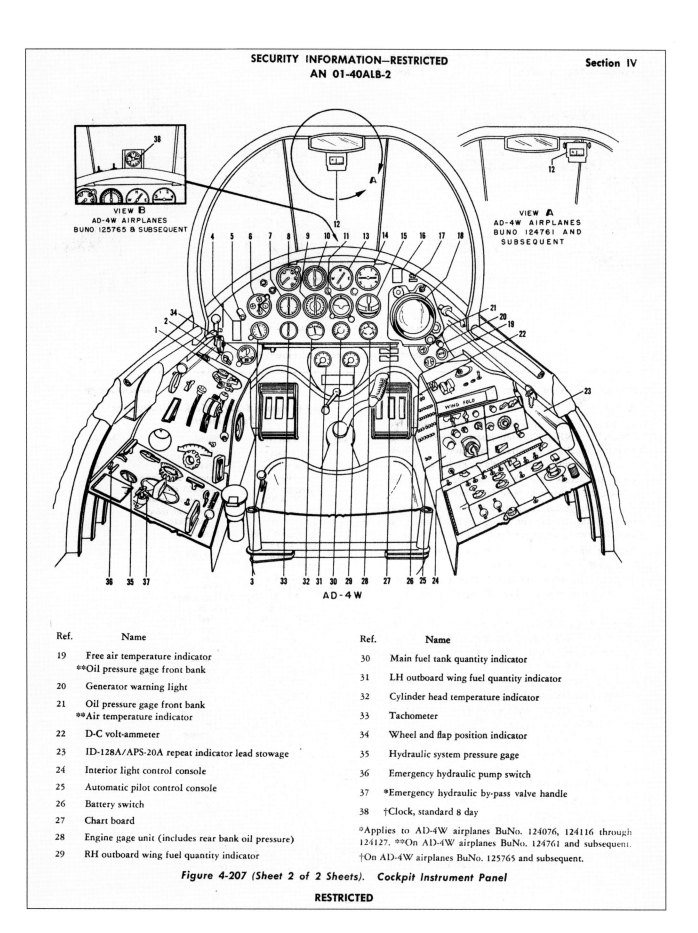

VIEW B
AD-4W AIRPLANES
BUNO 125765 & SUBSEQUENT

VIEW A
AD-4W AIRPLANES
BUNO 124761 AND
SUBSEQUENT

AD-4W

Ref.	Name	Ref.	Name
19	Free air temperature indicator **Oil pressure gage front bank	30	Main fuel tank quantity indicator
20	Generator warning light	31	LH outboard wing fuel quantity indicator
21	Oil pressure gage front bank **Air temperature indicator	32	Cylinder head temperature indicator
22	D-C volt-ammeter	33	Tachometer
23	ID-128A/APS-20A repeat indicator lead stowage	34	Wheel and flap position indicator
24	Interior light control console	35	Hydraulic system pressure gage
25	Automatic pilot control console	36	Emergency hydraulic pump switch
26	Battery switch	37	*Emergency hydraulic by-pass valve handle
27	Chart board	38	†Clock, standard 8 day
28	Engine gage unit (includes rear bank oil pressure)		
29	RH outboard wing fuel quantity indicator		

*Applies to AD-4W airplanes BuNo. 124076, 124116 through 124127. **On AD-4W airplanes BuNo. 124761 and subsequent.
†On AD-4W airplanes BuNo. 125765 and subsequent.

Figure 4-207 (Sheet 2 of 2 Sheets). Cockpit Instrument Panel

RESTRICTED

Chapter Four

Wright R-3350 engine

Born out of competition with rivals Pratt & Whitney, who had developed their Twin Wasp from the popular Wasp Radial, Wright needed a competitive engine if it was to win more government contracts. They created the Twin Cyclone and a larger development of this engine, which became the R-3350 engine.

OPPOSITE **The impressively large Wright R-3350 radial engine on the Skyraider.** *(Author)*

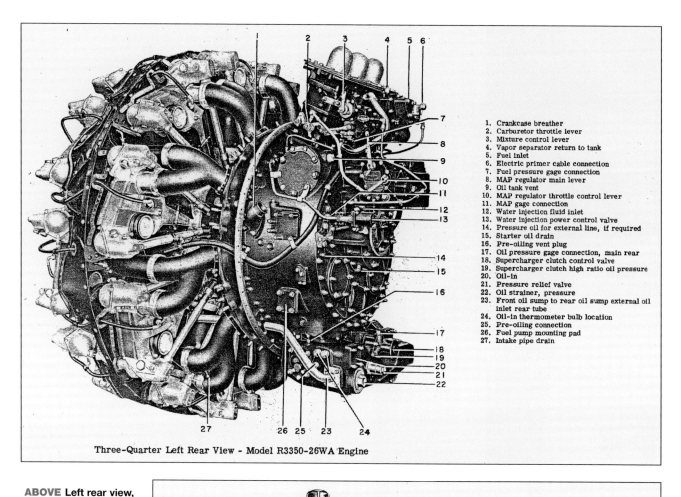

1. Crankcase breather
2. Carburetor throttle lever
3. Mixture control lever
4. Vapor separator return to tank
5. Fuel inlet
6. Electric primer cable connection
7. Fuel pressure gage connection
8. MAP regulator main lever
9. Oil tank vent
10. MAP regulator throttle control lever
11. MAP gage connection
12. Water injection fluid inlet
13. Water injection power control valve
14. Pressure oil for external line, if required
15. Starter oil drain
16. Pre-oiling vent plug
17. Oil pressure gage connection, main rear
18. Supercharger clutch control valve
19. Supercharger clutch high ratio oil pressure
20. Oil-in
21. Pressure relief valve
22. Oil strainer, pressure
23. Front oil sump to rear oil sump external oil inlet rear tube
24. Oil-in thermometer bulb location
25. Pre-oiling connection
26. Fuel pump mounting pad
27. Intake pipe drain

Three-Quarter Left Rear View - Model R3350-26WA Engine

ABOVE Left rear view, Model R3350-26WA engine. *(US Navy)*

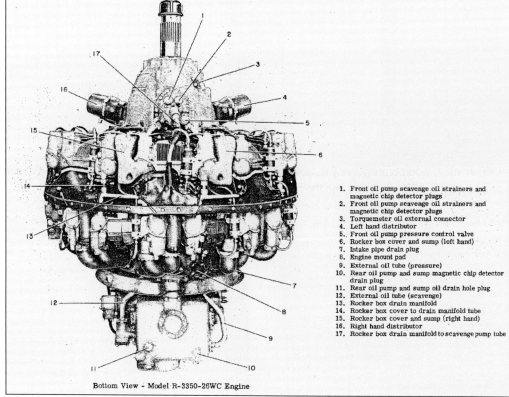

1. Front oil pump scavenge oil strainers and magnetic chip detector plugs
2. Front oil pump scavenge oil strainers and magnetic chip detector plugs
3. Torquemeter oil external connector
4. Left hand distributor
5. Front oil pump pressure control valve
6. Rocker box cover and sump (left hand)
7. Intake pipe drain plug
8. Engine mount pad
9. External oil tube (pressure)
10. Rear oil pump and sump magnetic chip detector drain plug
11. Rear oil pump and sump oil drain hole plug
12. External oil tube (scavenge)
13. Rocker box drain manifold
14. Rocker box cover to drain manifold tube
15. Rocker box cover and sump (right hand)
16. Right hand distributor
17. Rocker box drain manifold to scavenge pump tube

RIGHT Bottom view, Model R-3350-26WC engine. *(US Navy)*

Bottom View - Model R-3350-26WC Engine

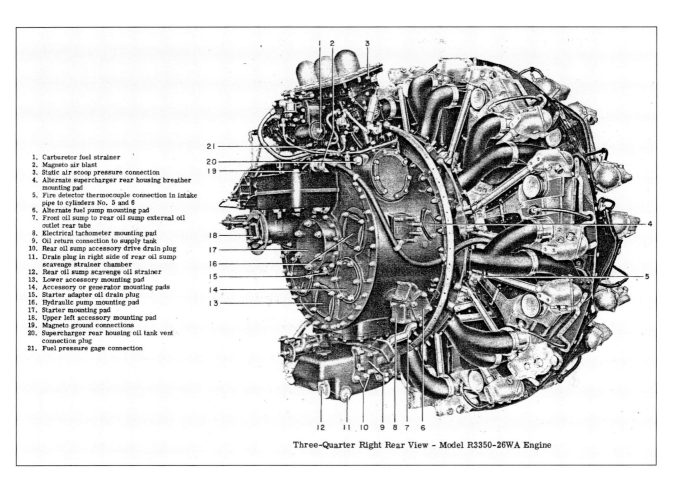

1. Carburetor fuel strainer
2. Magneto air blast
3. Static air scoop pressure connection
4. Alternate supercharger rear housing breather mounting pad
5. Fire detector thermocouple connection in intake pipe to cylinders No. 5 and 6
6. Alternate fuel pump mounting pad
7. Front oil sump to rear oil sump external oil outlet rear tube
8. Electrical tachometer mounting pad
9. Oil return connection to supply tank
10. Rear oil sump accessory drive drain plug
11. Drain plug in right side of rear oil sump scavenge strainer chamber
12. Rear oil sump scavenge oil strainer
13. Lower accessory mounting pad
14. Accessory or generator mounting pads
15. Starter adapter oil drain plug
16. Hydraulic pump mounting pad
17. Starter mounting pad
18. Upper left accessory mounting pad
19. Magneto ground connections
20. Supercharger rear housing oil tank vent connection plug
21. Fuel pressure gage connection

Three-Quarter Right Rear View - Model R3350-26WA Engine

ABOVE Three-quarter right rear view, Model R3350-26WA engine. *(US Navy)*

The Wright R-3350 engine was forever dogged with cooling problems and it wasn't until it was redesigned post-war for the Lockheed Constellation airliner that many of the long-term issues were sorted out. It was fairly simple by design, however, and its manufacture quite 'agricultural', which meant it was quick to build and spares were never a problem, even to this day.

Wright began the development of the R-3350 in 1937, incorporating many established Cyclone model R-1820 attributes into the new engine. The R-3350 is an air-cooled duplex engine with 18 cylinders arranged in two radial rings of nine surrounding the crankshaft. The cylinder heads radiate outward where they can be cooled by the airflow from the propeller blades. The design created an engine with twice the power of the R-1820 as used on the B17, but with the same frontal area. Early use of the R-3350 was in the Boeing B-29 Superfortress, and in an attempt to decrease the drag of these massive engines, Boeing had encased the engine in a snug cowl. Unfortunately, although

aerodynamically efficient, it limited airflow which led to cooling problems. To counter this, Wright's engineers increased the number of fins on each cylinder from 40 to 54 to vastly increase the cooling area on the cylinder. The much improved engine didn't initially prove reliable with the Skyraider; however, increasingly bigger versions of the engine did iron out some of the early development problems, and the engine continued to give relatively reliable service, although cooling issues never did fully go away. Problems continued throughout the engine's life with the rear cylinders due to a lack of cooling airflow. When a cylinder overheated it could burn the lubricating oil off the valves, which then stuck, resulting in the engine 'eating' its valve – this could sometimes even lead to a fire. Another problem was the tendency of the engine to backfire through the carburettor causing a gasoline fire. This was eventually

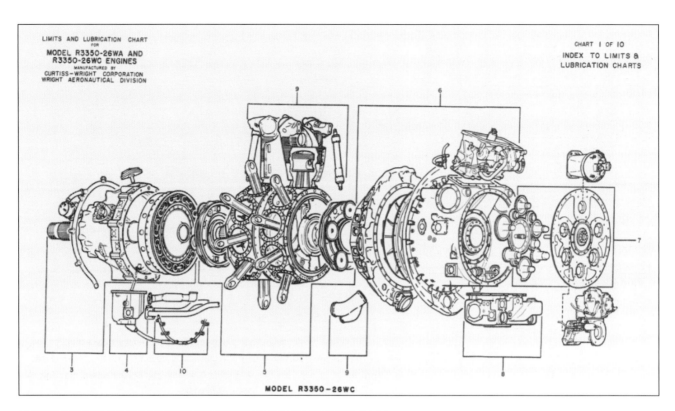

LIMITS AND LUBRICATION CHART
FOR
MODEL R3350-26WA AND
R3350-26WC ENGINES
MANUFACTURED BY
CURTISS-WRIGHT CORPORATION
WRIGHT AERONAUTICAL DIVISION

CHART 1 OF 10
INDEX TO LIMITS &
LUBRICATION CHARTS

MODEL R3350-26WC

solved with the fuel-injected -57 and -59 model engines, although these were never fitted to Skyraiders. The constant design changes required to correct problems as they arose or to improve the performance produced an amazing 6,427 design changes, each involving groups of parts and these in turn needed 48,500 engineering releases and change notes to implement. The engine itself is relatively simple, being split into four main sections:

Nose section

This contains the planetary type reduction gears that reduce the speed of the propeller shaft to .35 that of the crankshaft speed. It also contains an oil sump at the bottom with a combination scavenger and pressure pump.

LEFT Engine nose section shown prior to fitting to the engine power section. The starboard distributor mounting point can be clearly seen. The governor mounts to the top of the nose case (seen here on the left), while the forward oil sump mounts to the lower mounting are shown here on the right. *(Author)*

ENGINE TECHNICAL SPECIFICATIONS

Number of cylinders	18
Bore	6.125in
Stroke	6.312in
Compression ratio	6.70:1
Impeller ratio low	6.46:1
Impeller ratio high	8.67:1
Engine rotation	Anti-clockwise
Max cylinder temp	260°C
Overall diameter	55.84in
Overall length	80.81in
Total dry weight	2,907lb
Oil sump	Dry
Oil pressure @2,600rpm	70psi
Max hp take-off (5 mins)	2,700bhp
Max hp combat (30 mins)	2,700bhp
Max hp normal (continuous)	2,300bhp

ABOVE Engine nose case planetary gears. The planetary gears pick up from the power section and provide the reduction gearing to the propeller shaft. Distributor and governor gearing are driven directly by the power section and are not affected by the planet gears. *(Author)*

The propeller governor and ignition units are mounted externally to the nose case, driven by quill shafts that are in turn driven by internal gearing from the crankshaft output.

Power section

This contains the 18 cylinders staggered in two rows of nine. Valve actuating rods extend externally, activated by four-lobe cams rotating at ⅛ crankshaft speed at the nose and supercharger sections to valve rocker boxes on the front and rear row cylinder heads respectively. At the base of each actuating rod is an individual hydraulic tappet and roller assembly. Each row of cylinders connects to the crankshaft via a master

RIGHT Crankshaft gearing and forward cams. The large gear at the top picks up on the planet gears to provide reduction gearing from the crankshaft to the propeller shaft. The lower gears provide the necessary timing links for the distributors and governor with the output for the port distributor seen here at an angle of approximately 80° to the main gear. Below the gears are the two smooth cam gears that control the forward tappets. *(Author)*

ABOVE Hydraulic tappet and tappet guide shown disassembled. The roller follows the cam gears and the sprung tappet head moves the pushrod to the valve. There are 36 hydraulic tappets all exactly the same. *(Author)*

con rod and eight articulating rods. The master rod is attached to the No. 1 cylinder on the rear row and the No. 10 cylinder on the front row. Changing the No. 1 master cylinder was rare and required special care. As the cylinder was lifted off the piston, it was necessary to rig a holder to keep the master rod centred in the open port. All eight articulating rods for that row are connected to the base of the master rod. If the master rod tilted beyond certain boundaries, attached articulating rods would pull pistons too far into the crankcase and the piston rings would pop to full expansion, making it impossible to put them back without stripping the engine. Both rows of cylinders exhaust rearwards, some pairing up with adjoining cylinders to exit the cowlings in four banks of three exhaust ports, two banks each side of the cowling.

Supercharger section

The R-3350 has a single-speed centrifugal distribution, impeller-type supercharger with a vane-type diffuser plate geared to run at 6.06 crankshaft speed. The impeller has a 13in diameter and is located forward of the supercharger rear housing. Fuel and air are directed to the impeller where they are centrifugally compressed and distributed to the individual cylinder intake pipes. The impeller boosts the pressure of the fuel/air mixture by approximately 17in Hg at 2,400rpm.

ABOVE The unpainted engine power section mounted to the painted induction ring. The power section is bolted to the induction ring by 17 large bolts that are all torques and wire-locked for security. *(Author)*

RIGHT Exhaust outlets. *(Author)*

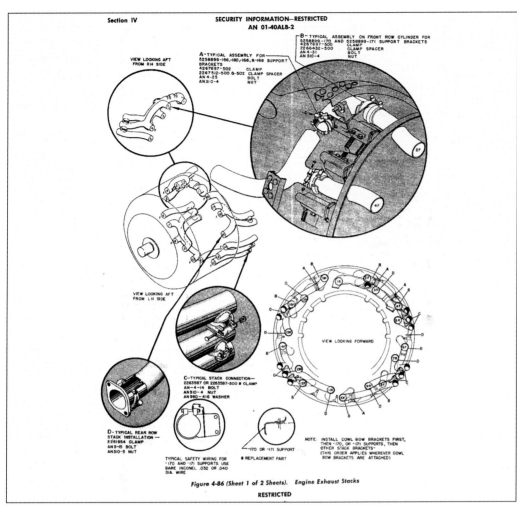

VIEW LOOKING AFT
FROM RH SIDE

A—TYPICAL ASSEMBLY FOR
5258899-156,-160,-166,&-168 SUPPORT
BRACKETS
4267697-502   CLAMP
2267512-500 &-502   CLAMP SPACER
AN 4-25   BOLT
AN310-4   NUT

B—TYPICAL ASSEMBLY ON FRONT ROW CYLINDER FOR
5258899-170 AND 5258899-171 SUPPORT BRACKETS
4267697-500   CLAMP
2266432-500   CLAMP SPACER
AN 4-31   BOLT
AN310-4   NUT

VIEW LOOKING AFT
FROM LH SIDE

C—TYPICAL STACK CONNECTION—
2263587 OR 2263587-500 & CLAMP
AN-4-14   BOLT
AN310-4   NUT
AN960-416 WASHER

D—TYPICAL REAR ROW
STACK INSTALLATION—
2261954 CLAMP
AN5-15 BOLT
AN310-5 NUT

TYPICAL SAFETY WIRING FOR
-170 AND -171 SUPPORTS. USE
BARE INCONEL .032 OR .040
DIA. WIRE

-170 OR -171 SUPPORT

* REPLACEMENT PART

VIEW LOOKING FORWARD

NOTE: INSTALL COWL BOW BRACKETS FIRST,
THEN -170, OR -171 SUPPORTS, THEN
OTHER STACK BRACKETS.
(THIS ORDER APPLIES WHEREVER COWL
BOW BRACKETS ARE ATTACHED)

Figure 4-86 (Sheet 1 of 2 Sheets).   Engine Exhaust Stacks

RESTRICTED

BELOW LEFT

The supercharger impeller seen through the opening in the supercharger for the input of the fuel/air mixture from the carburettor. *(Author)*

BELOW Supercharger unit. The supercharger is largely an empty case with a small impeller mounted in the very centre. Most of the void in the rear section shown here is taken up with accessory section gearing. *(Author)*

Engine accessory section

This contains a series of gear trains for the starter and accessory drives such as the generators and the fuel, oil and vacuum pumps.

Water injection

Although G-RADR is no longer fitted with its water equipment, the system is included here for interest.

The water injection system consists essentially of a tank for water supply, a water pump and a water injection power control assembly. In some Skyraiders, the water injection tank is utilised for anti-icing fluid.

The position of a manually operated selector valve – which is accessible through the forward equipment compartment access doors – determines whether the flow of fluid is to the water injection system or the anti-ice system. Water injection safeguards the engine from detonation and makes it possible to develop combat power. Combat power ratings represent an increase over the present prescribed military power ratings and should be used in emergencies only. The water tank consists of an aluminium alloy tank of 20 US gallon service capacity which is installed in the fuel cell compartment, below and to the starboard side of the fuel tank cell. The water tank is supported in the aeroplane by a cradle and strap assembly. The starboard engine mount stiffener furnishes additional support to the bottom of the tank. Damage to the tank from chafing is averted by means of synthetic rubber strips which prevent direct contact between the strap and the tank surfaces. The water tank filler cap is accessible through a door on the starboard side of the fuselage just above the wing. The

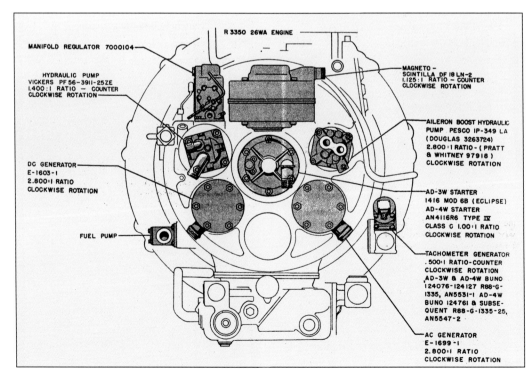

RIGHT Engine accessories. *(US Navy)*

RIGHT **Water injection system.** *(US Navy)*

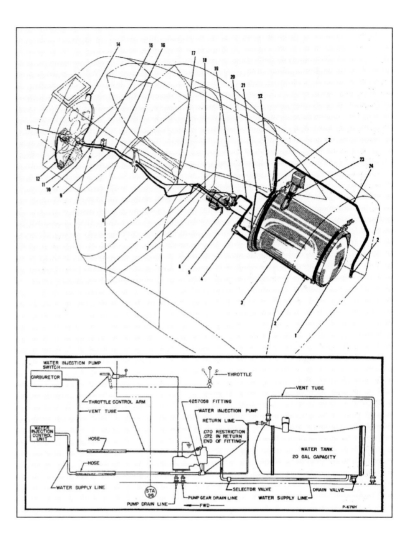

access door is designed so that the door can't be latched without the filler cap being locked in place. A tube on the top of the tank just forward of the filler assembly serves as a point of attachment for the water tank vent line. The vent line is directed aft over the top of the tank and then downward, where it exits on the bottom of the fuselage. The tank outlet fitting is on the bottom of the tank near its aft end. This fitting supports a finger screen directly above it, inside the tank, and can be removed by merely removing the snap ring from its retaining groove in the bottom of the tank. Directly aft of the tank outlet fitting is a drain valve. Both the tank outlet fitting and the drain valve are accessible through a cover on the bottom of the fuselage. The master switch for the water pump is located on the landing gear control panel directly above the engine control quadrant. When the master switch is 'ON', the water pump is automatically energised as soon as the throttle lever in the quadrant is moved approximately ⅛in forward beyond its point of contact with the take-off power stop. This automatic action results from the operation of a microswitch installed on the forward side of the upper firewall.

The water injection power control assembly is installed on the outboard side of the manifold pressure regulator adapter. This assembly is designed to control engine combat power and water injection operation for both low- and high-speed supercharger ratios. The water is metered as a function of engine manifold pressure and separate schedules are established for low- and high-blower operations. These separate schedules are automatically controlled by a metering bellows shift control-operated by engine high-blower oil pressure.

Ignition system

The standard R-3350-26WA engine is equipped with a high-tension dual ignition system. This system consists primarily of an ignition switch, a duel magneto, two individually driven distributors, an ignition harness and 36 spark plugs. The magneto generates high-

BELOW **The single drive twin magneto unit, blanked ready for fitting. The large rubber bungs protect the fittings for the distributor leads, whereas the red plugged ports are the grounding points for controlling its operation.** *(Author)*

tension current which is conducted through wires to the individual distributors and contact-breaker units. The distributors are connected by a high-tension ignition lead to each individual spark plug.

The dual magneto is mounted on the top centre mounting pad of the supercharger rear housing cover. The magneto provides true double ignition from a single unit. It employs the principle of the rotating magnet and stationary coils. One eight-pole rotating magnet is mounted between two pairs of pole shoes and produces simultaneous reversal of flux through the core of each coil at each 45° of rotation. Consequently, eight current impulses are produced in each coil for every revolution of the magneto driveshaft. Since the ignition requirements are nine current impulses per revolution of the engine crankshaft, the magneto is driven 1⅛ times the engine crankshaft speed. The pivotless breaker assembly consists of two contact-point assemblies operated by one compensated cam. The cam has 18 lobes spaced at unequal intervals to compensate for the slight top dead centre variation of each piston which is characteristic of radial type engines. The unequal spacing between the cam lobes causes the contact points to open at the exact predetermined firing position of each cylinder. Each contact point assembly of the breaker assembly supplies current through a high-tension, radio-shielded cable, to one of the two distributors. The right-hand coils of the magneto serve the right-hand distributor and consequently the front spark plug in each cylinder. The left-hand coils therefore serve the left-hand distributor and the rear spark plug in each cylinder. The magneto is enclosed in a split housing which has an inlet for cooling air. The four holes in the mounting flange are slotted to allow the magneto to be rotated during installation. Two terminals for switch connections and two high-tension terminals for connections to the distributors are provided.

The ignition harness and the two distributors are installed as a unit on the nose case of the engine. The high-tension lead from the magneto enters through a cap clamped on the top of the distributor and makes contact with the distributor finger through a coil spring. From the distributor finger the current passes to each of the 18 electrodes in turn. The harness portions of the spark plug leads are connected to the electrodes by piercing screws. As mentioned previously, the starboard distributor serves the front spark plug and the port distributor serves the rear.

Low-tension system

The optional low-tension ignition system is used for predominantly high-altitude operations and similar to the high-tension system described above, it incorporates

the same essential components but with an additional coil pack per cylinder, which boost the low-voltage current to high-voltage current, which is transmitted down a short lead to each plug. The magneto operates in the same way as the one for the high-tension system; however, it, and the distributors, are different models to reflect the difference in current carried.

Engine controls

The engine control quadrant is installed in the port side cockpit control panel. Included as its integral parts of the quadrant assembly are levers to operate throttle, mixture, propeller governor and supercharger controls. A retractable static throttle grip for catapult operations is directly forward of the fully advanced position of the throttle. An adjustable take-off power stop is incorporated in the quadrant assembly and an adjustable friction control knob is installed on the inboard side of the quadrant.

The supercharger control lever – marked 'blower' is the furthest outboard lever on the engine control quadrant. It is of the conventional rigid push-pull type and can be placed in either of the two indicated positions 'LOW' (forward) position and 'HIGH' (rear) position. The supercharger control lever guide incorporates a detent at both positions, which,

when combined with a shoulder on the lever, prevents inadvertent movement of the lever. The supercharger control lever is independent of the friction control, and connects via a series of bellcranks and control rods, directly to the supercharger control mechanism on the aft side of the rear oil sump.

The throttle lever is the next inboard lever from the supercharger controller. Also of the push-pull type, it can be set in any position from 'CLOSED' (fully aft) to 'OPEN' (fully forward). The throttle handle incorporates a microphone switch for radio operation. The throttle lever

ABOVE LT ignition coils mounted to each cylinder. Fed directly from the distributors, the coil then feeds both spark plugs on that cylinder. *(Author)*

LEFT Engine control quadrant in G-RADR. The open recess to the rear of the throttle unit is where the aileron trim control normally is fitted but was removed for servicing at the time of this photo. *(Author)*

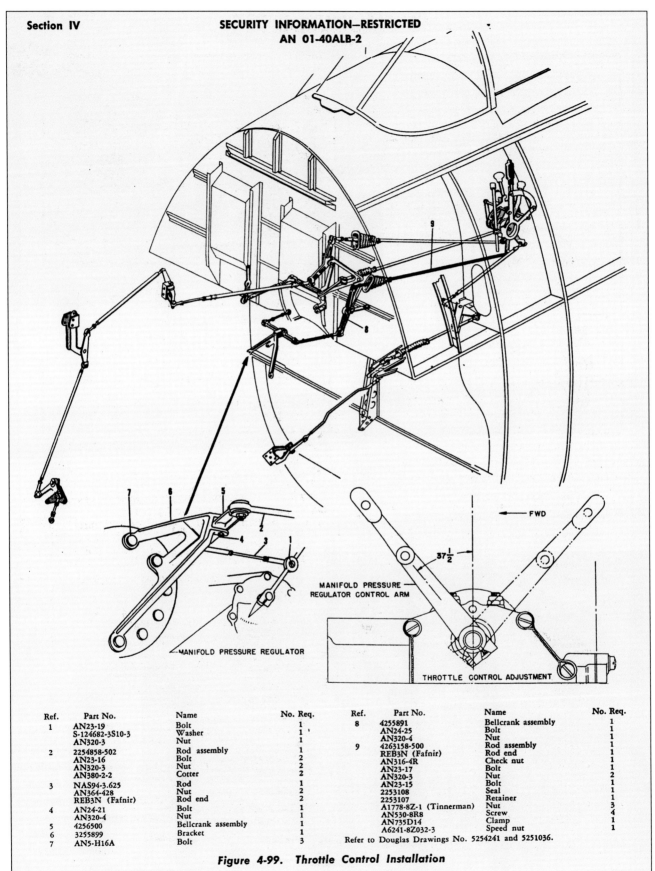

Ref.	Part No.	Name	No. Req.	Ref.	Part No.	Name	No. Req.
1	AN23-19	Bolt	1	8	4255891	Bellcrank assembly	1
	S-124682-3S10-3	Washer	1		AN24-25	Bolt	1
	AN320-3	Nut	1		AN320-4	Nut	1
2	2254858-502	Rod assembly	1	9	4263158-500	Rod assembly	1
	AN23-16	Bolt	2		REB3N (Fafnir)	Rod end	1
	AN320-3	Nut	2		AN316-4R	Check nut	1
	AN380-2-2	Cotter	2		AN23-17	Bolt	2
3	NAS94-3.625	Rod	1		AN320-3	Nut	2
	AN364-428	Nut	2		AN23-15	Bolt	1
	REB3N (Fafnir)	Rod end	2		2253108	Seal	1
4	AN24-21	Bolt	1		2253107	Retainer	1
	AN320-4	Nut	1		A1778-8Z-1 (Tinnerman)	Nut	3
5	4256500	Bellcrank assembly	1		AN530-8R8	Screw	4
6	3255899	Bracket	1		AN735D14	Clamp	1
7	AN5-H16A	Bolt	3		A6241-8Z032-3	Speed nut	1

Refer to Douglas Drawings No. 5254241 and 5251036.

Figure 4-99. Throttle Control Installation

(US Navy)

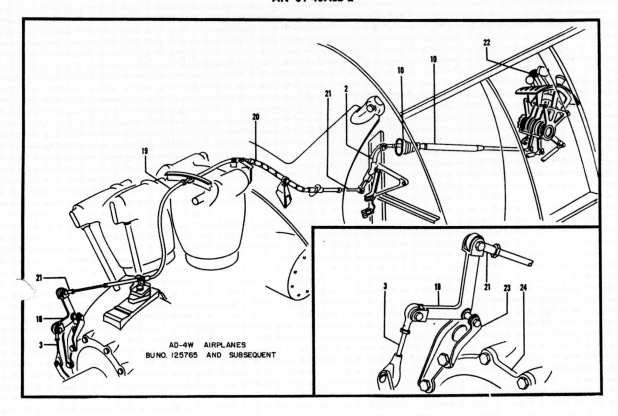

AD-4W AIRPLANES
BU NO. 125765 AND SUBSEQUENT

Ref.	Part No.	Name	No. Req.		Ref.	Part No.	Name	No. Req.
1	3252879	Bracket	1			AN530-8R8	Screw	4
	S-1029679P10-14	Bolt	2			AN735-D14	Clamp	1
	S-1029679P10-10	Bolt	1			‡‡4263158-506	Rod assembly	1
2	*4252881	Bellcrank assembly	1		11	NAS354-4-300	Rod	1
	AN24-23	Bolt	1			AN364-428	Nut self locking	3
	**4267641	Bellcrank assembly	1		12	2386233	Spring	2
	†4267641-500	Bellcrank assembly	1		13	S-124682-4D13-3	Washer	8
3	2272435	Rod	1		14	S-124682-4F16-6	Washer	2
	RE4F5 (Fafnir)	Rod end	2		15	2386222	Right bracket friction attach	1
	AN24-19	Bolt	2		16	2386220	Sector—friction attach	1
4	2265672	Bellcrank assembly	1			NAS229-33	Screw	1
	AN4-14	Bolt	1			NAS229-18	Screw	1
	‡2270276-500	Idler assembly	1			AN365-1032	Nut self locking	2
5	‡2272432	Rod assembly	1			AN960D10	Washer	2
	AN23-16	Bolt	2		17	2386221	Left bracket—friction attach	1
	*2255826-502	Rod assembly	1			NAS229-20	Bolt	1
6	‡2271374-500	Idler assembly	1			AN960D10	Washer	1
	AN5-12	Bolt	1			AN365-1032	Nut self locking	1
	*2265673	Bellcrank assembly	1		18	†3432729	Idler assembly	1
7	2267007	Rod assembly	1		19	†4388412	Propeller pitch flexible control assembly	1
	AN23-16	Bolt	1		20	†5435546-7	Asbestos tape	1
	AN23-15	Bolt	1		21	†REB 3N (Fafnir)	Rod end	1
8	‡4271637-502	Bellcrank assembly	1			AN316-4R	Nut	1
	AN5-33	Bolt	1		22	....	RPM control lever	Ref
	NAS43HT5-84	Spacer	1		23	†4433357	Bracket assembly	1
	*4263775	Bellcrank assembly	1		24	....	Crankcase forward section	Ref
9	*2254861-500	Rod assembly	1					
	REB3N (Fafnir)	Rod end	1					
	5251036-2	Rod	1					
	5251036-4	Collet	1					
	AN23-15	Bolt	1					
	5001-1 (Ideal)	Disconnect	1					
	REB3N (Fafnir)	Rod end	1					
	AN23-18	Bolt	1					
	4272433	Rod assembly	1					
10	*4263158-502	Rod assembly	1					
	REB3N (Fafnir)	Rod end	1					
	AN23-17	Bolt	1					
	2253108	Seal	1					
	2253107	Retainer	1					
	A1778-8Z1 (Tinnerman)	Nut	3					

*Applies to AD-3W airplanes.
**Applies to AD-4W airplanes BuNos. 124076 through 124777.
†Applies to AD-4W airplanes BuNo. 125765 and subsequent.
‡‡Applies to AD-4W airplanes.
‡Applies to AD-4W airplanes and AD-3W airplanes service changed in accordance with BuAer Change No. 143.
Refer to Douglas Drawings No. 5254241, 5251036, and 5267959.

Figure 4-102 (Sheet 2 of 2 Sheets). Propeller Control Installation

is connected via multiple rods to a bellcrank and lever arm fitted to the outboard side of the manifold pressure regulator. The control quadrant incorporates an adjustable take-off power stop which prevents accidental operation with water injection. The stop consists of a thin metal plate with an offset shoulder. When the lever is moved forward from the closed position and contacts the shoulder, the maximum manifold pressure for take-off power has been reached. When during flight it is necessary to increase the throttle

RIGHT The prop
control linkage
passes from the
cockpit through the
firewall, then the
upper port engine
frame leg before
routing down through
the cylinder and a
bracket mounted on
the governor plate,
and finally to the
regulator control arm.
G-RADR has the later
type Teleflex cable
control, whereas
earlier Skyraiders have
mechanical linkages,
bellcranks and levers
throughout. (Author)

opening beyond this point, the throttle lever can be pulled inboard and moved further forward. In this situation, a microswitch (the water injection system automatic switch) installed on the forward side of the upper firewall, is actuated by the throttle control bellcrank. When the throttle is moved $\frac{1}{16}$in beyond its point of contact with the take-off power stop, the switch is closed by the movement of the throttle control bellcrank and the water injection pump is energised, provided that the water injection master switch has been placed in the 'ON' position. The throttle can be prevented from automatically retarding itself by use of the throttle friction knob located on the inboard side of the quadrant. Increased friction is applied by twisting the knob in a clockwise direction.

The lever second from inboard is the propeller governor control lever. Labelled 'RPM', fully forward to 'INCREASE' puts the propeller into the fully fine position, and moving the lever aft to 'DECREASE' coarsens the blades. This is the last lever to be affected by the throttle friction control as the lever can be set anywhere between the two extremes of propeller travel. This has by far the largest control run of all the engine controls in that by a series of levers, bellcranks, rods and a flexible control line, actuation of the propeller governor control lever forward of the nose case of the engine can occur.

The mixture control is the inboard control lever and can be adjusted to any variation of three main positions: 'IDLE CUT OFF' (fully aft), 'NORMAL' and 'RICH' (fully forward). The mixture control lever guide is notched so that the lever cannot be moved aft to a leaner mixture unless the spring-loaded latch is freed by depressing the release in the centre of the lever knob. Therefore, the friction control does not affect the mixture control lever operation. Again of the push-pull type, this lever connects to the port side of the carburettor via a system of rods and bellcranks.

Carburettor air control is controlled by an electrically operated door.

Engine cowlings

The cowlings consist of multiple sections, namely a fixed nose section, removable hinged side cowls, the cowl bow, the cowl side flaps and the accessory cowlings. Nose cowl flaps are mounted internally in the fixed nose section.

The fixed nose section forms the forward end of the anti-drag ring. It consists of an aluminium alloy outer skin riveted to aluminium alloy ribs. Six nose cowl flaps are hinged to fittings attached to the nose section structure. The nose cowl flap actuating system is mounted on brackets attached to the perimeter of the cowl.

A finger-type flap position indicator coloured red is linked to the upper starboard flap. The indicator projects through the fixed nose section outer skin when the nose cowl flaps are closed. Twelve nose section support links, two of which incorporate sockets to support the side panels in the open position, are bolted to brackets around the engine front row rocker box studs. The forward ends of the support links are bolted to the aft end of the fixed nose section. A hook-shaped extrusion riveted along the aft outer

ABOVE Mixture control on carb with the green lever arm attached. Situated high on top of the supercharger and tucked in tight behind the engine frame, access to the carburettor for servicing can be somewhat awkward. *(Author)*

LEFT The impressively large cowlings on the Skyraider dominate the view forward of the pilot. Although in simple appearance from the outside, the cowlings actually contain an awful lot of equipment and accessories and to remove from the aircraft completely will take the best part of a working day for several workers. *(Jelle Hieminga)*

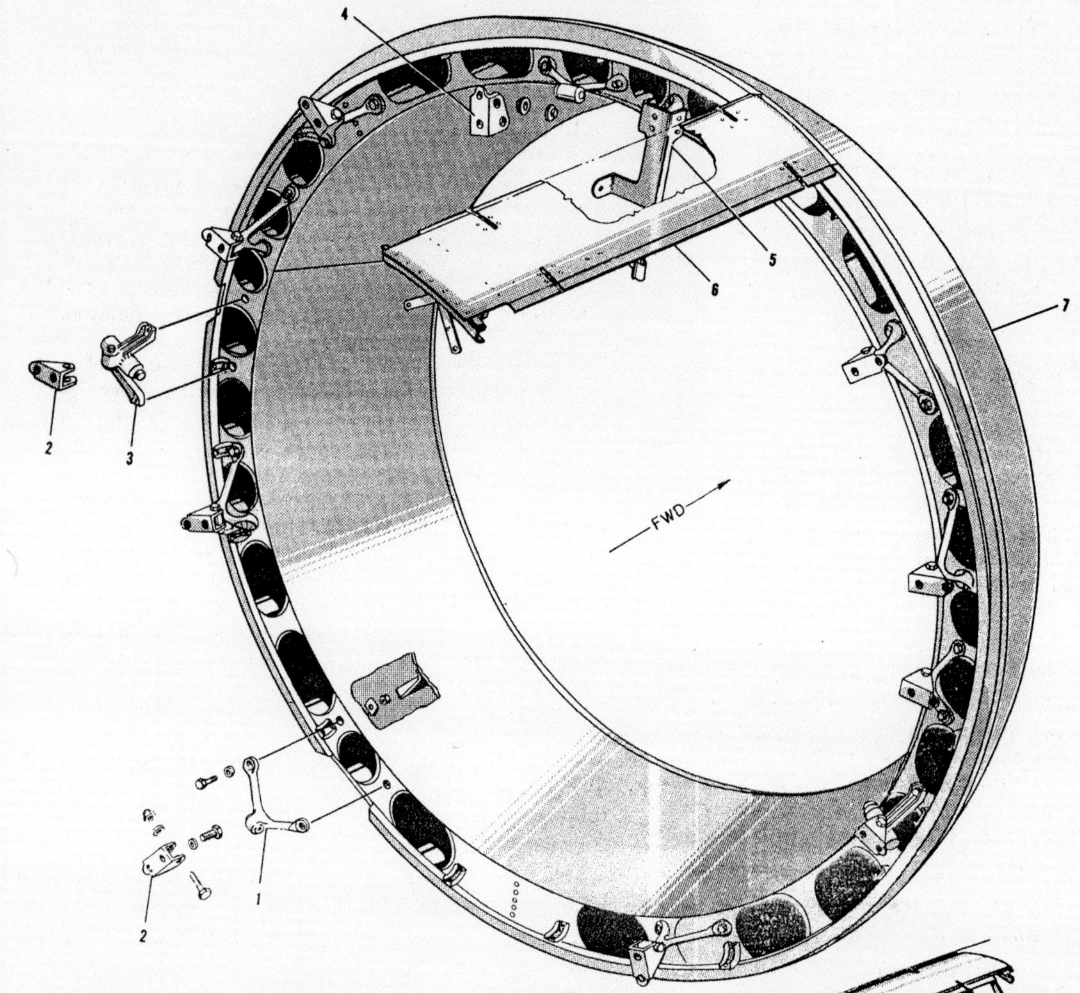

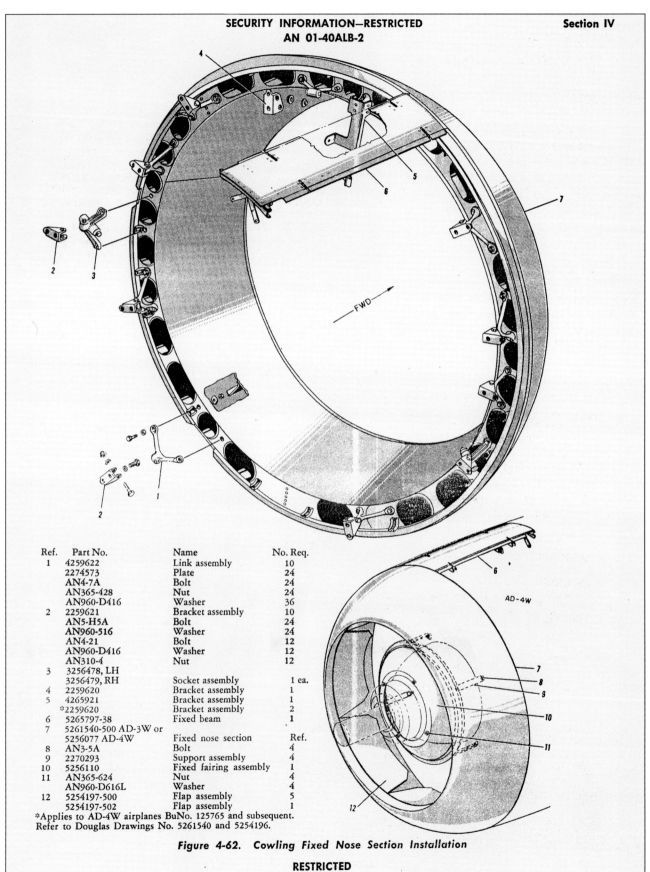

Ref.	Part No.	Name	No. Req.
1	4259622	Link assembly	10
	2274573	Plate	24
	AN4-7A	Bolt	24
	AN365-428	Nut	24
	AN960-D416	Washer	36
2	2259621	Bracket assembly	10
	AN5-H5A	Bolt	24
	AN960-516	Washer	24
	AN4-21	Bolt	12
	AN960-D416	Washer	12
	AN310-4	Nut	12
3	3256478, LH		
	3256479, RH	Socket assembly	1 ea.
4	2259620	Bracket assembly	1
5	4265921	Bracket assembly	1
	*2259620	Bracket assembly	2
6	5265797-38	Fixed beam	1
7	5261540-500 AD-3W or		
	5256077 AD-4W	Fixed nose section	Ref.
8	AN3-5A	Bolt	4
9	2270293	Support assembly	4
10	5256110	Fixed fairing assembly	1
11	AN365-624	Nut	4
	AN960-D616L	Washer	4
12	5254197-500	Flap assembly	5
	5254197-502	Flap assembly	1

*Applies to AD-4W airplanes BuNo. 125765 and subsequent.
Refer to Douglas Drawings No. 5261540 and 5254196.

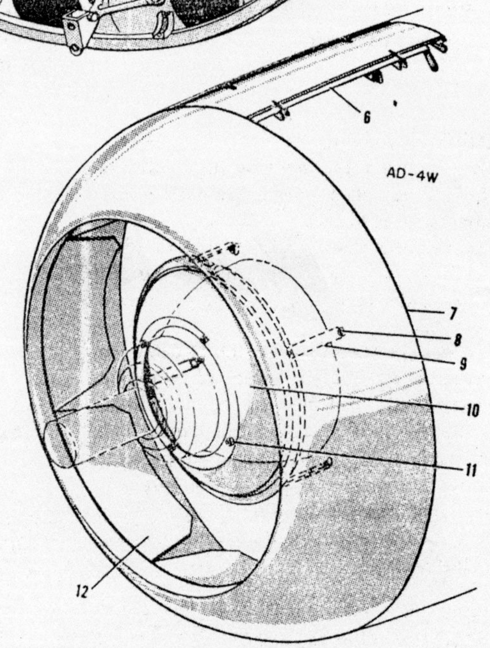

Figure 4-62. Cowling Fixed Nose Section Installation

(US Navy)

RIGHT The nose cowl awaiting fitment. Clearly shown here is the green-coloured nose cowl flap motor and the nose flaps. *(Author)*

outside edges of the nose section engages an angle along the edges of the side panels when the panels are in the closed position. At the top of the nose section (just to the starboard of the centreline) the hook-shaped portion of the extrusion has been eliminated to allow permanent attachment of the side panel fixed beam by means of a hinge. The side panel fixed beam hinges from the fixed nose section, and is

RIGHT The red indicator pin protrudes from the upper starboard side of the nose cowl in the pilot's line of sight to indicate that the nose doors are closed. Here the fixed beam has been removed for work. *(Author)*

BELOW Maintenance workers perform a task on the Wright R-3350 engine. The protection that the side cowlings give the maintenance personnel here is clearly evident. *(Public Domain)*

BELOW RIGHT Cowl bow with cowl flaps removed. The rubber bushes that support the rear of the side cowls in the closed position can be clearly seen. *(Author)*

Ref.	Part No.	Name	No. Req.
1	5258888-502	RH anti-drag ring side panel assembly	1
2	2129782 AD-3W or 2270821 AD-4W	Hook	2
	1215723	Trunnion	2
3	S-1199965-8500	Seal	2
4	3259439-500	Latch assembly	1
5	5258882-500	LH anti-drag ring side panel assembly	1
	3259439-502	Latch assembly	1
6	AN43-16	Eyebolt	2
	AN310-4	Nut	2
	AN960-D416L	Washer	4
7	AN23-14	Bolt	2
	AN320-3	Nut	2
	AN960-10	Washer	2
8	4259667-500	LH anti-drag ring support tube assembly	1
	4259667-502	RH anti-drag ring support tube assembly	1
9	5265797	Anti-drag ring fixed beam installation	1
10	AN25-19	Bolt	4
	AN320-5	Nut	4

Refer to Douglas Drawings No. 5265797, 5258882, and 5258888.

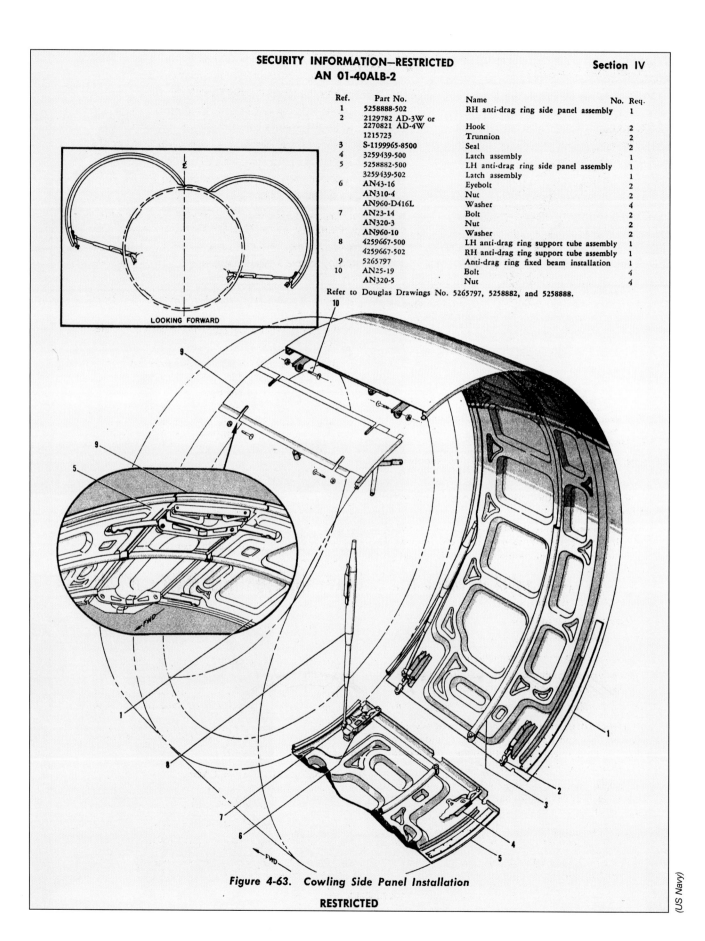

LOOKING FORWARD

Figure 4-63. Cowling Side Panel Installation

RESTRICTED

(US Navy)

allowed to open by the removal of two bolts which secure it to the cowl bow.

The two side panels are installed on the beam between the nose section and the cowl bow. Each side panel is hinged to the beam at two points and the two panels are latched together at the bottom. A support tube attached to the inside of each panel is provided to hold it in the open position.

The cowl bow is installed just forward of the aft end of the side panels. It consists of upper and lower 'C' channel lengths of equal sizes. These segments join to form a complete

circle. The cowl bow supports the aft end of the cowling side panels and also serves as a point of attachment for the aft cowl flaps. There are two sets of cowl flaps, six in total split port and starboard. These flaps control the amount of cooling air which passes between the engine cylinder fins and consequently control, to a great extent, the cylinder head temperature. Each flap is hinged at two points and is actuated by a jack screw attached to a supporting bracket, mounted to the engine frame. The jack screws for each set of cowl flaps are interconnected and operated by flexible shafts through a

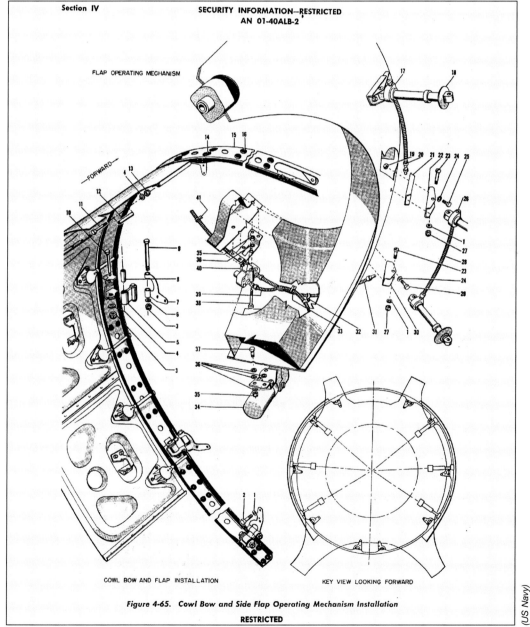

SECURITY INFORMATION—RESTRICTED
AN 01-40ALB-2

FLAP OPERATING MECHANISM

FORWARD

COWL BOW AND FLAP INSTALLATION

KEY VIEW LOOKING FORWARD

Figure 4-65. Cowl Bow and Side Flap Operating Mechanism Installation

RESTRICTED

(US Navy)

gearbox which is in turn connected by a flexible line to an electric actuator.

The operating mechanism for both the aft cowl flaps and the nose flaps is controlled by a single switch on the port side instrument panel in the cockpit. By means of this switch combined with a temperature control unit, both sets of cowling flaps can be operated either manually or automatically as desired. When the flaps are operated they do so in sequence. During the closing sequence the aft cowls close first and then the nose flaps. In the opening sequence, the cycle is reversed.

ABOVE Cowl flap operating switch situated on the lower left cockpit panel. Situated below the throttles, this switch shares the same panel with the oil cooler door switch and the aileron trim. *(Author)*

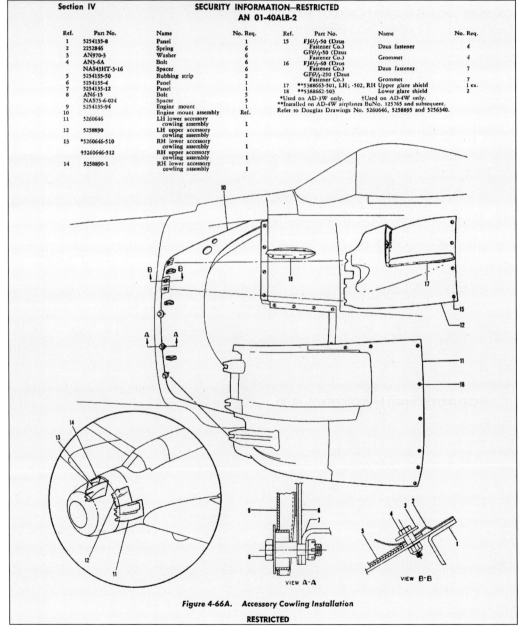

Section IV

SECURITY INFORMATION—RESTRICTED
AN 01-40ALB-2

Ref.	Part No.	Name	No. Req.
1	5254135-8	Panel	1
2	2252846	Spring	6
3	AN970-3	Washer	6
4	AN3-6A	Bolt	6
	NAS43HT-3-16	Spacer	6
5	5254135-50	Rubbing strip	2
6	5254135-4	Panel	1
7	5254135-12	Panel	1
8	AN6-15	Bolt	5
	NAS75-6-024	Spacer	5
9	5254135-94	Engine mount	1
10		Engine mount assembly	Ref.
11	5260646	LH lower accessory cowling assembly	1
12	5258890	LH upper accessory cowling assembly	1
13	*5260646-510	RH lower accessory cowling assembly	1
	†5260646-512	RH upper accessory cowling assembly	1
14	5258890-1	RH lower accessory cowling assembly	1

Ref.	Part No.	Name	No. Req.
15	FJ6½-50 (Dzus Fastener Co.)	Dzus fastener	4
	GF6½-50 (Dzus Fastener Co.)	Grommet	4
16	FJ6½-60 (Dzus Fastener Co.)	Dzus fastener	7
	GF6½-250 (Dzus Fastener Co.)	Grommet	7
17	**5388663-501, LH; -502, RH	Upper glare shield	1 ea.
18	**5388662-503	Lower glare shield	2

*Used on AD-3W only. †Used on AD-4W only.
**Installed on AD-4W airplanes BuNo. 125765 and subsequent.
Refer to Douglas Drawings No. 5260646, 5258895 and 5256340.

VIEW A-A

VIEW B-B

Figure 4-66A. Accessory Cowling Installation

RESTRICTED

(US Navy)

RIGHT Exhaust glare shields can be clearly seen here above the protruding exhaust stacks. The forward glare shields are attached to the removable rear cowling panels, while the rear shields are attached directly to the fuselage. *(Matt R. Kyle)*

The accessory cowlings consist of four panels which provide a streamlined cover for the engine accessory section. The panels can easily be removed to permit the accessories at the aft end of the engine to be reached. Exhaust glare shields are installed on both the port and starboard upper accessory cowlings. The upper panels are secured in place by springs along the leading edge and by Dzus fasteners along the trailing edge. The retaining springs are a part of the engine mount assembly. The lower panels are secured in position by pre-installed bolts and spacers on the leading edges and Dzus fasteners again on the rear section. Corrosion-resistant steel sheet is used in the areas adjacent to the exhaust stack outlets to prevent exhaust gases from damaging the panels. A hinged door in the upper aft corner of the lower starboard panel permits access for filling the oil tank. The door is secured in the closed position by two Dzus fasteners.

Engine quick-change unit

The engine quick-change unit, procured as a 'spares' item, consists of all the equipment forward of the firewalls (not mounted on the firewalls) with the exception of the oil cooler front and rear fairings and the cowling. In order to facilitate aeroplane engine changes, quick-change units are procured in complete sets for replacement. At no time in military service except in emergency should parts or other accessories be removed from these sets for other use. Should any part be removed, a replacement part should be requisitioned immediately and restored to the set as soon as received. In the civil world, most operators do not have this luxury and therefore the splitting of engine quick-change units is quite commonplace.

Engine quick-change units should be maintained in readiness for immediate installation. All openings should be closed by suitable plugs or covers to prevent the entrance of foreign matter.

ABOVE Engine change unit ready to fit. In service, the oil cooler would also have been fitted, but here is left off for better access to the rear of the engine for the firewall connects. The engine is shown here devoid of cowling rails and the drive system for the cowl flaps. *(Author)*

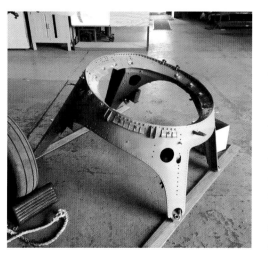

LEFT A refurbished engine frame awaiting fitment to the Wright 3350. The frame is made up of multiple thick aluminium sections and strong forgings. Few repairs are actually permitted and is therefore a critical part of the Skyraider's structure. *(Author)*

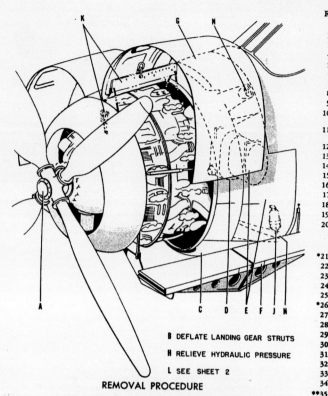

B **DEFLATE LANDING GEAR STRUTS**

H **RELIEVE HYDRAULIC PRESSURE**

L **SEE SHEET 2**

REMOVAL PROCEDURE

Step A If facilities do not permit ready handling of an engine quick change unit on which the propeller is installed, remove the propeller (see paragraph 4-605).

Step B Deflate the main landing gear shock struts.

Step C Remove the oil cooler scoop front and rear fairings, remove the oil cooler drain plug, and drain the cooler.

Step D Drain the oil from the supply tank.

Step E Remove the accessory section cowling and the left-hand side panel. (See paragraphs 4-380 and 4-348).

Step F Install the engine work platforms (see figure 3-10).

Step G Remove the carburetor air scoop (see paragraph 4-515).

Step H Operate the wing flaps to relieve any pressure in the hydraulic system.

Step J Place the fuel tank selector valve in the "OFF" position, then drain the fuel supply lines at the fuel strainer drain valve.

Step K Disconnect the propeller pitch control bracket just forward of the cowl bow and install the engine hoisting sling. (Utilize the sling attach holes as indicated on the sling beam.)

Step L Disconnect engine lines and conduit as illustrated on sheet two of this illustration.

Step M Engage the hoisting sling hook to the engine sling ring and raise the hoisting gear to support the engine weight.

Step N Using special wrench (Douglas Tool K-38903), remove the two engine lower mount bolts. Using special wrench (Douglas Tool K-38902), remove the two engine upper mount bolts.

Step O Carefully remove the engine quick change unit from the airplane.

Ref.	Name	Type Connection
1	Oil dilution line	B-nut
2	Oil dilution valve conduit	Plug and receptacle
3	Engine vent and drain line	Clamp
4	Auxiliary fuel pump conduit	Plug and receptacle
5	Hydraulic pressure line	B-nut
6	Fuel supply line	B-nut
7	Hydraulic supply line	Quick disconnect fitting
8	Oil supply line	Fitting
9	Hydraulic blast tube	Clamp
10	Hydraulic reservoir pressure relief tube (AD-4W)	B-nut
11	Generator blast tube (remove for access to generator leads)	Clamp
12	Supercharger control rod	Quick disconnect fitting
13	Generator leads	Terminals
14	Throttle control rod	Quick disconnect fitting
15	Ignition conduit	Plug and receptacle
16	Carburetor vapor vent lines	B-nut
17	Propeller governor control rod	Quick disconnect fitting
18	Mixture control rod	Quick disconnect fitting
19	Engine priming valve conduit	Plug and receptacle
20	Fuel pressure gage line	B-nut
	Front oil pressure line	B-nut
	Rear oil pressure line	B-nut
	Manifold pressure line	B-nut
*21	Starter booster conduit	Plug and receptacle
22	Aileron boost pressure line	B-nut
23	Starter ground strap	Terminal
24	Engine temperature control conduit	Plug and receptacle
25	Hot air ducts	Clamps
*26	Engine thermocouple	Plug
27	Starter cable	Terminal
28	Oil return line	Fitting
29	Oil tank vent line	B-nut
30	Power plant J-box conduit	Plug and receptacle
31	Voltage regulator blast tube	Clamp
32	Hot air exhaust duct	Clamp
33	Starter booster conduit (AD-3W only)	Receptacle
34	Engine thermocouples (AD-3W only)	Receptacles
**35	Engine starting vibrator conduit	Plug and receptacle
**36	Conduit carburetor temperature to firewall	Plug and receptacle

*References 21 and 26 are replaced by 33 and 34 respectively on the AD-3W firewall.
**Used on AD-4W airplanes only.

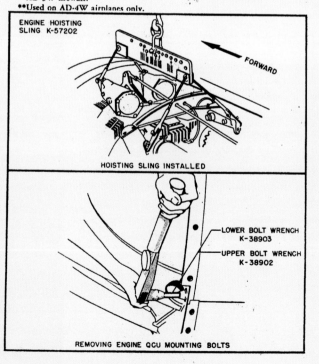

ENGINE HOISTING SLING K-57202

FORWARD

HOISTING SLING INSTALLED

LOWER BOLT WRENCH K-38903

UPPER BOLT WRENCH K-38902

REMOVING ENGINE QCU MOUNTING BOLTS

Figure 4-90 (Sheet 1 of 2 Sheets). Removal of Engine Quick Change Unit

(US Navy)

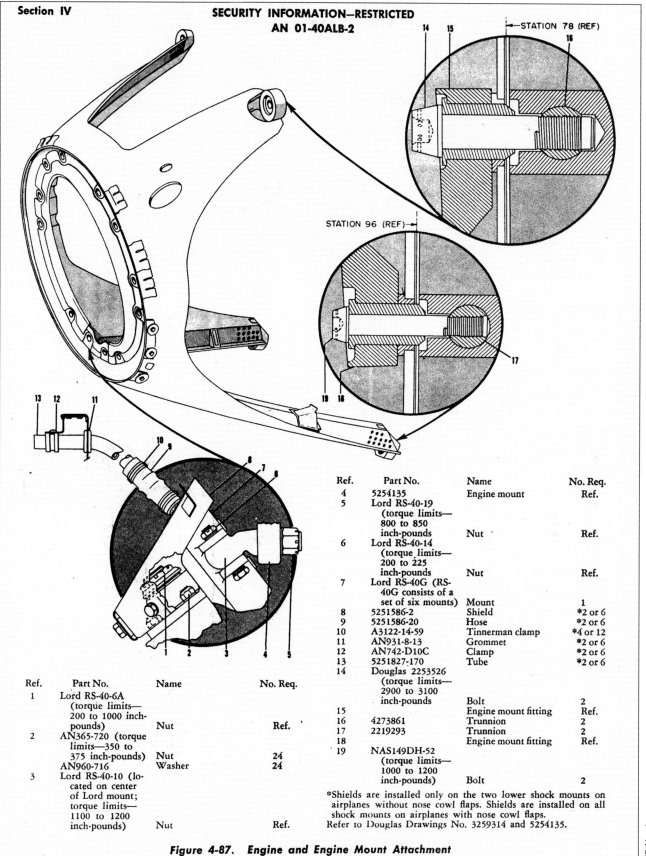

Ref.	Part No.	Name	No. Req.
4	5254135	Engine mount	Ref.
5	Lord RS-40-19 (torque limits— 800 to 850 inch-pounds)	Nut	Ref.
6	Lord RS-40-14 (torque limits— 200 to 225 inch-pounds)	Nut	Ref.
7	Lord RS-40G (RS-40G consists of a set of six mounts)	Mount	1
8	5251586-2	Shield	*2 or 6
9	5251586-20	Hose	*2 or 6
10	A3122-14-59	Tinnerman clamp	*4 or 12
11	AN931-8-13	Grommet	*2 or 6
12	AN742-D10C	Clamp	*2 or 6
13	5251827-170	Tube	*2 or 6
14	Douglas 2253526 (torque limits— 2900 to 3100 inch-pounds)	Bolt	2
15		Engine mount fitting	Ref.
16	4273861	Trunnion	2
17	2219293	Trunnion	2
18		Engine mount fitting	Ref.
19	NAS149DH-52 (torque limits— 1000 to 1200 inch-pounds)	Bolt	2

Ref.	Part No.	Name	No. Req.
1	Lord RS-40-6A (torque limits— 200 to 1000 inch-pounds)	Nut	Ref.
2	AN365-720 (torque limits—350 to 375 inch-pounds)	Nut	24
	AN960-716	Washer	24
3	Lord RS-40-10 (located on center of Lord mount; torque limits— 1100 to 1200 inch-pounds)	Nut	Ref.

*Shields are installed only on the two lower shock mounts on airplanes without nose cowl flaps. Shields are installed on all shock mounts on airplanes with nose cowl flaps.
Refer to Douglas Drawings No. 3259314 and 5254135.

Figure 4-87. Engine and Engine Mount Attachment

Chapter Five

Skyraider weaponry

The Skyraider was a war machine that was intended to be an accurate bombing platform. It was reputed that the Skyraider could make dive-bombing attacks at angles of up to 70°, which was considerable for an aircraft of its size and weight. Its payload was extensive and variable, with no real 'standard' load for any particular role. In this chapter we explore the ordnance known to have been used in Skyraider operations.

OPPOSITE Fully-armed and ready for action – A-1H Skyraider, 'Anita Michelle', of the 602nd Special Operations Squadron, 56th Special Operations Wing. The 602nd was flying out of 'Naked Fanny' in the extreme north-east of Thailand when this photograph was taken in 1968. Nakhon Phanom (the 'City of Hills') was affectionately known as 'Naked Fanny' or NKP by the Americans. *(G. Merrit)*

ABOVE A Skyraider of VA-115 with an ordnance load ready to go on a mission. *(Cliff Johns)*

It is widely known that the Skyraider could carry significant external stores to a target – after all that's what it was invented for. Designed with 15 external stations on which jettisonable fuel tanks and weapons were carried, the Skyraider had the ability to lift externally, 8,000lb of ordnance (this being the equivalent of carrying a complete P-51 Mustang underneath it). As a comparative example, a land-based Second World War B-17 bomber could only carry 5,000lb of ordnance in total. The ability to carry vast stores meant a Skyraider could push home an attack repeatedly and, depending on its load, this meant up to 100 passes on a target in a single sortie. Not all its external stores were for weapons – it was common for the Skyraider to

TOILET BOMB

A most interesting payload was delivered by Skyraider on 4 November 1965. On the final mission of VA-25's deployment to Vietnam, Commander Clarence W. Stoddard Jr, Executive Officer of the unit, flying an A-1H Skyraider, NE/572 'Paper Tiger II', from Carrier Air Wing Two aboard USS *Midway* carried a special bomb to the North Vietnamese. It was to commemorate the 6-millionth pound of ordnance dropped. This bomb was unique because of the type . . . it was a toilet!

The following is an account of this event, courtesy of Clint Johnson, Captain, USNR Ret.:

BELOW A-1H 'Paper Tiger II' carrying the toilet bomb in October 1965 *(US Navy – unknown sailor)*

If my memory serves me right, 572 was flown by Commander C.W. 'Bill' Stoddard. His wingman in 577 was Lieutenant Commander Robin Bacon, who had a wing station mounted movie camera (the only one

remaining in the fleet from WWII). The flight was a Dixie Station strike (off South Vietnam) going to the Delta. When they arrived in the target area and Commander Stoddard was reading the ordnance list to the FAC, he ended with 'and one code name Sani-flush'.

The FAC couldn't believe it and joined up to see it. It was dropped in a dive with Lieutenant Commander Bacon flying tight wing position to film the drop. When it came off, it turned hole to the wind and almost struck his airplane.

It made a great ready room movie. The FAC said that it whistled all the way down. The toilet was a damaged toilet, which was going to be thrown overboard. One of our plane captains rescued it and the ordnance crew made a rack, tail fins and nose fuse for it. The squadron flight deck checkers maintained a position to block the view of the Captain and Air Boss while the aircraft was taxiing onto the catapult. Just as it was being shot off we got a 1MC message from the bridge, 'What the hell was on 572's right wing?' Possibly one of the most famous photographs taken of the Skyraider in service featured this unusual ordnance, the tale became legend, and is often the subject of military scale modelling!

Captain Johnson was one of the two VA-25 A-1 Skyraider pilots credited with shooting down a MiG-17 on 20 June 1965.

LEFT An E model
Spad ground crew
pulling safety pins
from the ordnance
prior to a mission.
(Barry Rowland)

carry more fuel in external tanks (3,000lb) than
was carried internally (2,000lb). Therefore, its
fantastic range and power meant it could deliver
its load cruising to the target at 140kts indicated
airspeed at a maximum altitude of approximately
10,000ft. This equated to approximately 3 miles
per minute over the ground.

Some elements were dated, though, and
didn't always prove to be the most reliable.
Primarily this was noticed with the four M-3
20mm cannon which used percussion primed
(as opposed to electric primed) ammo. This
ammo had to be drawn from Korean War
surplus since it was no longer produced during
the Vietnam War era.

The ordnance carried for a search and
rescue (SAR) mission was: 720 rounds of
20mm for the M-3 cannon, 1,500 rounds of
7.62 ammo for the SUU-11 Minigun, 4 × CBU-25
canisters with high-explosive bomblets,
2 × CBU-22 canisters with smoke bomblets,
2 × AN-M47 white phosphorus smoke bombs,
2 × LAU-3 pods with 19 HE (high-explosive)
rockets each, 2 × LAU-59/68 pods with 7 WP
(white phosphorus) marking rockets each.

CBU-25 (cluster bomb unit)

These odd-shaped dispensers are CBU-25s
(cluster bomb units). Each of the six tubes
contained baseball-sized bomblets which
were dispensed out of the rear of the tube.
The CBU was dispensed one tube per press
of the pickle button. Since the A-1 often
carried four CBU-25s, this was good for up to
24 passes alone without regard to the rest of
the ordnance!

BLU-32 napalm

These 500lb class stores happen to be
finned, which allowed for a more accurate and

LEFT A Spad wing
loading from left to
right. The six triangular
tubes are SUU-14 CBU
dispensers, the two
outboard are normally
anti-personnel CBU-
25s and the inner one
a CBU-22. Next the
M47 WP bomb, then
LAU-3, LAU-68 and
SUU-11 Minigun.
(Barry Rowland)

LEFT BLU-32 Napalm awaiting loading for the next mission. Just a single napalm bomb could decimate up to 2,500 sq yards of ground. Initially napalm was intended for use against buildings, but soon its devastating effects were used in anti-personnel missions. *(Public Domain)*

predictable trajectory. If the fins were removed, the canisters would tumble haphazardly after release, which created a wider dispersion pattern for the napalm. Napalm was used as an incendiary-type weapon.

Guns

The AD-1 Skyraider was equipped with two integrated 20mm (0.79in) M3 cannon, one on each wing. Each M3 carried 200 rounds of ammunition (2 boxes of 100). Three types of ammunition were available: HE, HEI (high-explosive incendiary) and AP (armour piercing). Later Skyraider models were equipped with an additional outboard M3 on each wing, for a total of four on the aircraft.

LEFT M3 20mm cannons in the gun shop and pylon storage at Nakhon Phanom Royal Thai Air Force Base in 1970. These particular guns were spares that were either assembled from new parts or were repaired or rebuilt guns that had been salvaged. *(Barry Rowland)*

RIGHT An occasional alternative to the M3 was the 20mm GE Gatling and 7.62 Minigun, seen here in the servicing bay.
(Barry Rowland)

AN ARMOURER'S TALE – BARRY ROWLAND

Barry Rowland grew up in Arma and Elkhart, Kansas, and served 4 years in the US Air Force from 1969 to 1973, of which 18 months were spent in Thailand and a year in Vietnam. His entire military career was as a weapons mechanic and he had attained the rank of staff sergeant by the time of his discharge. He graduated from Kansas State University in 1977 and owned a small apple orchard in western Colorado, as well as becoming a construction manager for over 36 years. He is now semi-retired and lives on Lake Norman in Sherrills Ford, North Carolina, with his wife Donna.

My work on the A-1s was strictly concerned with the M-3 20mm wing guns. The mini-gun shop was separate although we did assist them at times such as with the bore-sighting where we used Perkins-Elmers lasers. This was new for the Air Force and I was one of the guinea pigs who had a baseline scan of my eyes before doing laser work, during and after but my med records were destroyed in the St Louis fire of 1978. The weak spots of the M3s were the firing pin assembly that consisted of a large sliding structure that had a tendency to crack after a short service life. If a gun fired out its complete complement of ammunition more than five times it was a pretty successful event! After all these years I can't recall the ammunition capacity as the weapons crews actually filled the boxes with 20mm and torqued the belts into the gun feeders. The inboard guns were easy to change out, although they required the wings to be folded to access them, which was good because it meant you could stand on the ground and work on them. The outboard guns however required you to be on the wings and in misty or rainy weather the wings were as slick as ice and most of us made the slip and slide to the PSP tracking or concrete below more than once. It seemed to be a rare event that a plane would come back with all four guns still serviceable, so we were usually not lacking work and were always covered with oil and grease from a combination of the lubricating oil from the guns, combined with the Skyraider's character oil and hydraulic leaks.

Being at NKP [Nakhon Phanom] from June 1970 to June 1971, I was present when Col. Bull Simmons crew took over the base and the raid on the Son Tay prisoner of war camp took place. None of us knew what the hell was going on, but we watched from the sidelines since we were on the night shift anyhow. I also recall the teamwork of every unit when a search and rescue mission was in progress and no one worried about staying at work until it was over so we could keep planes flying as long as they were needed. The Skyraiders were the backbone of these operations escorting and providing low air support for the rescue helicopters. I recall some of the planes returning with incredible battle damage but were quickly repaired to fly again.

ABOVE Barry Rowland attending to the SUU-11 A mounted on a Douglas A-1 at Nakhon Phanom. *(Barry Rowland)*

BELOW Working on the M3 20mm cannon. *(Barry Rowland)*

ABOVE SUU-11A Minigun with covers removed.
(Public Domain)

BELOW Testing the Minigun at the firing range.
(Barry Rowland)

Ordnance

Typically a Skyraider load could consist of most of the inventory of the US forces, this included bombs, torpedoes, mine dispensers, unguided rockets and gun pods.

SUU-11/A Minigun pod

General Electric GAU-2/A six-barrelled machine gun. Uses 7.62 × 51mm NATO ammunition in a 1,500-round magazine. It could deliver a fixed rate of fire of 4,000 rounds per minute.

M-47 100lb white phosphorus bomb

White phosphorus (WP) aka 'Willy Peter' is a colourless to yellow translucent waxlike substance with a pungent smell similar to garlic. When exposed to air, it spontaneously ignites, bursting into a yellow flame and producing dense white smoke.

White phosphorus can be used for signalling, screening and incendiary purposes.

The M-47 bomb was developed to meet the requirements for a chemical bomb for 'bombardment' purposes. It is a thin case bomb whose design and construction is intended to provide maximum efficiency after being released from a plane.

This particular bomb (AN-M47-A1) has a thin steel case 1⁄16in thick. It has an 8in diameter and is 45in long, excluding the fuse. The fuse in this case is an M108 (nose) with an M4 burster using a tetryl charge.

RIGHT An M47-A2 with napalm charge.
(Public Domain)

Mk 82 500lb low-drag general-purpose bomb

Fitted with M904 mechanical impact (nose), it had the ability for selectable arming and a functional delay with 'daisy cutter' extension.

The explosive was tritonal (80% TNT, 20% aluminium powder) coming in at 192lb (87kg) which made it 18% more powerful than TNT.

Dimensions:
Length: 87.4in
Diameter: 10.75in

SUU-14A/A sub-munition dispenser

The SUU-14A/A dispenser consisted of six metal tubes strapped together. Each of the tubes were filled with sub-munitions. These would be ejected out of the rear of the tubes while flying over the target area.

A colour-coded stripe just behind the forward end cap would indicate the type of sub-munition being carried in the dispenser.

Dimensions:
Length: 6.7in
Width: 9.4in
Height: 11.3in

BLU-17/B smoke bomblet

Functioning essentially like an M-15 smoke grenade, this was delay-fired. Its main chemical agent is white phosphorus. These were mostly deployed so that a Skyraider could lay down a smokescreen to help downed aircrews evade the enemy until they could be extracted by helicopter. One CBU-22A/A cluster bomb consisted of 72 BLU-17/B bomblets in an SUU-14A/A dispenser.

Dimensions: 2.74in × 5.73in

BLU-3/B pineapple bomblet

Consisting of a fragile aluminium bomb body with embedded steel fragmentation balls, the RDX [research department explosive] explosive scattered the balls at detonation, causing horrific injuries to anyone in its path. It was

BELOW BLU-3/B.

(Ordata Online)

stabilised in its descent by drag vanes and detonated on impact. Painted bright yellow with a gold anodised end cap, they were commonly loaded in CBU-14A/A cluster bombs.

Dimensions: 2.75in × 3.75in, before drag vanes deployed

BLU-24/B 'jungle' bomblet

Similar in construction to the pineapple bomblet and with exactly the same purpose, the jungle bomblet consisted of a cast-iron bomb body for greater penetration in jungle environments. It was fin-stabilised, spin-armed and delay-fired. The bomb contained the explosive cyclotol.

One CBU-25A/A cluster bomb consisted

of 132 BLU-24/B bomblets in an SUU-14A/A dispenser.

Dimensions: 2.80in × 3.70in

BLU-24C/B 'jungle/all-terrain' bomblet

Exactly the same as the normal jungle bomblet, but this one could either be delay-fired, or fired on impact.

One CBU-25A/A cluster bomb consisted of 132 BLU-24C/B bomblets in an SUU-14A/A dispenser.

Dimensions: 2.80in × 3.70in

'Gravel' minelet

These mines consisted of a small green or brown camouflage fabric pouch filled with explosive and 30g of coarse ground glass between two sheets of plastic.

To allow them to be handled and dropped from the air, the mines were stored soaked in Freon 113. Once released from their container, the Freon would evaporate within 3–8 minutes, thereby arming the mines. No fuse was required because the RDX explosive became shock-sensitive when dry.

There are reports that the SUU-14A/A dispenser was used to deliver 'gravel' minelets. No details are available. It is unknown which type and how many 'gravel' mines would fit into one SUU-14A/A dispenser.

A Skyraider could lay down a carpet of

'gravel' minelets behind a downed aircrew on
the run to block pursuers.

Anti-personnel

The minelets came in quadrant, square and
rectangular shapes and in various sizes. The
XM40E5 and XM44s did not carry an explosive
charge. They were designed to provide an
audible warning of enemy forces entering an
area that could be detected from a distance by
acoustic sensors.

Mark 7 'Thor' (or Mk-7)

This was the first tactical fission bomb adopted
by US armed forces. It was also the first
weapon to be delivered using the toss method
with the help of the low-altitude bombing
system (LABS). To facilitate external carriage
by Skyraiders, the Mark 7 was fitted with
retractable stabiliser fins. The Mark 7 warhead
(W7) also formed the basis of the 30.5in
(775mm) BOAR rocket, the Mark 90 Betty
nuclear depth charge, MGR-1 Honest John
rocket and MGM-5 Corporal ballistic missile.
The Mark 7 was in service from 1952 to 1967
with 1,700–1,800 having been built.

The Mark 7 nuclear weapon weighed
approximately 1,600lb with a diameter of
30in (760mm). The Mark 7 was a dial-a-
yield capsule-type weapon with fissile (or
fissionable) elements (uranium 235) stored in a
separate container. This bomb used a 92-lens

implosion system, meaning that the uranium
235 would be compressed into critical mass
by a combination of fast and slow explosions.
To ensure the plutonium core would go critical
and detonate, it had to be evenly compressed,
which was achieved by the 5in-thick HE shell.
The missile was capable of either airburst
detonation (above the target) or to detonate on
contact with the target.

BELOW A full load on a mission-ready Spad at NKP. With every hard
point full, and the pilot's helmet hanging from the cockpit awaiting its
owner, this aircraft is close to returning to the conflict once more.
(Barry Rowland)

A common evolution for an Air Force Skyraider pilot was first to fly missions in Northern Laos supporting General Vang Poa, leader of the Hmong tribe who sided with the United States to fight communism in South-East Asia. The second step of the theatre check out involved flying at night over the Ho Chi Minh Trail to stem the flow of supplies headed south. Finally, after about six months, a pilot could be expected to join the Search and Rescue forces as a Sandy pilot. I was based at Nakhon Phanom Royal Thai Air Force Base (NKP) from May 1970 to May 1971 as a Squadron Pilot. Our standard area of operations was normally Laos, North Vietnam and Cambodia. Although we staged (sat alert) in South Vietnam I personally never dropped ordnance in South Vietnam. During other time frames of the Vietnam War USAF Skyraiders operated extensively in South Vietnam. By May of 1970 most 'in country' operations were performed by VNAF A-37s and Skyraiders.

In September 1970, while receiving my initial night check out I was assigned to fly as flight lead with an instructor sitting in the right seat and acting as aircraft commander. Our wingman was a newly minted 'night pilot' with only one previous mission in the dark. After a routine briefing and engine start we found our way to the run-up/arming area where we checked the engine operation and signalled the arming crew we were ready for them to inspect the ordnance load security and remove the safety pins. While the ground crew scurried about beneath the wings, the pilots were required to sit with hands on the canopy rails so as not to accidently discharge any of the weapons. It was also a time to sit quietly, gather your thoughts and contemplate the mission ahead. That night we were facing east and had a good look toward the general target area. It was the rainy season and there were large but widely scattered thunderstorms over the central region of Laos. My concerns about flying at night, in mountainous terrain, and during the rainy season were eased by the cool flow of air swept through the open cockpit by the propeller. I began to think about this first mission over the trail and that most enemy gunners that protected the supply trucks with AAA weapons had been doing it for years. Much to my relief, it was a very dark night with no moon. I heard horror stories about the 'gunner's moon'. Enemy gunners had a distinct advantage when there was a high, thin, overcast cloud layer backlit by a full or nearly full moon. In today's parlance, think of it this way, 'It's hard to miss a fly crawling across your computer screen.' The ground crew leader waved his arms at me and jolted me back to the present. With a thumbs-up we moved to the runway and were cleared for take-off. Take-off at night with ordnance on board was done single ship with about 8 seconds spacing. The wingman joined up at about 1,500ft above the ground and we visually checked each other as best we could in the darkness. As we crossed the Mekong River we turned off all our exterior lights and the wingman maintained his position by referencing the glow of our engine exhaust. We settled into extended route formation and made our way to the rendezvous point to meet up with a C-123 Forward Air Controller, Candlestick 25.

Candlestick FACs had a variety of target marking devices for night operations. The Candlestick crew were equipped with the early version of night vision goggles. They were keenly adept at finding and marking supply trucks moving down the trail in total darkness. This particular night as we checked in with the 'Candle' they informed us that a convoy of trucks was backed up at the Dog's Head. This was a prominent landmark known to pilots operating in Laos. They marked the target area with a 'log', an incendiary device that burned slowly on the ground after impact. Candle gave

BELOW Skyraider 803 in front of the tower at NKP in 1970.
(Barry Rowland)

LEFT Skyraider 803 again at NKP – note the small size of the nationality markings compared to those worn in the Second World War just a few years earlier. (Barry Rowland)

us directions to the target by referencing the ground marker.Because we were flying without exterior lighting, the standard procedure was to strike targets as single ships. As flight lead we descended to 7,000ft and the wingman climbed to 8,000ft. That night we were loaded with 'Funny Bombs'. I don't know how they got their name, but they were the same type of bomb used during the night raids on Tokyo at the end of the Second World War. The bomb had a clamshell casing that opened above the ground and expended smaller thermite bomblets that could cover an area the size of a football field. These devices were excellent for killing trucks or artillery as thermite burned extremely hot and would melt most metals. I completed my weapons delivery and destroyed a couple of the trucks while no more than scaring the remainder. Fortunately on this particular night there must have been gunner training in progress because the enemy gunners came nowhere near me as we attacked the trucks. That said, the first time I saw a clip of 37mm go dancing across the sky it did cause a certain seizing in my lower intestinal tract. It was the wingman's turn to have a go at the remaining trucks, so we traded altitudes and I settled down to watch the show as my instructor bantered away about what I had done right and mostly done wrong during the strike. At one point during my strike the instructor had to correct my armament switch selection to prevent me from dropping my centreline fuel tank instead of a bomb when I pushed the 'pickle' button! Kindly he just passed it off as a rookie mistake. As the wingman rolled in for his first pass on the trucks he called, 'FAC's in sight, in hot.' We expected a pause as he descended toward the bomb-release altitude and were anticipating his next call which would tell us he was pulling away from the target and the direction he was turning. Instead what we heard next was, 'OOPS!' For a moment both the instructor and I sat in stunned silence then the Candle pilot said, 'OOPS. . . . What the hell do you mean OOPS?' The wingman quickly explained he had failed to pickle the bomb away while diving at the target and had accidently depressed the pickle button as he was climbing out at a 45° angle. HOLY CRAP! This was not good . . . somewhere out there over Laos was a 600-pounder sailing unguided through the darkness. It didn't take long for the truth to be told and we saw an initial explosion of thermite about two clicks (2,000m) from the target area. What happened next was truly amazing . . . amid the burning thermite a secondary explosion occurred that looked like a small nuclear device had been set off. Of all the crazy things to happen, that bomb landed in the middle of a previously unknown enemy petroleum oil & lubricant (POL) storage area. For the next half hour we lost count of the smaller secondary explosions. According to the flying command post responsible for collection of such data, the site smouldered for nearly two days. There's an old pilot saying, 'I'd rather be lucky than good any day.'

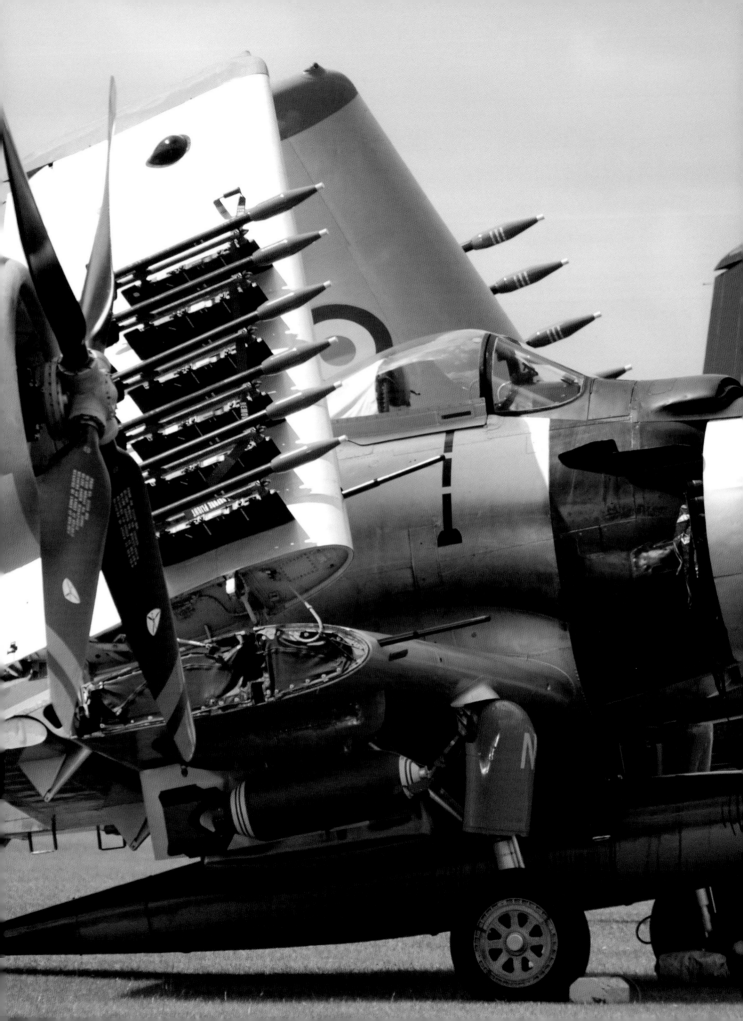

Chapter Six

Operating the Skyraider

If you've got an airworthy Skyraider, then in the sky is where it belongs. They are so rare in Europe that those which are capable of flight have quite an appeal for airshow organisers and as such have a popular following among enthusiasts. It is certainly not the sort of aeroplane one would take out to enjoy a pleasant day's flying, nor does it make a particularly good trainer for any other aircraft types, but it does bring pleasure to both pilots and spectators alike.

OPPOSITE Christophe Brunelière's Skyraider parked in between G-RADR and F-AZDP at Duxford. *(Phil Glover)*

An owner's and pilot's view

Christophe Brunelière

Christophe is a current commercial pilot, qualified on B747, B777 and is both a Type Rating Instructor and Supervising Type Rating Examiner. Having gained 4,000 flight hours as a pilot in the French Navy, Christophe has now amassed around 25,000 flight hours in a variety of types. He has been the proud owner of Douglas Skyraider F-AZHK since 2009 and flies regularly at many European airshows. Alongside being a pilot, Christophe is a Consultant in Aviation Safety and Human Factors.

Getting started with the Douglas Skyraider

It is not easy to summarise the handling of such a gigantic brick of a machine by just a few lines on the aircraft, covering the reason for its existence and the way in which it is best piloted. Owning and operating a Skyraider is a way of life, a choice, a commitment. I explained to a Slovak pilot recently that to own a Skyraider is like getting married to a top supermodel – it is a life full of lots of happiness, but also an equal amount of questions and many nights of insomnia.

The first part of your life is devoted to fulfilling the dreams you have for your adult future. The second part of your life, when the first part is successful, is dedicated to realise your dreams as a child.

The big question has to be how can you find yourself one day, sitting at a height of 3m, behind a huge windscreen, a huge propeller and in command of the last, the biggest and one of the most powerful single-piston engines ever built? I can't explain it rationally! Just like the top supermodel!

The Skyraider is the aeroplane of all superlatives. You do not climb in a Skyraider, you just climb it! It is not big, it is huge! It is not 'sexy' as our American friends say but it has 'rugged looks', it immediately seduces you with its unique face.

It is akin to a ploughing horse – a real draught animal. It's needy, a wrestler, a mover, a shadow worker. Powerful, agile but watch you do not get in its way or in the way of its rear hooves!

To some it doesn't hold the perceived glory of its older brothers or cousins. It's unfair because it seduces, it attracts affection to the point that its pilots always end up finding it a nickname suited not only to its multiple talents, but also to the affection they bear it.

That list of nicknames is long:

Sandy, Zorro, Spad, Able Dog, Destroyer, Firefly, The Big Gun, Guppy, Old Faithful, Old Miscellaneous, Fat Face, Flying Dumptruck or Crazy Water Buffalo. In my home, it's 'Gros Minet'!

However, back to our question. By what circumstances are we sitting on the back of the plough horse? To be honest, it's not quite the plane I dreamed of. ...

My more reasonable aspirations, those I consider in my dream category, were oriented towards a US naval aeroplane, but rather one of those whose name is made up of a 'Cat' or a 'Hell' or both at once. Why? It's simple! The Battle of Midway is the book I have read more than a hundred times. It marks the spirit of my childhood! I had a few other fantasies like the A26, but that's another story.

Then an opportunity came in the spring of 2009. I saw this Skyraider. It was parked and maintained in one of the hangars next to the hangar I was renting in Avignon for another of my toys. My fantasy was close at hand, should I seize the opportunity? There was no hassle to bring the plane from the other side

BELOW Christophe Brunelière with his Skyraider F-AZHK. (Christophe Brunelière)

of the Atlantic, it was perfectly maintained, the engine was already at Mr Anderson's home in the United States to be upgraded and overhauled to 3350-26WD standard. All the indicators were in the green, the deal was concluded.

The aircraft was thoroughly restored. Complete renovation of the hydraulic, electrical, oil and fuel systems had just been finished. Everything had been redone from the propeller up to the firewall.

Meanwhile, in order for my dream to come true, I had to be sure that I could make the whole thing fly, if possible in order. That is to say, to control these thousands of pieces in tight formation around me in the cockpit and not the opposite!

My experience at the time with warbirds was limited to a few hundred hours of DC-3 and the only single-engine tailwheel was in my Rallye 235! Don't laugh – this is one of the most difficult planes I have had the opportunity to master on the ground. So I made an appointment with Thom Richard in Kissimmee, Florida, for a week of intensive flying on the T-6. Thom created for me a custom programme based on formation, aerobatics and a lot of 'emergencies'.

Thom! If you read this, you are a sadist, but your advice and briefings have been and still are very valuable. On my first flight on the Skyraider, it seemed your voice was in my helmet: 'Chrissstoooophe, put the bloody stick in the corner!'

The preparation of the plane takes a good half-day. The exhausts and intake pipes of the bottom cylinders are equipped with removable plugs screwed into the pipes. They are removed after each flight so that the oil that drains down to the bottom cylinders can flow into the appropriate tray cleverly put in the right place under the plane. These plugs must be put back in place before flying, then close the cowls and pass a last rag around with a pout of satisfaction. The oil that is now in the tank under the aircraft will therefore not be expelled by the exhaust at start-up, which has two advantages: the aeroplane remains clean and the cleaning session after flight is greatly facilitated.

Radial engines are quite oil-intensive. It is, it seems, a sign of good health, or more accurately – gluttony! The average consumption is between 6 litres and 12 litres per hour, depending on the use. Beyond 20 litres, it is necessary to examine the reason for such gluttony.

Fuel is adjusted according to the flight undertaken. The Wright's appetite with 18 cylinders and 55 litres of cylinder capacity can be monumental and ranges from 300 litres per hour in a very economical mode to a good cubic metre per hour at take-off power.

The use of 100LL fuel imposes a limitation of the maximum intake pressure of 46in. In period operations with 115/145, the intake pressure could reach 56in or even 62in with the injection of water. The power on the propeller shaft then reached more than 3,050hp. Nowadays, since the thickness of the wallet is not extensive, I rarely use greater than 42in on take-off. Anyway, the plane is in the air long before!

The pre-flight visit begins with the left side and the battery connection is located in the back of the rear compartment. A first ascent of the beast can verify two or three important things in the first instance. The most important being the extinguished particle lamp. If it is turned on, the pre-flight visit stops here and a check of the magnetic chip detectors is required to find the reason for future potential engine hassles.

The pre-flight is the same as on any plane. It consists in taking a long and considered look at the machine while trying to verify that everything is in its place and that no defect has escaped the watchful eye of Pascal, my engineer. If nothing is missing and the weather is suitable, one can consider the ultimate climb to settle in the cockpit.

Right away it feels perfect. Not too vast, like a cockpit of a modern American fighter, nor too cramped as in an old English fighter. Then there is a real floor unlike the T-6. One can therefore drop his pencil, his drinking bottle, his glasses, his card or the whole wallet, without undertaking an acrobatic expedition to recover them. We find the smell so characteristic of old planes, a subtle blend of hydraulics, gasoline, burnt oil, old rubber

along with I do not know what. An addictive scent that permeates the flight suit and takes you back home with images and sounds memorised during the flight.

It is strongly recommended to start with external power. Indeed, the aim of the game is to keep fire inside the engine and not outside. In the event of a flamer at start-up, the only solution to reduce the flame and continue the start-up is to keep cranking the starter. With a low battery, the success of this operation is compromised.

The check before starting begins on the left and ends on the right. It's a bit like the pre-flight check. It is used to ensure that everything is in its place and that each switch and lever is in the right position. Check that the ash tray is empty, that all the lamps that are switched off are not burnt out and vice versa, all those that need to be turned on are well on. The electric seat is adjusted. Yes! An electric seat, this plane is full of useful and intelligent things.

A few signals with the mechanic, bottom left, to tell him that it is the time to wake the animal. Some back and forth, from left to right, some more looks to my mechanic to reassure and give courage. In any case, you

have taken the precaution of attaching your harness which serves only to prevent the pilot from escaping from the plane before the starting of such a machine. If you were told the harness was for anything else, you were lied to! Joking aside, now we have to go.

It is necessary to pressurise the hydraulic circuit with the electric auxiliary pump so as to have pressure for the brakes in order to avoid cutting the external power unit or the mechanic into bits when starting up.

Again a sign to the mechanic, elbow raised and thumb towards the mouth, to warn him of the pressurisation of the fuel system and the filling of the carburettor. When the overflow flows under the aeroplane through the main drain, the mechanic raises his hand. The mechanic is always in charge and one interpretation of his actions is simply: 'Do not touch anything until I have my hand up'. One often imagines that the pilots of warbirds are a breed of Martian with three hands and 20 fingers. On the Skyraider, it is from now on that the third hand is perfectly useless, two hands and two fingers are adequate enough.

When the plane has not been run for more than 48 hours, pre-oiling is essential. An

electric pump is dedicated to this operation. It involves sending oil to the engine at every place that will be moving and therefore needs it. Running the pump for 1 minute 30 seconds is sufficient, but it is recommended to finish with 20 more seconds to reach the 40psi which guarantees that the oil arrives at the top cylinders.

My preference is to turn the engine with the starter 16 blades, which will ensure the absence of hydraulic locking by oil that may have accumulated in a cylinder. If this is the case, the starter will automatically disconnect. At this stage, uninformed observers can be grieved and amazed that after so many propeller turns, the engine has still not started. No, it has not broken down, of that they can be reassured – it is just the correct procedure.

As for throttle position, open it two fingers: no more, no less. A little more, it starts rich and you risk the fire escaping the engine in a bid for freedom on the outside, a little less, it does not start.

Now select fuel pump ON, left hand on magneto selector, right index finger on starter. At the second blade, the magneto selector is set to 'Both' and at the same time the right middle finger injects fuel using the primer. At the fourth blade, it coughs and the 18 cylinders wake up in a cloud of smoke.

With the exhaust being about 1m in front of the cockpit, when it starts the Wright symphony is launched in Dolby stereo. No special effects genius can replace the sensations and emotion that seize the pilot in that moment. The 'beast' comes to life, vibrates, snorts and a wicked spirit will make you feel that the aircraft loves it.

The wings are unfolded, the safety of the external power and the mechanic are gone – we must go. The journey to the runway is not initially a disconcerting feeling. The visibility in front of the enormous cowling is excellent for a plane with the classical tailwheel design, but one then becomes aware of the size of the plane and its inertia related to its mass. A little more than 6 tons under the buttocks wants to go places.

Your last stop is the hold to check the propeller regulation and the magnetos and it is then time for the moment of truth. Once aligned with the centreline and the vital actions performed satisfactorily, it is necessary to concentrate for a few seconds. On a plane as big and powerful as the

Skyraider, your best friends for the next stage are your leg muscles on the rudder pedals. At power-up, the nose will try to leave the runway to the left and the plane will tend to quickly follow it. It is exactly the reverse when reducing power and speed during landing. It is therefore preferable, if the wind is not directly down the runway, to take off with the wind from the right and land with the wind across from the left.

Given the size and power of the beast, the best practice is to apply full rudder and stick to the right before powering up, and then remove the excess during acceleration. It accelerates very hard, and the noise escalates tremendously. Barely in the first stages of flight, the characteristic 'clacclac' noise of the landing gear indicates that the plane is already leaving the ground. This does not mean that it is already flying. The shock absorbers have a very long stroke; it is better to wait to be in the air properly before getting in the wheels. The take-off run will rarely exceed 300m. The aircraft must be allowed to accelerate to 150kts, optimum speed for a better climb. The adjustment of the throttle, mixture and prop controls are refined and the take-off loading on the engine is relieved. Everything is safe when the climb parameters of 2,500rpm and 36in are displayed.

There are two important instruments that I consult very often. Cylinder temperature and the triple instrument: gasoline, oil pressure and oil temperature. The Wright 3350 is a very cold engine. Once the take-off path is stabilised, it is essential to close the cowl flaps and part close the front ring to ensure a minimum cylinder temperature of 180°. The oil temperature is regulated by the automatic radiator flap, which does not mean that this temperature shouldn't be checked regularly to be regulated manually by the pilot if the automation system goes on strike.

For cruising, the adjustment of the throttle and mixture depends mainly on the thickness of the wallet. A cruise at 240kts will generate a consumption of almost 450 litres per hour. I prefer to use the curves of the US Navy, which advise an intermediate cruise at 180kts. The engine speed is then set to 1,800rpm, which gives 900rpm of the propeller. Given the size of the blades, it is almost possible to count them. This would only happen if you get bored during flight – and that chance never arises!

The aircraft is very manoeuvrable in a speed range of between 150 and 240kts for very basic figures. However, you must not forget that you are flying a fighter/bomber and not a hunter. It is akin to trying to win the 'Great America Prize' with a farm horse! Of course, the aircraft can pass all the basic aerobatic figures except the negative G flight, however, I do not dance acrobatic rock with a 60-year old lady. The tango or waltz is more suitable with this lady. When it is your Skyraider – it is your choice!

I do not forget that this aircraft was designed primarily as a ground-attack aircraft, a truck essentially. It has an enormous inertia with its trajectory that must be constantly in mind. Forgetting it and letting yourself be dazzled by the power and size of the machine can quickly lead to the fatal hoof strike and you'll dig a big hole in the ground.

I enjoy formation flight most, it is magical. The aircraft responds immediately to the slightest pressure on the controls or the throttle, plus it looks and sounds great on the ground!

Below 200kts, the canopy can be opened completely. This is good as it cleans the cockpit of all dust, navigation charts, navigation log and other unnecessary papers. . . . Above 200kts, it can be opened a few centimetres. Paradoxically, the noise in the cockpit decreases and greatly improves the radio exchanges. It seems that a closed canopy creates the phenomenon of an echoing sound box.

The return to the airfield and the downwind circuit before landing pose only one problem. The plane is very slow to decelerate; inertia wins again! The landing gear can be taken out below 200kts but it is necessary to be patient to reach the 130kts allowing the operation of flaps. The trouble with these big radial engines is that they do not support low torque operations. At 2,600rpm, there is no question of descending below 24in of pressure at the intake, otherwise the propeller will drive the engine and that is not advised for engine health!

The landing is straightforward – 90kts on finals, again the visibility throughout the approach and roll-out is excellent. The reduction in speed must be slow to avoid torque-rolling to the right. The three-point landing is very easy, like flying a big Piper Cub that only wants to stay in the air and it is only the 'clacclac' of the landing gear on the ground which lets you know that the wheels are in contact with the runway. This is not a time to relax however; the landing is not finished until the beast has stopped. The plane is still considered to be in flight and wants to fly; a surprise for the pilot is always possible. It oscillates from left to right. You catch this with the rudder but do not brake unless it is an emergency! The brakes are powerful but without any form of anti-lock so you could find yourself easily with flat-spotted tyres on hard runways.

When arriving back at the hangar, do not forget to fold the wings, it is much easier to put the plane away when it is more compact. The engine is allowed to run at 1,000rpm for a minute to allow the scavenge pumps to draw the oil back to the tank and then the engine can be switched off.

The silence is striking, a burst of happiness and sensations invade you: the odours of hot oil and the 'tic-tic' of the engine as it cools.

We must now descend from the cockpit and the plane and leave thoughts of your flight behind. To leave the plane is easier than leaving your memories of your flight. It can take a lifetime to forget a Skyraider flight. The Skyraider means a lot to me, I spent my childhood reading articles on the subject. I was fascinated that all these young people gave their youth and their lives so that we could have freedom. Continuing to fly these planes pays tribute to the genius of the men who built them and to all those young people who gave their youth for us.

The Skyraider, like many of its warbird stablemates, is a vaccine against gloom. Not only for the pilot who took advantage of these special moments, but also for those who stayed on the ground. It is thanks to them that these thousands of pieces of metal manage to work together in perfect harmony. It is the engineers and mechanics – the healers and surgeons if you like – who listen to, repair and pamper the beast. You understand that to fly a Skyraider, a Spitfire, Yak, Mustang or similar, it is above all a question of having a team of enthusiasts. Let them all be thanked for this.

BELOW Christophe takes his Skyraider to the runway threshold at Duxford's Flying Legends display in 2010. Pilot caution is advised, as not to keep it fully under control can lead to the Skyraider taking a route of its own. *(Peter Arnold)*

Buying a Skyraider

Although few Skyraiders survive compared to the numbers built, it isn't actually too unusual for them to come up for sale sporadically, although hardly ever in Europe. At the time of writing there is one AD-4W project and one airworthy AD-4NA Skyraider for sale, both in America. A good complete Skyraider project suitable for return to flight should fetch in the region of $250,000, while an airworthy flyer would retail in the region of around $600–700,000.

Spare parts as always can add a vast amount to the value of a Skyraider, and many owners hoard the common parts when they arise. Obviously the restoration costs of a Skyraider are pretty much an 'open cheque book' undertaking – and could range from a few hundred thousand dollars, to in excess of a million dollars, depending on the level of work required. If you can afford the restoration of such a machine, then the running costs are equally significant.

RUNNING COSTS

Running costs depend very much on how many hours you fly your aircraft, but as a rough guide the following applies:

Oil	Approximately £6.45 per litre, approximately £930.00 to fill to full. Usual oil burn is approximately 3 US gallons an hour, so budget £80.00 in oil for each flight hour.
Fuel	At the time of writing, 100LL is approximately £1.78 per litre, so to fill the main tank of the Skyraider would cost approximately £2,700; if the maximum three external tanks were included, filling a Skyraider right up would be in the region of £5,900! Typically, with a mix of cruising and mild display flying, you can expect to burn around £600 per flight hour in fuel.
Hydraulic fluid	At around £8.75 per litre, to fill the hydraulic system costs around £200. Use per hour on a properly serviced Skyraider is negligible.
Tyres	Tyres are still commercially available in the United States to fit the Skyraider. To purchase one and to import it to the UK will cost in the region of £1,400 per tyre.
Engine	Not surprisingly, due to the popularity of the engine, overhauled units are available almost off-the-shelf from several engine workshops, with around a 12-week lead time. In 2016 the price of a ready-to-install R-3350-26WD shipped to the UK was approximately £140,000 without accessories (starter, magneto, carburettor, generators, etc.). Accepted engine life depending on country of operation is around 1,500–1,800 hours in a non-combat role. Therefore approximately £100 per engine hour ought to be set aside for the overhaul fund.
Propeller	The Aeroproducts propeller carries a finite life of 1,500 hours of operation, with intermediate servicing periodically between, again differing depending on the country of operation. It is not possible currently to buy a spare propeller from the usual suppliers. Typically a major overhaul of the propeller is in the region of £30,000.
Servicing	On average, one would expect a Skyraider in private hands to fly around 30 hours per year, which allows for relatively straightforward servicing. The biggest check takes place approximately every 16 years. A normal yearly service would take two people around 2 months to complete properly, with the major servicing taking around 6 months at the end of the 16-year period. Therefore, you should budget around £700 per flight hour towards maintenance.

Summary: Direct operating costs are therefore somewhere in the region of £1,500 per flight hour, with a UK season costing around £45,000. This is before paying to insure it and paying for somewhere to keep it!

The pilot's view

John Beattie

John Beattie MBE has been a stalwart of the UK air display circuit for nearly 45 years. His first display took place in 1973 while on an exchange tour with the Army Air Corps flying the Scout AH.1. As the Senior Pilot of 705 Naval Air Squadron, he led the renowned Sharks Helicopter Display Team in 1982 flying the Gazelle HT.2. John joined the Royal Navy Historic Flight (RNHF) in 1986, having already accrued a large number of tailwheel hours flying Chipmunks while aero-towing for the RN Gliding Club since 1979. An initial season displaying the Swordfish in 1986 subsequently led to him stepping into the Firefly AS.5 in 1987 and both the Sea Fury FB.11 and T.20 in 1988. He took over as the Flight Commander of RNHF in 1991 where he remained until he retired from the Royal Navy in 1994. After life in the Royal Navy, John took up a career with the airlines, but this never deterred him from display flying and throughout the 1990s and even currently he can be seen displaying historic rotary and fixed-wing aircraft at air displays all over the UK. While continuing to mentor pilots of the RNHF in his retirement, John is also the Chief Pilot of Kennet Aviation.

It is quite definitely a BIG aeroplane! When you first see it it's an impressive sight and when you read a little of its history you appreciate that it is also a very impressive performer. For the pilot it is a delight to fly, being comfortable, stable, light to the touch and the power-to-weight ratio very good indeed. It features well-harmonised controls with ailerons power-assisted by hydraulics and everything balanced by three trim tabs, the elevator trim being electric. It has electric raising and lowering of the pilot's seat and a hydraulically operated canopy, but believe it or not it doesn't have a parking brake, one assumes to save weight!

Powered by a Wright 3350 supercharged 18-cylinder air-cooled radial engine producing 2,700hp, it uses a modest 75 US gallons per hour in cruise but this goes up to around 120 gallons per hour when at display powers. The internal fuel is 380 US gallons

LEFT **John Beattie, Chief Pilot of Kennet Aviation seated in the Kennet Aviation Seafire XVII.**
(John Beattie)

LEFT **Typical Skyraider exhaust staining seen here on the Planes of Fame Collection's AD4-N.**
(Dai Ngo)

**ABOVE Skyraider on
take-off.**

(Dries Embrechts)

or 1,440 litres, giving an endurance of
about 4½ hours. To cope with the
10½-hour endurance obtained with three
drop tanks plus internal fuel, it has a 32
gallon oil tank, necessary because rather like
English engines the Wright spits quite a bit
of oil out. The maintenance manual states
'when oil consumption gets to 19 gallons
per hour the cause should be investigated'!
I usually have to top up our aircraft with 5
gallons of oil every couple of hours' flying
time. In fact oil on the outside of the airframe
has taken a considerable amount of my time
over the past 9 years, getting it looking good
to present to the public. Most pictures of
it in service show a dirty curved path over
the fuselage sides following the wing shape,
caused by oil and exhaust mixing and
caking on.

Wing folding, flaps, canopy and
undercarriage operation are hydraulic from
a main system and power-boosted ailerons
and brakes from separate hydraulic sources.
The boosted ailerons give a very nice feel,
but stick force becomes four times heavier
without the boost and it is a VERY different
aircraft to fly! I only flew it in manual once

and while controllable, particularly at slower
speeds, you certainly wouldn't entertain
aerobatics. In order to bury the wheels in the
wing, the main gear legs turn through 90°
during operation. The tailwheel has a solid
tyre which is locked fore and aft for take-off
and landing but can be unlocked to swivel
through 360° for manoeuvring. The flaps are
high-drag when fully down and very effective
at achieving short landings at the limited
weights we tend to operate at. Somewhere
around a 600m landing run is achievable.

Before starting the engine the prop
is pulled through twelve blades by hand
to ensure no oil has pooled in the lower
cylinders, which would result in engine
damage if a start is attempted. It is a very
heavy engine to turn and should be part of
every pilot's fitness programme! Starting is
achieved by the electric starter turning the
prop ten blades with fuel turned off, then
selecting ignition on and priming with fuel.
When the engine starts, select 'Rich' mixture
and allow the engine to warm through slowly
at 1,100rpm. Cooling shutters are fitted to
the rear of the engine cowls and these are
closed part way at this stage. There are

also a set of 'iris'-like shutters at the front of the engine to maintain temperature in very cold climates, but we don't use these in the English summer. Taxiing is easy using rudder and toe brakes and you can just about see forward over the nose. Before take-off the propeller pitch change mechanism is exercised at 1,700rpm and mag drops checked at 2,000rpm. The engine is a little fickle and occasionally spits back during this check, but can be fixed by running in lean mixture for a minute or two.

Prior to take-off the tailwheel is locked and five divisions of right rudder trim set. The aircraft has a strong tendency to turn to the left under propeller, torque and gyroscopic effects, so lots of right rudder is needed until at about 50kts the tail is lifted and rudder eased a little. She flies at around 100kts, after which brakes are pressed, undercarriage raised and cooling gills closed allowing a fast acceleration to climb speed of 145kts. Climb is impressive and taking off straight into display is very achievable, though of course vertical manoeuvres aren't possible until a little speed has been built up. To loop the aircraft 250kts is needed, but barrel, aileron and slow rolls can be started around 200kts, which coincidentally is cruise speed. The stick forces are relatively pleasant unless you let it get out of trim and to that end my left hand spends more time trimming than adjusting the throttle.

A 'standard' display appears below, but may be modified to suit venue or weather:

Run in from behind the crowd at 90° to the display line but off to one side to complete a curved pass at about 45° of bank and 200ft to show the top surface to good effect. At this stage the engine would be at 2,600rpm and 38–40in boost; speed MUST be 250kts or more. Adjust to parallel to the display line and just off the airfield boundary fence pull a 4G ½ Cuban (¾ loop, rolling out upright when upside down on the 45 down line), followed by a straight pass and again at the other end another 4G ½ Cuban. Fly past again to wingover by pulling the nose up to at least 45° and rolling over 90° to reverse direction and dive into a barrel roll. The aircraft climbs to about 1,500ft in

the barrel roll, but this can be tweaked to be higher or lower to suit the cloud conditions or venue. Another wingover followed by a slow roll (or rather a level aileron roll which is easier to perform than a true slow roll and complies with the instruction 'no intentional negative G'). Depending on the length of the slot, while running in at 45° towards the display centre, throttle back and slow to below the gear limit of 200kts, put the gear down and make a 360° turn, selecting gear back up when at 45° going towards the crowd again. Throttle back up to 40in boost, which sounds terrific and you very soon have enough speed to complete another barrel roll the other way. Wind up the speed to 260kts and complete a ¼ clover, which is effectively a loop with roll through 90° while pointing vertically upwards. From this manoeuvre a straight fly-by waggling wings to say goodbye followed by a rolling 'break' to land or depart. The whole thing will be over in about 8 minutes and is intended to be smooth, the relatively low-energy manoeuvres showing off the aeroplane to its best advantage. It is also more fun for the pilot than those watching!

The longevity of the aeroplane and engine are fairly important, so we limit the engine power output to a maximum of 42in boost from its operational limit of 52in. Cruise

BELOW Skyraiders **F-AZFN and F-AZHK in close formation at a European air show.** *(Dries Embrechts)*

is achieved at about 1,800rpm and 28in boost in lean mixture which gives a speed of 200kts. 350kts is VNE (Velocity Never Exceed). The rear compartment is extremely useful, if only to carry someone with you to help clean the airframe and the rags and release agent needed to do it. When parked with the wings folded, bracing struts are put in to stop them being blown down in adverse winds and these are carried in the rear too.

Gary Schaffer

Gary Schaffer served in the USAF from 1969 to 1975. In addition to the Skyraider, he flew as aircraft commander on the C-5A Galaxy. His aviation experience includes military, corporate, production flight test and airline. He is retired and lives in Virginia with his wife Mary Ann who flies for a major US airline. After more than 50 years he remains close to general aviation and his love of flying, owning a 1946 Luscombe 8E and a Vans RV-3B. Recently, while talking on the phone with his wife, she stated, 'You've been out flying!' He asked how she came to that conclusion and she replied, 'I can hear the happiness in your voice.'

As an undergraduate student at Parks College of Aeronautical Technology in Cahokia, Illinois, I was a member of Phi Alpha Chi fraternity. During homecoming 1966 a Chi brother returned to regale us with his exploits flying the Douglas Skyraider, or AD (Able Dog) as the Navy called it. I was hooked! The big round motor, sliding canopy and tailwheel all harkened back to a bygone 'scarf out the window' flying era. I made up my mind right then and there that I was going to join the Navy after graduation and fly the Skyraider. The Air Force ROTC office constantly badgered me about joining, but I informed them that I intended to fly Skyraiders and they were only in the Navy's inventory. Little did I know the Navy was beginning to transfer Skyraiders to the Air Force for development of a special operations capability. One morning I opened my mailbox to find a note from the Air Force ROTC commander that read, 'If you want to fly Skyraiders, you better hot-foot-it to my office ASAP.' That afternoon I raised my right hand to join the Air Force and the journey began!

I carried out my Skyraider training at

BELOW 440A-1E 52-133858, 7th Combat Crew Training Squadron, Hurlburt Field, Florida, USA, pictured in December 1969. *(Gary Schaffer)*

Hurlburt Field, Florida, between October 1969 and March 1970, where all of the 4407th CCTS instructors were SEA [Southeast Asia] combat veterans and long-time special operations pilots. Little did I know then, but Hurlburt Field would see me again from June 1971 to October 1972, but this time as an Instructor Pilot myself. Then it was my turn to pass my knowledge to both USAF and VNAF pilots and help them transition to the Skyraider. Many of my instructors for my own training had T-28 experience in SEA as military assistance advisors stationed with indigenous units in Laos and Vietnam. Skyraider training was not simply about how to fly the airplane. The instructors went out of their way to make sure you were prepared for the demanding task ahead. Tactics learned by my instructors and passed on to me during training saved my life. My instructor made sure that I not only hit the target, but lived to fight another day.

I heard stories about the torque and right rudder requirements of the Skyraider, but I had been flying taildraggers since I was 15 years old, so I was not intimidated. I found the Skyraider to be a stable, predictable platform. One wore it like a glove and flying it became second nature, allowing the pilot to focus on the more complicated aspects of the mission.

My experience in the Skyraider includes all versions operated by the Air Force. A-1E, A-1G, A-1H and A-1J and what I appreciated about all these types was the structure. It was strong and solid, and it could take a hit that would seem fatal then continue to fly. I have friends that are alive today because as they said, 'she just kept flying'. However, what I loved most about the Skyraider is also what I cursed most . . . the four forward-firing M3 20mm guns mounted in the wings. There were two on each side. The M3 was an automatic combination gas/recoil operated belt-fed, air-cooled cannon. We carried about 800 rounds of ammunition. There was nothing more powerful than the thunder of the four guns operating simultaneously, yet nothing more impotent than the pop-pop-pop of a single gun firing after the other three

ABOVE A-1H 52-139820 of the 4407th Combat Crew Training Squadron. *(Gary Schaffer)*

jammed. In the years before I was in South-East Asia, the M3 had a bad habit of blowing itself up and damaging large portions of the Skyraider's wing. This happened when a round failed to fire and was not properly extracted. As the next round was chambered it would detonate the unextracted round and cause extensive damage. By the time I was in SEA, the problem was limited mostly to jamming of the guns. There was nothing more frustrating than working to extract a team from a fire fight and have all or most of your guns fail. I recall one mission when this happened to both me and the wingman as we worked to extract a recon team that encountered resistance shortly after their insertion into central Laos. Two of the team's indigenous troops were wounded within moments of setting foot on the ground and the bad guys had moved dangerously close. My wingman and I immediately went after the enemy troops with the 20mm guns and after firing only a few rounds from each of our aircraft, all eight guns jammed! But you work with what you have and fortunately, we also carried on the left stub pylon a SUU-11 A/A pod which contained a 7.62mm GAU-2B/A mini-gun. We carried 1,500 rounds of ammunition, so at 6,000 rounds per minute we each had about 15 seconds of firepower. By working closely together and firing short bursts, we were able to bring enough firepower to bear on the enemy that the CH-3 helicopter was able to swoop in and rescue the struggling recon team.

Chapter Seven

Maintaining the Skyraider

The Skyraider is a big machine to operate on a Permit to Fly. In the UK only two companies carry the CAA approval to restore and maintain such an aircraft. Although the airframe itself is fairly straightforward, its systems and engine are not. Specialist knowledge of large radial engines is dwindling and it takes a certain dedication and knowledge-set to keep these nearly 70-year-old aircraft flying.

OPPOSITE G-RADR under maintenance in spring 2017. The aircraft is raised ready for gear swings and landing gear leg servicing. The Skyraider takes up a lot of floor space, but equally an engineer needs to be aware of the roof space when it comes to raising the tail. *(Author)*

155

MAINTAINING THE SKYRAIDER

Maintenance schedule

Inspection periods established for the Air Force and Navy service organisations are not identical. Therefore flying-hour inspection periods specified in the manuals fall into two categories depending upon the operator. The Air Force period between inspections was always less than the Navy, with the Air Force being multiples of 25-hour inspections, and the Navy being multiples of 30 flight hours. The most in-depth for the Air Force was the 100-hour inspection, while the equivalent Navy inspection was at 120 hours. Repetitive major inspections, *ie* 200/240-hour, 300/360-hour, and 400/480-hour, carried essentially the same inspections, but with increasingly bigger components to be removed for overhaul. The only difference being that a Navy aeroplane on a 120-hour inspection would carry out all items listed in the 30-hour, 60-hour and 120-hour, whereas an Air Force machine would exclude the 25-hour servicing requirements, and include only those of the 50-hour and 100-hour.

A differentiation also existed with the daily and pre-flight inspections as made by the Air Force. Navy service personnel considered that their daily inspection covered both checks made by the Air Force personnel.

BELOW Pulling through the propeller. *(Author)*

Personnel safety

The important thing with any aeroplane is that it can almost always find a way to kill you. Any aeroplane, not just the Skyraider, should be treated with great care; to this end you should hopefully not hurt it, and it shouldn't hurt you. Firstly, externally, it is important to be very aware of all protrusions from the aircraft, be these edges of control surfaces, external drop tank fittings and, in many ways the most obvious, the propeller. Propellers should always be treated with caution, and every care must be taken not to walk through the arc of the blades always on the ground. Propellers are the things most likely to kill you, so should always be avoided when somebody is in the cockpit. Turning the Skyraider engine over is not an easy task to achieve on your own, and if attempting this as part of a pre-flight, make very sure the magnetos and fuel are both turned to 'off' before attempting this. The Skyraider is a big aircraft, and working on the wings and engine involves being a considerable distance from the ground. Close attention needs to be paid when getting aboard the aircraft in wet conditions. Something as simple as a slip or trip will give you a rapid descent to earth, due to the angle of the wing. If clambering into the cockpit, first check all pockets for loose items. Although the floor is fairly solid throughout the cockpit of

the Skyraider, it is still possible for small items to work their way behind the rudder pedals, or into the gaiter around the control stick. Not always a problem on the ground, but any loose item in the cockpit of an aircraft that has taken to flight has the potential for fatal consequences.

Tools and working facilities

The Skyraider is a large machine, and conventional hangars struggle to

Recommended lubricants and fluids

The following fluids and greases are recommended for use on the Douglas Skyraider:

Hydraulic fluid = MIL–O–5606 Red
Propeller hydraulic fluid = MIL–O–5606 Red
Oil = MIL–O–6082
Grease = MIL–L–7711/MIL–G–7118/MIL–G–7187/MIL–L–3545
Fuel = MIL–F–5572

LEFT While its engine idles, Douglas A-1E Skyraider 52-132649 is rearmed in South Vietnam during 1966. Rearming is no longer a required task today, but the perils of working on such an awkward surface are evident, let alone doing so while being close to the prop wash. *(USAF)*

ABOVE Gear swings being carried out in the hangar. The steps are in place to inspect the hydraulic system on the firewall for any signs of hydraulic leak when operating at pressure. *(Author)*

BELOW The landing gear oleos contain both fluid and nitrogen and both require servicing periodically. First the nitrogen pressure is removed from the leg and the fluid level is checked and replenished if required. The leg is then inflated with nitrogen to the required level. If the engine of the aircraft is to be removed, the nitrogen pressure should be relieved from the leg to stop the aircraft springing up when the weight of the engine comes off the firewall. *(Author)*

BELOW RIGHT Lifting eyes fitted in the outer wing panels ready for them to be lifted back into place. The same lifting eyes are also used to remove the centre fuselage fuel tank. *(Author)*

accommodate its large dimensions. Needless to say, a maintenance facility tasked with servicing a Skyraider needs to accommodate the aircraft safely, both in the wings folded and wings unfolded configuration. Larger-than-normal jacks are required to lift the Skyraider for gear swings, but otherwise little in the way of specialist tooling is required to carry out the majority of tasks. Special lifting eyes are about the only major requirement, and these double for many jobs – an example being that the lifting eyes for the outer wing panel can also be used to remove the centre fuel tank.

Obviously being built in America, the tools as standard are American AF imperial tools, so sufficient stock of these will be necessary. Tool control on working on aircraft is absolutely critical, with good records kept of which tools enter the aircraft, and a count carried out to ensure all tools come back out of the aircraft at the end of maintenance.

As G-RADR is a Navy specification AD4-NA, Kennet Aviation's Approved Maintenance Schedule (AMS) follows the original Navy servicing requirements, with the inclusion of some extra inspections required to comply with operating an aircraft of its weight in the United Kingdom and Europe.

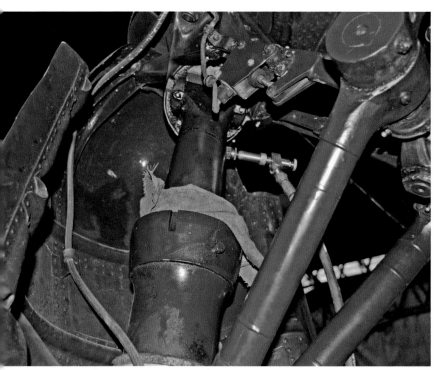

Approved maintenance schedule

- Daily Inspection
- Pre-flight inspection
- 30-hour inspection
- 60-hour inspection
- 120-hour inspection (R1)
- 240-hour inspection (R2)
- 360-hour inspection (R3)
- 480-hour inspection (R4)

Daily inspection requirements

Obviously the Skyraider was intended to be prepared by a team of assigned mechanics prior to operations. Many will have been specialists in their particular field and the practice will have been well known to those carrying out their duties every day. Today, these aircraft are used on a far less regular basis, and so the daily inspection is particularly thorough with regard to the systems in place. Although those who regularly carry out checks on aircraft will recognise the significance and necessity of the checks called for here, perhaps the scale of work required to undertake these checks is lost. Essentially, one does not attempt to prepare a Skyraider for flight without a good set of steps, tools for removing cowlings and panels and normally at least one other person to assist!

- Open cowlings and inspect engine for oil leaks, and fuel components for fuel leaks
- Inspect all components of cowling and cowl flaps for cracks and security of attachment
- Inspect exhaust stacks for cracks, misalignments and security
- Check ease of movement of engine controls, their security and for 'slack' in the system
- Inspect all accessible nuts and screws for presence, locking and security
- Inspect propeller regulator for oil leakage
- Inspect alignment stripe for slippage of nut on hub
- Inspect propeller hub oil level and top up as necessary
- Inspect blades for scratches, nicks or other damage
- Inspect ignition harness conduit for good coupling, and all connections for security and locking
- Inspect insulated portions for nicks and cracking
- Inspect magneto and distributor housings for excessive oil leakage

- Inspect underside of aircraft for fuel leaks
- Inspect fuel tank caps for security
- Inspect top of main fuel cell for leaks around attachment of fuel quantity condenser
- Inspect fuel vent lines for obstructions
- Drain small amount of fuel from fuel cell drain point – inspect for contamination
- Inspect oil cooler core for debris and remove dirt or obstructions
- Inspect oil system for leaks
- Inspect engine rocker box covers for leaks
- Check oil tank quantity and replenish as required. Inspect cap for security
- Ensure all wing and fuselage access covers closed and secure
- Inspect aircraft skins for obvious damage
- Inspect upper surface of wings and tail for dirt, oil or frost deposits
- Ensure rear compartment doors are properly installed and jettison handle is present and can be used if necessary. Ensure doors can be closed and secured
- Check tyres for correct inflation
- Check brakes for operation
- Inspect shock struts for leakage
- Inspect tyres for cuts, chafing, slippage and tread wear
- Inspect wheels for cleanliness, cracked or distorted rims, security of nuts and bolts
- Check operation of enclosure control
- Check full and free movement of ailerons, rudder, elevator and stabiliser trim
- Check full operation of aileron trim
- Check full operation of wing flaps
- Inspect instrument panel and instrument glass for condition and security
- Check cockpit seat operation
- Check arm rest attachment and operation
- Inspect all lap belts and shoulder harnesses for condition and operation
- Check headrest for security and adjustment operation
- Ground-test VHF comms as required
- Check cockpit indicating lights for operation
- Check oil cooler door motor for operation
- Check pitot heater for operation
- Check hydraulic reservoir for quantity
- Inspect hydraulic system accumulator for correct air charge
- Inspect enclosure air bottle for correct charge
- Check operation of emergency hydraulic pump.

RIGHT Tony Hoskins, author and engineer.
(Author)

BELOW An engine frame on engine. The frame sits on mounts fitted to the induction ring, with the supercharger passing through the centre of the frame. The rear sump is fitted after the frame is mounted to the induction case.
(Author)

The engineer's view

Tony Hoskins

It is not often one gets the opportunity to work such a rare aircraft in Europe – the type never really made it in vast numbers to the shores of the UK, and those that did grace mainly the museums of our country. With just two other flying examples in Europe, it was an absolute privilege to get to know the Able Dog and form what is honestly a love/hate relationship.

To summarise, it is an engineer's dream – but only if that dreaming engineer is supported by the resources and spares holding you would expect is held by military forces during active service. Having come from a considerable general aviation and airline maintenance background, some aspects of the design are just fantastic for quick turnaround repairs, but less so for deeper maintenance checks. For example, to change the engine is a fairly straightforward exercise – 21 disconnects on the firewall, remove the propeller, and four big bolts later, the whole unit from the firewall forward is hanging as one engine change unit (ECU). In military service, hang another ECU on the front, 21 reconnects and re-hang the propeller and you are away flying. This is my love aspect of the design!

Winding on the clock 65 years, few operators have the luxury of having a spare ECU, and to replace the core components of one is not a straightforward job. Before you can get the engine into a stand, you need to remove the engine mounting frame; to remove the frame you need to remove most of the accessory equipment and systems along with the carburettor, and lower oil sump/pump module. All in all, to remove from the aircraft takes three people a matter of hours, to break down the ECU, the same three people about two further days. Not the aeroplane's fault at all, nor the designer's, more a factor of an increasing shortage of spare parts.

Here lies the biggest problem with maintaining the Skyraider today – particularly in the UK. There are still a few stockists of ex-military airframe parts across the mid- and eastern regions of the USA, but these tend to hold the essentials – tyres, wheels, instruments, voltage regulators and such. It

RIGHT A common fault on the Skyraider is a broken rudder stop bracket. Although not possible to repair – due to the regularity of these becoming damaged – new old stock items are fairly easy to find. *(Author)*

is the bigger parts, such as castings, large structural assemblies and the like which are getting more difficult to come by. With most other aeroplanes of this era, if you had to change a major assembly, you probably would have encountered serious issues with your aeroplane to get to this stage, but the Skyraider is different. There are very strict damage limits listed in the Navy repair manual, which appears to be more of a guide to 'field repairs to battle damage' rather than actual proper structural repairs. The Douglas repair papers call for either complete replacement of the damaged component, or return damaged item to the Douglas factory for repair. Today this isn't really practical as Douglas no longer exists and the Boeing archives don't reveal much more than the manuals that are still readily available. Therefore finding new old stock (NOS) is on the objectives list of any Skyraider owner.

The casual observer will notice when – on the odd occasion that a Skyraider does come up for sale in the world – it is normally accompanied by a considerable spares package. Unlike a Spitfire, where drawings exist for nearly every part, to the point where pretty much anything can be bought 'off-shelf' for the popular marks, there are few Skyraider drawings available with the necessary material specifications, processes and dimensions to remanufacture these parts. So far we have been lucky with G-RADR, in that we have managed to source original parts from around the globe to keep her in top condition – but it will not be too many years into the future when the process of reverse engineering through

RIGHT Some parts are not held as spares, and certain items are listed in the book as being able to be fabricated from raw stock. Cables and pipework are most common and the Skyraider manuals do include quite considerable information for the military engineers on how to make basic components. *(US Navy)*

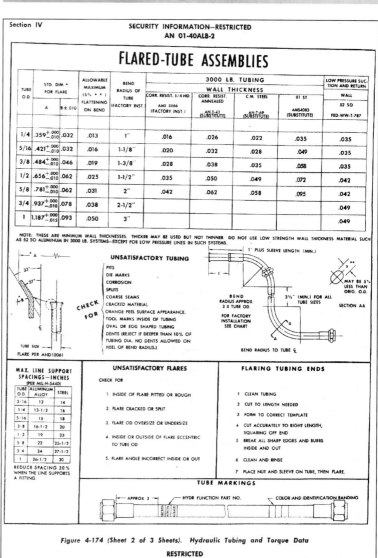

Figure 4-174 (Sheet 2 of 3 Sheets). Hydraulic Tubing and Torque Data

RIGHT When running any old aircraft, spare engines are a welcome necessity. Again, a fairly common engine, it makes sense to have two for spares, or at least spares recovery in case something untoward was to occur during operations. *(Author)*

BELOW Hanging the propeller takes great care and many hands. With the tail on the ground, the propeller has to be angled rearwards considerably to mate on the splines – once the threads on the propeller shaft make with the propeller nut in the hub, the propeller can be drawn in on to the rear cone by tightening the nut. *(Author)*

approved companies will have to take place to keep these monsters in the air.

Engines will never be a problem. The Wright 3350 was built in such huge numbers that massive quantities of parts for overhaul or servicing are available from a number of reputable companies across the USA; however, the propeller is becoming more of a difficult component to maintain. There are few types running in the world with the Aeroproducts propeller – mainly the Skyraiders and Bearcats that survive to this day corner the market. There are a number of Aeroproducts repair centres across the USA and Canada, and although you can get the regulator overhauled almost by return of post, the willingness to do propellers is another matter. As with most variable-pitch propellers, there is very specific tooling required to assemble and disassemble components, most of which is unavailable and has to be locally manufactured against the item it is designed to work with. On top of this, the rubber seals from within the propeller hub deteriorate with age and finding those suppliers that stock replacements that are willing to sell abroad are few. The blades themselves are hollow, made up from two formed sheets and are welded together at their edges – these require very careful non-destructive testing to ensure their integrity is sure before they go back on the aircraft.

Other than that, the airframe is essentially the same as any other aircraft – its enormous size lets it dominate most hangars, and the volume of space it takes up when unfolding the wings and conducting gear swings has to be seen to be believed. Being an ex-Navy machine, the level of corrosion inhibiting and therefore the preservation of the structure is among the best I have ever seen. Panel edges are meticulously sealed from the elements to keep the interior dry, plus the amount of oil the engine throws out does its best to keep the paintwork preserved. Nobody is ever short of work to do if the Skyraider needs cleaning!

Considering this aircraft could be flown by any pilot with suitable differences training, working on the aircraft is like working on an airliner, where tools are transported around the aircraft in small carry boxes as once you are in the fuel tank bay, it's a long way firstly to climb out, and then climb down from the aircraft if you need a different spanner from your toolbox on the ground.

Despite the challenges of working on aspects of the aircraft, and procuring the spare stock to keep everything working, she is certainly a machine of character. Even after long man hours struggling to access items deep in the bowels of the electronics bay – to stand back with a mug of tea and admire the machine as she rests does bring a huge sense of pride.

The Wright R-3350-26WD: my mistress and my enemy (sometimes)
Caleb Carpenter

I'll lead off with the powerplant because, well, it's the heart of the 'Raider, and it is the specific component of her which I've spent the most time working on and getting to know. I must say that I can be having the worst of days in the shop but the second I hear 'The Beast' (my nickname for the AD-5) roar to life it instantly puts me in a better mood. Hearing the rumbling gallop of the 3350 thrum away soothes my mind, as I'm sure it does for other mechanics and warbird/ radial enthusiasts alike. Although my daily work involves nearly 20 operational aircraft in my immediate vicinity, 'The Beast' is the only one that draws everyone in the neighbouring hangars outside to see what the hell that monstrous, beautiful noise is all about. It's like a mass exodus of all nearby hangars. This happens only for my mistress – not the P-51, F4U, B-25, DHC-4 . . . only her.

Getting more into the technical side of things, I can say without doubt that the 3350 (at least our two) can be quite needy. When I first came across the Skyraider

in 2014, the AD-5, and specifically the powerplant, is what I and other maintenance personnel attended to the most. Damn near after every flight it seemed like something else was breaking. Part of that I'm sure is due to the fact that we have very irregular operation schedules. There are times when we may put 15 hours on her in less than 2 months, and then other times she'll sit for 4 months for various reasons such as winter maintenance, lack of scheduled rides, airshows, etc., etc. These birds need and want to be flown, but due to the reality of operational costs, it isn't always that this can occur. Thankfully, through many hours and hard work the AD-5's powerplant is now much more reliable. To this date, she has been running strong for 11 months and roughly 25 hours on the Hobbs meter since the last major work was done on her.

Let's change a jug, or three . . . Nos 9, 10 and 11

I still have vivid memories, or nightmares, of struggling to hoist and hold a 50lb jug above my head in position while another mechanic is frantically trying to reposition the piston ring compressor tool over the last ring, so I can then push the jug up to the case and seat it. I then hold it in place – suspended on

RIGHT A piston fitted and oiled prior to the fitting of the cylinder. All pistons are measured and matched to prepared cylinders of given sizes. Care must be taken in compressing the rings when fitting into the base of the cylinder so as not to snap one. *(Author)*

the back of my head and shoulders, while he desperately tries to thread in by hand two cylinder hold-down bolts before I lose all strength and it comes crashing down on me! That was only one jug – we still had two to go, and all together they are the three jugs a mechanic hopes and prays he never has

to change on a 3350 (or any twin row radial for that matter): Nos 9, 10, and 11. No. 10 is precisely at the 6 o'clock position in the front row when looking at the power plant, and No. 9 and No. 11 flank it on either side on the rear row. Changing a jug up top or on the side of the motor is enough work alone, but when you must change the bottom cylinders and are forced to work above your head, with the constant annoyance of oil dripping on your head, in your hair and in your eyes at times, is when morale can get pretty low, pretty fast. What I learned very quickly when performing this type of work is that there are NO shortcuts. No EASY way. Tearing into one of these engines is just like peeling away layers of an onion and not a fraction of an inch of space was spared in regards to how the components all fit and interlock together. Hazards for the engineer are the induction system piping, ignition system leads and transformer coils, upper and inner cylinder baffles and their supporting brackets, rocker drain manifold/scavenge system, front oil sump and pump and piping, push rod tubes, exhaust system piping, clamps and supporting brackets that attach to the

RIGHT Three cylinders in place on the power section. Cylinders are bolted to the case which is threaded. Bolts are torqued and then either a pressed locking plate is forced over the bolt heads, or are wire-locked to secure these critical items. Obvious here is the great increase in cooling fin size towards the head in order to take away the heat as fast as possible. *(Author)*

cylinders and in some places are sandwiched underneath or on top of the cowl flap ring supports. You can see why engine change units were common in the field – today we have to break these things down.

Not only that, but in order to get to these jugs we had to remove additional baffling, intake piping, exhaust and cowl flap parts from Nos 8 & 12 and the lower half of the cowl support ring and oil cooler intake scoop just to grant us sufficient access to the cylinder base bolts; many hours of work just to get access. At the end of the disassembly/demo phase of the job I clearly remember looking at the four or five 3 × 6ft tables we had set up that were each completely filled with the hundreds of parts we had removed. It was crazy to think that all of those parts would soon, in a methodical, precise order, be going back in.

Now, about those cylinder base bolts . . . to my best estimate, those bolts had not been removed since the last time our engine had been overhauled some 30+ years ago, and let me be the first to tell you that we had one hell of a time removing them. We damn near rendered useless one of our Curtiss-Wright wrenches trying to remove them and finally resorted to building our own wrench by heating up and bending a 30in long ½in breaker bar extension to the same curvature as the factory wrench and then welded on a high-strength ½in drive ½in head impact socket on the end and ground it down so it would just barely fit on the bolt heads, yet fit between the cylinder skirt flange and first cooling fin. We call it our 'Curtiss Left Wrench' or 'Curtiss Wrong Wrench' – whichever you prefer. Worked like a charm once we could attach a pneumatic impact gun to it to break the bolts loose. . . . Installing them was not any easier given that there is minimal room to get your wrench in there to tighten and torque them to 600in/lb, let alone your hands or pliers to safety wire them properly afterward.

Going back in with all of those parts and pieces is where things get inevitably more tricky, especially with regard to induction system and inner baffling components, which are the first items installed after one

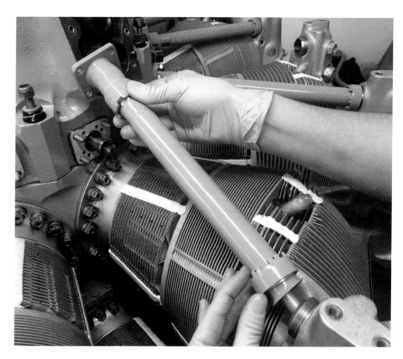

is done fighting with the base bolts. I can't exactly tell you the magic trick I performed while installing the first section of induction piping (the S-pipe that attaches to the front cylinders and connects to the Y-pipe which bolts to the blower housing section), but I seem to recall the trick involving a dead blow hammer! A wretched design, but oh so beautiful when completely together!

One thing I feel is very important to discuss here is the sometimes constant uncertainty with which a mechanic must deal with while working on a 'Raider. How many times do you think I went back and double checked, tripled checked, quadruple checked the work I was doing when changing the jugs? Or consulted the 3350 maintenance or overhaul manual to make SURE I have done things right? How many times did I hope to God that I did not miss something somewhere out of all the hundreds of parts, or had a piece of hardware fall down into the case or blower section I was unaware of. . . . The consequences of failure will be disastrous. There's no room for error or mistake. Errors and mistakes can destroy a valuable engine or an irreplaceable airframe in a matter of seconds. More importantly, it could cost someone their life. . . . Now, any aircraft mechanic must deal with this mental stress, but for guys like me I feel it

ABOVE Pushrods are fitted once the cylinders and hydraulic tappets are fitted and secure. It is important to ensure the rocker arms are free and wound out completely to allow the rods to be fitted. A delicate exercise as even at the extremes, the clearances to fit are minimal. *(Author)*

*more times than not it'll be rear plugs on
the bottom cylinders (jugs Nos 7–13) on the
left mag, which fires all rear plugs. We've
had instances in the LT [low-tension] ignition
system where a malfunctioning transformer
coil (there are 18, one per cylinder) caused
a jug to go dead. Another time one of the
Y-harness leads that completes the circuit
from the main harness to the coils frayed and
began shorting out. We've also had issues
with some of the shorter high-tension leads
(coil to spark plug). So when you consider
that there's 18 cylinders, 18 transformer
coils, 36 spark plugs, 36 high-tension
leads, 9 Y-leads with 37 connection points,
you start to understand the magnitude of
troubleshooting an ignition problem. Douglas,
Wright, Bendix recognised this and took steps
to help maintenance personnel be able to
troubleshoot in the form of an onboard ignition
analyser receptacle that one could connect an
ignition analyser box to but unfortunately we
do not have that equipment now and it's not
even hooked up on the airframe anymore. I
do wonder though how effective it was for the
boys back in the day. . . .*

*Speaking of those boys, quite often I find
myself thinking about how things were for
them back during wartime. In some respects,
I believe it may have been a little more
straightforward and simplistic for them in their
approach to maintenance simply because
it was wartime and good old Uncle Sam
was footing the bill. If you look through the
maintenance manuals you'll see the pages
and pages of troubleshooting charts (which
can come in handy and be quite useful, by
the way!) where the recommended solution
to a problem is quite simple; replace the
part. It was OK back in period – there was
an abundance of spare parts and manpower
to boot! I've spoken with a few gentlemen
who worked on 'Raiders in Vietnam and they
marvelled at how we can operate all our
aircraft with such a small group of mechanics
– back then they had entire teams of guys
who worked on each airframe, and they
were subdivided into powerplant, airframe,
electrical, instrumentation and hydraulic
specialists. They didn't all need to know how
to do everything. One gentleman who worked*

*is a little different in some ways because
an 18-cylinder 3350 is inherently more
complicated than a small four-cylinder
continental in a Cessna 150. The aircraft
itself as a whole is incredibly complex and
robust in its design and systems. It is old
technology; electro-mechanical. No computer
diagnostic systems. When they break you
have no choice but to put on your detective
hat, troubleshoot and go to work. We're not
just parts-changers here; we do not have
that luxury.*

*One recurring problem we've experienced
quite often with the AD-5 is ignition issues. We
pull her out to go fly and next thing I know my
mistress is taxiing back from the run-up area
and the pilots report a 150rpm drop on the
mags (the book says 100rpm is acceptable)
accompanied with banging and popping. . . .
Often times, if you're lucky, it is just a spark
plug or two. But it can be three or four and*

on them at NKP in Thailand related that they typically had between 10 and 15 freshly overhauled 3350s fashioned as engine change units in the shop ready to be installed on an airframe in short order, and at least as many if not more 3350s sitting in their respective cans ready to be built up into ECUs. Often they'd simply replace the powerplant on an airframe with a new one during inspections to save down time so the 'Raiders could get back in the air faster. It made more sense for them to do tasks such as removing, cleaning, testing and installing 36 spark plugs with the engine on a stand. Just that alone is a lot of time-consuming work!

One impression I gathered from talking to some of these men – something that we both shared in common – is that they didn't know what they were doing really any much more than I do. They were not all masters of their trade and didn't know exactly what to do in every situation. They were young and constantly learning on the fly just like me! Mostly everything was a big mystery and they dealt with the same mental battles that cause one to go over and recheck something 100 times hoping they didn't miss something that could spell disaster. Where our stories and experiences differ, though, is that while I perform my work in a no- to low-pressure environment, these men did the same work in places where the conditions made things incredibly difficult and inherently more dangerous. How must it have been trying to change a jug on an aircraft parked on the hangar deck of a carrier that is pitching and rolling 15ft constantly? Something as mundane and routine as removing the large and bulky left-hand accessory cowl to check and service the accumulator pressures and hydraulic system. There have been times where I've almost lost my balance on the ladder trying to step down backwards with it because it is so awkward. Today the cowl piece I'm gripping weighs only 15lb maybe? Their accessory cowl pieces must have weighed at least 3–4 times more because they had plates of armour attached to them! Now imagine trying to keep your balance and not fall off the stand while doing that on a pitching and rolling carrier deck. Men

would have done this multiple times every single day their aircraft were operating. You could be seriously injured or killed working in environments like that within seconds doing the most routine of things. And how about the USAF maintenance crews who did their jobs in constant 90–100+ degree weather and humidity with the added bonus of mosquitoes and bugs ceaselessly harassing you . . . I suppose I have no right to complain anymore do I?

BELOW Provisions were made for working on the Skyraider in the field. Portable maintenance platforms could be mounted on the sides of the engine installation to aid servicing. Quite how easy this would have been on a rolling, pitching carrier can easily be imagined. *(US Navy)*

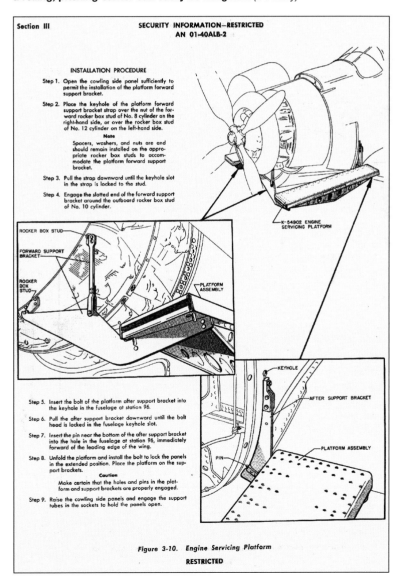

SECURITY INFORMATION—RESTRICTED
AN 01-40ALB-2

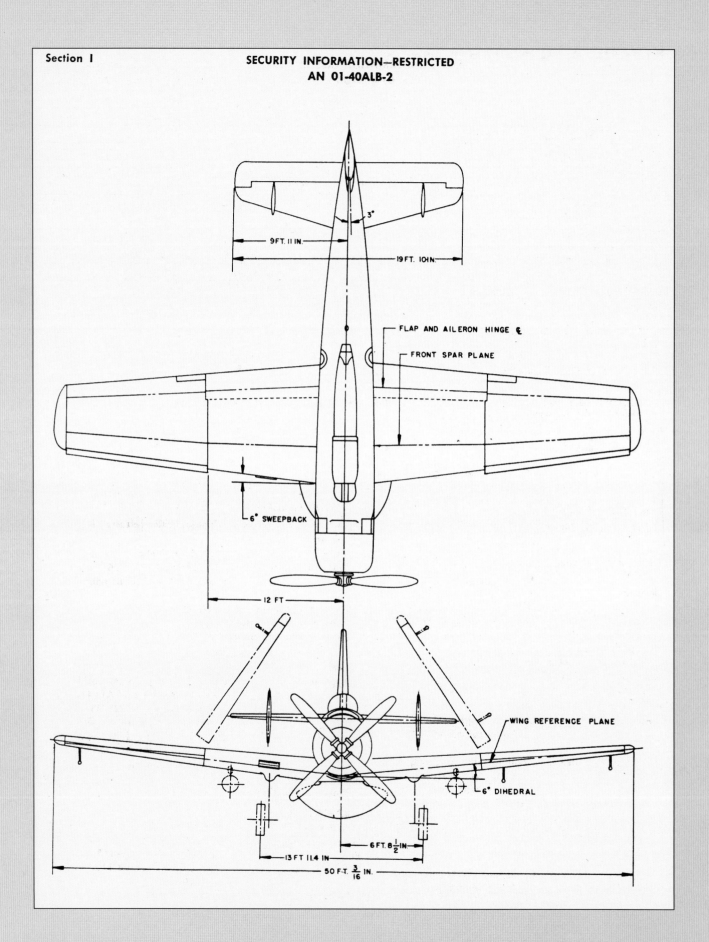

SKYRAIDER LEADING PARTICULARS

Wingspan unfolded	50ft ¼in	Wing aerofoil section	NACA 2417 & NACA 4413
Wingspan folded	23ft 10½in	Dihedral	6°
Height (tail down)	15ft 8in	Incidence at root	3° 45'
Height (wings folded)	16ft 8in	Incidence at tip	-0° 25'
Max height while folding	19ft 4½in	Wing sweepback	6°
Propeller clearance (tail up)	6⁹⁄₃₂in	Wing area	368.68sq ft
Fuselage length	39ft 2¾in	Horizontal stab span	19ft 10in
Fuselage width	5ft 0in	Stab incidence range	4° up to 6° down
Rudder range	50°	Elevator range	25° up, 15° down
Flaps range	40°	Aileron range	17° up, 13° down
Fin offset from fuselage	3°	Landing gear track	13ft 10¾in
Landing gear leg pressure	900psi	Tyre inflation pressure	95psi
Tailwheel leg pressure	650psi	Tailwheel range	360°
Fuel main tank	380 US gallons	External fuel tanks	450 US gallons
Oil tank capacity	36 US gallons	Hydraulic tank capacity	5.8 US gallons

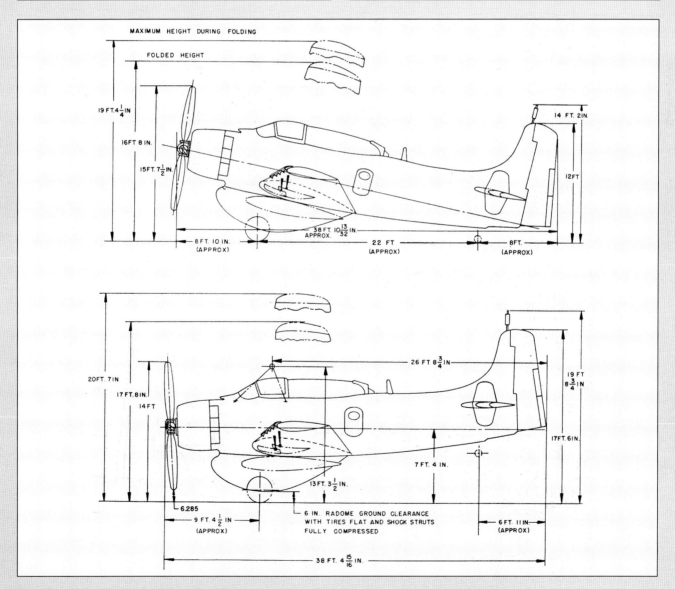

Chapter Eight

The Skyraider major inspection

It is not possible for an aircraft to fly indefinitely; periodically there is a need to take time out to completely gut the aircraft in question and overhaul all the systems to ensure its longevity into the future. Be it a Lancaster, Spitfire, T-6 or pretty much any other type of aircraft that graces our skies, it will at some point disappear into the back of a workshop to emerge many months or years later, fresh-faced and ready for the next decade and more of service. The Skyraider is no exception.

OPPOSITE G-RADR nearing the end of its major check in the spring of 2017. *(Author)*

the 75th anniversary of the Battle of Britain – but in a workshop in Essex, the major check of G-RADR was starting.

When the aircraft was accepted on to the UK register, the operator limited the engine installed to a maximum TBO (time between overhauls) of 800 hours and therefore as G-RADR's Wright engine was nearing the end of its service life, it was due to be exchanged with one of the spare engines held for the aircraft. The overhaul life of the propeller and the replacement of the fuel lines had aligned, and the latter required the removal of the fuselage fuel tank. There is no particular fatigue life published for the Skyraider, so the decision was taken to employ the services of a specialised non-destructive testing company to check the integrity of the major critical points. The outer wings were removed to allow the hinge and actuator pins to be inspected, which at the same time permitted extensive internal inspections and the reapplication of corrosion protective treatments to be carried out.

In the fuselage, with the fuel tank removed, thorough detailed inspections could be carried out of the bulkhead structures and the main fuselage longerons. Control cable runs that are normally inaccessible with the tanks in place could be inspected in detail and all the hydraulic lines and electrical looms could be completely examined over their entire runs. Being a Navy aircraft, the level of corrosion protection was excellent, and for an aircraft of its age, the minor level of corrosion present was surprisingly welcomed.

With the aircraft relatively empty, the opportunity was taken to entirely clean out the lower fuselage and the whole machine got a complete polish to preserve its paintwork.

The usual annual inspection elements were carried out, with minor blemishes to the paintwork being rectified. As with every major check, a few defects are found, and these, along with even fairly minor irritations, were worked to keep G-RADR on top form.

As ever, it was a team effort and for many months towards the completion of the work, everybody that could be spared was working away on aspects of the aircraft. From cylinder baffle refurbishment, to testing harnesses and

G-RADR had left the military to start its civilian life back in 1985, and hadn't had a major overhaul since. Its annual utilisation is not high, and had only accumulated a total of 707 hours in its civilian life. The summer season shows of 2015 in the UK were mostly to commemorate

LEFT Owning a Skyraider is most importantly a team effort. To share the enjoyment of the type is one of the benefits of ownership. *(Christophe Brunelière)*

BELOW G-RADR in the static aircraft park at Duxford. From 2018, this popular participant will once again perform at shows to the delight of those in attendance. *(Phil Glover)*

looms, from replacing tired bonding leads, to repainting creep marks, it all had to be done.

It is through this work and dedication that G-RADR joins the airshow season in fine fettle, her engineers and flight crew confident and safe in the knowledge that she is as good – if not better than – the day she left the Douglas factory. Her continued safe operation we hope will last for many years to come, and that her shape and noise entertains the thousands of spectators who will see her at shows across Europe from here on.

Skyraider survivors

O f the 3,180 Skyraiders made of all types, at the time of writing in 2017, just 50 survive, and of those only 17 are airworthy. The Korean War was the first costly campaign for the Skyraider, a total of 128 were lost, of which 27 were through accidents, mostly during landing on carriers. The Vietnam War accounted for 191 USAF Skyraider losses, of which 150 were in combat. Similarly the US Navy lost 48 and the Marines 81 Skyraiders. The rest are largely lost to time and the scrapman's axe. Once the pride of the Navy's carrier-borne fleet, their dispersal to other forces saw few survive into preservation.

Those aircraft shown in **bold text** below represent airworthy examples:

9102	XAD-1	USS *Intrepid*, New York City. Museum display
9257	**AD-1**	Skyraider Historic Military Aircraft LLC, Lake Forest, Illinois. Airworthy
122811	AD-3	Naval Inventory Control Point (NAVICP) Philadelphia, Pennsylvania. Museum display
123827	**AD-4**	Gerry Yegan, Virginia Beach, Virginia. Airworthy
124086	AD-4W	WV106 FAA Museum, UK. In storage
124121	AD-4W	WT141 FAA Museum, UK. In storage
124143	**AD-4N**	F-AZDP Jean-Baptiste Salis, France. Airworthy
124156	**AD-4N**	Sanders Aviation, Troy, Alabama. Airworthy
125716	AD-4N	F-AZFN Didier Chable, France
125739	AD4-NA	USNMAT, NCC China Lake (North) Ridgecrest, California. Museum display
126179	AD4-NA	Musée de l'Air et de l'Espace, France. Museum display
126867	**AD-4W**	Erickson Aircraft Collection in Madras, Oregon. Airworthy
126882	**AD-4NA**	Marine Aviation Museum in Houston, Texas. Airworthy
126922	**AD-4NA**	Kennet Aviation, Old Warden, Bedfordshire, UK. Airworthy
126924	AD-4NA	Yanks Air Museum in Chino, California. Museum display
126956	AD-4NA	National Museum of Naval Aviation, NAS Pensacola, Florida

BELOW Prototype Skyraider XAD-1 aboard USS *Intrepid*, New York, in 2016. *(Alan Wilson)*

BELOW 123827 belonging to Jerry Yeagan seen at Chino, California. *(Mark Peapell)*

ABOVE WV106 in external storage at the Fleet Air Arm Museum Reserve Collection, RNAS Yeovilton. *(Phil Glover)*

BELOW 126959 at Titusville Warbird Air Show in 2002. *(Jelle Hieminga)*

BELOW 132598 was delivered as a US Navy AD-5N night attack plane and was re-designated an A-1G in 1962. The aircraft is painted in the 1964–66 scheme used by the USAF in Vietnam. However, it wears the tail code of the 1st Special Operations Squadron ('TC'), which was applied only later on camouflaged Skyraiders. *(USAF)*

ABOVE 124143 now flying in France as F-AZDP, seen here at Duxford in 2009. *(Peter Arnold)*

BELOW 126997 takes off at the Planes of Fame Air Show in 2017. *(Dai Ngo)*

BELOW 139606 early in the day at an air show in 2010. *(Chad W. Veich)*

126959	AD-4N	East Iowa Air Inc., Bennett, Iowa. Airworthy
126965	AD-4NA	Heritage Flight Museum in Burlington, Washington. Airworthy
126997	AD-4	Chino Warbirds Inc., California. Airworthy
127002	AD-4NA	F-AZHK Christophe Brunelière, France. Airworthy
127007	AD-4N	Patriot's Point Naval and Maritime Museum, Mount Pleasant, South Carolina. Museum display
127888	AD-4NA	Air Zoo in Kalamazoo, Michigan. Museum display
127922	AD-4W	USS *Midway*, San Diego Aircraft Carrier Museum, California. Museum display
127945	AD-4W	Flygvapenmuseum, Sweden. Under restoration?
127947	AD-4W	Arlandasamlingarna, Stockholm-Arlanda Airport, Sweden. Status unknown
127960	AD-4W	Svedinos Bil-och Flygmuseum, Ugglarp, Sweden. Under restoration
132261	AD-4B	NAS Fallon, Nevada. Museum display
132436	A-1E	Vietnam Military History Museum in Ha Noi, Vietnam. Museum display
132443	AD-5W	Historic Aviation Memorial Museum, Tyler Pounds Field, Tyler, Texas. Museum display
132463	AD-5	Aerospace Museum of California, McClellan Air Force Base, California. Museum display
132532	AD-5Q	National Museum of Naval Aviation, NAS Pensacola, Florida. Museum display
132534	AD-5N	Evergreen Aviation & Space Museum in McMinnville, Oregon. Museum display
132598	AD-5N	Hurlburt Field Memorial Air Park, Hurlburt Field, Florida. Museum display
132649	AD-5	National Museum of the United States Air Force, Dayton, Ohio. Museum display
132683	**AD-5**	Greatest Generation Naval Museum, San Diego, California. Airworthy
132789	AD-5W	March Field Air Museum, March AFB (former) in Riverside, California. Museum display
134600	AD-6	National Museum of the United States Air Force, Dayton, Ohio. Museum display
134636	A-1H	Vietnam Military History Museum in Ha Noi, Vietnam. Museum display
135018	AD-5Q	Pima Air and Space Museum, Davis-Monthan AFB, Tucson, Arizona. Museum display
135152	**AD-5W**	Cavanaugh Flight Museum in Addison, Texas. Airworthy
135178	**AD-5W**	Midwest Wild Relics Refuge Inc., Saint Charles, Missouri. Airworthy
135188	**AD-5W**	Collings Foundation in Stow, Massachusetts. Airworthy
135300	AD-6	National Museum of Naval Aviation at NAS Pensacola, Florida. Museum display
135332	AD-6	National Air and Space Museum, Smithsonian Institution, Washington DC. Storage
137602	AD-6	NAS Lemoore, California. Gate guardian
139606	**AD-6**	Warbird Aircraft, LLC, in San Diego, California. Airworthy
139665	**AD-6**	Tennessee Air Museum in Sevierville, Tennessee. Airworthy
139674	A-1H	War Remnants Museum in Ho Chi Minh City, Vietnam. Museum display
139723	A-1H	Vietnam Air Force Museum, Bac Mai Airport, Ha Noi, Vietnam. Museum display
142072	AD-7	Royal Thai Air Force Museum, Thailand. Museum display

ABOVE 139674 in Ho Chi Minh City, Vietnam. *(Peter Arnold)*

ABOVE The wreckage of an unknown Skyraider in Ho Chi Minh City, Vietnam. *(Peter Arnold)*

BELOW 142072 at the Royal Thai Air Force Museum, Don Mueang International Airport, Thailand. This aircraft was accepted by the US Navy on 28 January 1957. It was retired on 27 February 1968 and passed to the US Air Force as 52-142072. It was damaged on a mission in December 1968 and made a gear-up landing at Udorn RTAF. It was then written off and put on display. *(Aeroprints.com)*

Index